Plate C
NASA Goggles and VPL Glove.
A "hair-raising" experience in artificial reality. *Courtesy of W. Sisler and S. Fisher, NASA Ames Research Center.*

Plate D
The Autodesk HiCycle in Artificial Reality.
Participants in this graphic world, if they pedal quickly enough, can take off and fly above a graphic landscape. *Courtesy of Autodesk.*

Artificial Reality II

Myron W. Krueger

Addison-Wesley Publishing Company

Reading, Massachusetts • Menlo Park, California
New York • Don Mills, Ontario • Wokingham, England
Amsterdam • Bonn • Sydney • Singapore • Tokyo
Madrid • San Juan • Milan • Paris

To Starry and My Parents

Sponsoring Editor: Peter S. Gordon
Assistant Editor: Helen M. Goldstein
Production Administrator: Sarah Hallet
Production Assistant: Genevra Hanke
Text and Insert Design: Jean Hammond
Electronic Production Administrator: Beth Perry
Composition: Jacqueline Davies
Manufacturing Manager: Roy Logan
Senior Manufacturing Coordinator: Judy Sullivan

Flying Mouse™ is a trademark of SimGraphics Engineering Corporation.
PowerGlove™ is a trademark of Mattel, Inc.
AutoCAD® is a registered trademark of Autodesk, Inc.
DataGlove™ is a trademark of VPL Research, Inc.
EyePhone™ is a trademark of VPL Research, Inc.
SPARCstation™ is a trademark of SPARC International, Inc., licensed
  exclusively to Sun Microsystems, Inc.

Many of the designations used by manufacturers and sellers to distinguish
their products are claimed as trademarks. Where those designations appear in
this book, and Addison-Wesley was aware of a trademark claim, the designations have been printed in initial caps or all caps.

Library of Congress Cataloging-in-Publication Data

Krueger, Myron W.
        Artificial reality / Myron W. Krueger. —2nd ed.
        p. cm.
        Includes bibliographical references.
        ISBN 0-201-52260-8
        1. Technology and the arts. 2. Man-machine systems. 3. Avant-garde
(Aesthetics) I. Title.
NX180.T4K7 1990   90-568
700'.1'05—dc20   CIP

1 2 3 4 5 6 7 8 9 10–DO–9594939291

Contents

Contents

Chapter 8
Controlling the Experience   151

Chapter 9
Applications   169

Chapter 10
Artificial Reality and the Arts   209

Chapter 11
Cybernetic Society   229

Preface

The central idea of this book is artificial reality, the ultimate form of interaction between human and machine. In an artificial reality, everything you perceive is generated by a computer that responds to your movements with sights and sounds designed to make you think you are in another world.

This book is an update of *Artificial Reality* (Addison-Wesley, 1983). Its content overlaps the original book. However, much that was presented as a vision in the early 1980s has now been implemented. The VIDEOPLACE concept has been realized as an art form. In addition, portable glasses that allow you to look around in a graphic world, as well as reality gloves and clothing that can inform a computer of your movements in that world, now also exist.

Unlike other books that deal with the implications of computers, *Artificial Reality II* is not a survey. Rather, it is a personal account, tracing the development of this powerful, culture-defining idea from original insight, to current prototype technology, to future broad application and ultimate social consequences.

Artificial Reality II is directed toward anyone with an interest in art or technology who is open to unexpected ways that the two may intersect. This audience would include anyone involved with computer–human interaction, computer graphics, video, psychology, or education. Indeed, the reader could be anyone who likes to keep up with new ideas.

Although the book does discuss technical issues, every effort is made to present this information in an intuitive way.

Acknowledgments

The long-term editorial assistance of Joan Sonnanburg was essential to writing this book. Sonnanburg also created the diagrams.

Over the years, many people contributed directly or indirectly to VIDEOPLACE and its antecedents. Some individuals volunteered thousands of hours of their time; others provided institutional support. The original encouragement and support for the book came from my doctoral advisor, Leonard Uhr, at the University of Wisconsin and from a Research Assistantship under a grant from the National Science Foundation (NSF) that ran from the late 1960s to 1974.

From 1974 to 1978, Thomas Haig and Verner Suomi provided an institutional umbrella at the Space Science and Engineering Center of the University of Wisconsin. Gilbert Hemsley provided assistance in securing financial support. The National Endowment for the Arts, the Brittingham Trust, and the Wisconsin Arts Board provided funding during this period.

From 1979 through 1985, I continued my research at the Electrical Engineering and Computer Science Department of the University of Connecticut, with support from the Connecticut Research Foundation in 1979.

Of the many individuals who have participated, several deserve special mention. In METAPLAY and PSYCHIC SPACE, Wayne Weber was responsible for the electronics and computer interfacing. Wayne Van Engen and Richard Gobeli worked on the software. At the Space Science Center, Charles Moore was instrumental in pursuing arts funding. At the University of Connecticut, Victor and Peter Odryna, Mark Duffy, James Kurdzo, John Rinaldi, Bruce Shay, Thomas Gionfriddo, and Katrin Hinrichsen made significant contributions to the development of the Artificial Reality Laboratory.

Since 1985, VIDEOPLACE development has continued independent of any institutional affiliation. Katrin Hinrichsen has remained with the project full-time and continues to make important contributions. The friendship and support of Wallace Bowley in the Mechanical Engineering Department at the University of Connecticut have also been crucial. In 1987, the NSF provided a six-month Small Business Innovation Research (SBIR) contract that we used to develop techniques for operating the VIDEODESK. Further thanks are due to Carl Rettenmeyer, the Director of the Connecticut State Museum of Natural History, which has served as home base for VIDEOPLACE for the last three years. Finally, a note of appreciation to Joy Mountford of Apple Computer for the loan of a MAC-IIx, which has made writing this book an education as well as a pleasure.

December 1990
Myron W. Krueger
Box 786
Vernon, CT
06066

Introduction

The world described in Genesis, created by mysterious cosmic forces, was a volatile and dangerous place. It molded human life through incomprehensible caprice. For centuries, the goal of human effort was to tame Nature's terrible power. Our success has been so complete that a new world created by human ingenuity has emerged.

To an overwhelming degree, our daily experiences take place in a reality of our own construction. We live our lives in the automobile, the home, the office, and the shopping mall. Through the spoken word, the written word, and the television broadcast, we experience a conceptual world that is every bit as real to us as the physical world. As the rate of technological change accelerates, it becomes increasingly difficult to understand the changing culture that technology defines.

This ignorance makes us uneasy. However, it is as foolhardy to yearn for a benign Nature, which never existed, as it is to accept technological developments that make us anxious. Rather, we must explore ways of shaping our environment that lead to psychological comfort and aesthetic pleasure, as well as to efficiency.

The practical concerns of technology and the humanistic concerns of aesthetics need not be estranged. In fact, during most of human history, artists were conversant with the advanced technology of their culture, and employed it in their art. Only the unprecedented rate of scientific and technological developments during the past century created the current chasm between technology and art. Today, however, these disciplines are coming together again with considerable force. This trend is part of a larger cultural implosion that is now well underway: the integration of all aspects of society by interconnected information, communication, and control systems. These networks and the computational power they bring will permeate our lives much as electricity does today.

The focus of this book is the interaction between people and machines, both in the immediate interface and in the broader cultural relationship. Although a significant fraction of the workforce spends much of its time dealing with computers, we rarely ask, "What are the various ways in which people and machines might interact, and which of these are the most pleasing?" In this book, the question is posed as a problem in aesthetics. The tool for exploring this issue is the artificial reality, which serves as a paradigm for our future interaction with machines.

An artificial reality perceives human actions in terms of the body's relationship to a simulated world. It then generates sights, sounds, and other sensations that make the illusion of participating in that world convincing. Since the complete repertoire of video, computer graphics, and electronic music are amenable to computer control, rich relationships can be established between an individual and the environment. The environment can be controlled by a preexisting program, or operators can intercede and use the computer to amplify their ability to interact with other people.

An artificial reality is a medium of experience. It is more akin to film or television than it is to mainframe computers. Thus, it should be considered in terms of the content it conveys rather than in terms of the technology that is used to implement it. In my own work, artificial reality is conceived as an art form. It represents a unique melding of aesthetics and technology in which creation is dependent on a collaboration among the artist, the computer, and the participant. The artist anticipates the participant's possible reactions and composes different response relationships for each alternative. The participant explores this universe, initially triggering responses inadvertently, then gradually becoming more and more aware of causal relationships.

The implications of artificial realities go beyond art. An artificial reality is a generalized concept that separates technology from any single application, enabling us to examine its broad implications. Thus, we can judge it in isolation from purely practical concerns or use it to expand our understanding of specific fields.

Artificial Reality Versus Virtual Reality Versus Cyberspace

When I coined the term *artificial reality* in the mid-1970s, I intended it to cover both my VIDEOPLACE technology and the head-mounted, three-dimensional viewing technology that originated with Ivan Sutherland. I considered them to be separate paths leading to the same goal. That goal was full-body participation in computer events that were so compelling that they would be accepted as real experience.

During the ensuing years, the terms *virtual worlds, virtual cockpits, virtual environments,* and *virtual workstations* were used to describe specific projects. Computer scientists apply the term *virtual memory* to the use of disk memory as though it were computer memory. In physics, a virtual image is created at the focus of one parabolic mirror when a real object is placed at the focus of a second such mirror facing the first. In 1989, Jaron Lanier, CEO of VPL, coined the term *virtual reality* to bring all of the *virtual* projects under a single rubric. The term therefore typically refers to three-dimensional realities implemented with stereo viewing goggles and reality gloves.

A third term was coined by currently popular science-fiction writer William Gibson, who started writing about *cyberspace* in 1984 [1]. He used the term to refer to a single artificial reality that could be experienced simultaneously by thousands of people worldwide. Although he is only the most recent in a series of science-fiction authors (including Ben Bova and Ray Bradbury) who have speculated about artificial realities, his terminology has appeal for people who first encountered the concept through his books [2, 3].

The promise of artificial realities is not to reproduce conventional reality or to act in the real world. It is precisely the opportunity to create synthetic realities, for which there are no real antecedents, that is exciting conceptually and ultimately important economically. The term *artificial reality* conveys this point to the layperson.

Personal Participation

My own participation in computer–human interaction began in one of the very first BASIC classes at Dartmouth College. Dartmouth's attitude was that knowledge of computers was part of a liberal arts education, and that anything we might do with these machines was likely to be instructive. I continued using computers in the Army, after which I entered graduate school in Computer Science at the University of Wisconsin in 1966.

I approached graduate work as a continuation of my liberal arts education. I saw the encounter between human and machine as the central drama of our time. I was puzzled by some of the concerns I found in the technical literature. What was all this talk about efficiency? What was the point of spending five years developing optimization techniques if the technology was going to be obsolete in three? It was clear that the human was the most important component in a computer system. Therefore, it followed that the human interface should be the central research problem in computer science. Indeed, its importance transcended computer science, for the computer–human interface is a permanent part of the human condition—as permanent as the laws of physics.

Humans are evolving slowly, if at all. On the other hand, computers are the most rapidly evolving technology in history. It seemed that study of the interface should focus on the static qualities of the human, rather than on the transient issues of computer technology. The computer should adapt to the human, rather than the human adapting to the computer. It was clear that the ultimate computer should perceive the human body, listen to the human voice, and respond through all the human senses.

It was this view of the human interface that distinguished my approach. Whereas the other early workers thought in terms of devices worn or held by sedentary operators, I was commited to unencumbered, full-body participation in artificial experiences. While they saw artificial reality as the next step in computer graphics or as the solution to a particular problem, I envisioned it as a general computer interface, as a form of telecommunication, and as a medium of expression.

My goal was to create *unencumbering, environmental* artificial realities. The realization of my goal has been an environmental technology called VIDEOPLACE. (Actually, I had originally hoped to implement both technologies.) It is unencumbering in the sense that people can experience it without wearing special instrumentation. It is environmental in the sense that the technology for perceiving the participant's actions is distributed throughout the environment instead of being worn. The alternative is a *wearable, encumbering* technology, in which the participants wear the sensors and the displays.

From the beginning, I have believed that artificial reality is not just another technology; it is a powerful idea with possible implications for every human transaction. Whether the technology will ever deliver on every promise is an open question. Even if the technology falls short, however, the *idea* is powerful. It will change the way we think.

The Rest of the Cast

While my own work developed outside the mainstream of both science and technology, there were important players in the mainstream. Their work took an alternative approach, using special goggles, gloves, and suits to monitor the movements of participants' bodies and to deliver computer-generated stimuli to the participants' senses.

A single towering pioneer, Ivan Sutherland, invented the first three-dimensional, head-mounted display in the late 1960s, but then left the field in the mid-1970s. Starting a few years later, Tom Furness led a series of long-term, secret research projects for the Air Force. This work was heavily funded, considered many technological options, made important discoveries about human perception, and developed display technology far superior to the current commercial goggles. In the mid-1970s, Fred Brooks directed a brilliant project at North Carolina that enabled a user to grasp and feel the weight of imaginary objects a decade before the contemporary touchless data glove.

The second wave received its impetus from NASA, whose efforts initially resembled guerrilla research more than a priority program. Both of the prime movers at NASA, Mike McGreevy and Scott Fisher, have backgrounds in the arts. A small company called VPL had been founded earlier by Tom Zimmerman and Jaron Lanier, currently the most visible cheerleader for the technology. The DataGlove they sold NASA was then reengineered for use in video games. Another company, Autodesk, became involved, and then a third, Sense8, joined in. Like particles in a fission reaction, the personnel from one project disband and reappear with new affiliations.

The third wave has already struck. America's scientific, business, and intellectual communities get their marching orders from the front page of *The New York Times* [4]. The headline "Artificial Reality" initiated the media monster of 1990. We have a myth that ideas are powerful, and that theory precedes practice. In fact, it was only after there was working technology that the intellectuals started thinking, the scientists saw the scientific implications, and the press started reporting. All that happened only after there was business. Extensive coverage did not occur until we could produce color pictures, suitable for publication in magazines and broadcast on television.

The third wave will be followed by cycles of excitement and despair. The small band of less than two dozen players will explode. Part of the momentum will come from the fact that people want to work on artificial reality—whether or not there is funding or investment or course credit or salary to support their efforts. Why is there so much excitement?

Imagine

Imagine that the computer could completely control your perception and monitor your response to that perception. Then, it could make any possible experience available to you. In fact, it could provide any *imaginable* experience.

In a sense, an artificial reality is the incarnation of imagination: a projection hallucinogen that can be shared by any number of people. It is a laboratory for philosophy where we can ask basic questions such as, "What is reality?" "What is perception?" "Who am I?" in fundamentally new ways.

Contemplate the limits of your own imagination. What can you dream that you cannot experience? Think now—or the answer will be provided as a *fait accompli*.

This book is the outgrowth of 21 years of research into the relationship between human and machine. Its premise is that in a world where technological innovation increasingly defines our experience, the quality of our interactions with machines will significantly affect the quality of our lives. One result of these efforts has been an artificial-reality art form that seeks to communicate the benign essence of technology before it has been attached to particular interests and applications. By making the technology both palpable and palatable, it seeks to engage people in a playful exploration of the coming fact.

References

1. W. Gibson, *Neuromancer*, ACE Books, New York, 1984.

2. B. Bova, "The Perfect Warrior," Conde Nast Publications, 1963.

3. R. Bradbury, "The Veldt," in *The Illustrated Man*, Doubleday, Garden City, NY, 1951.

4. A. Pollack, What is Artificial Reality?, *The New York Times*, Vol. CXXXVIII #47,836, 10 April 1989, p. 1.

1

Antecedents in Art and Technology

Introduction

Artists today are not technologists. Most are careful to maintain the distinction between the two roles and would be offended if they were considered technicians. Yet, art and technology once were inextricably intertwined. Prehistoric artists were using state-of-the-art technology when they ground their pigments. From the Middle Ages through the Renaissance, art was the most powerful means of communicating the beliefs of a culture to a largely illiterate public. The architects who built awesome cathedrals and the painters who invented systems for depicting perspective realistically were well versed in the technology of their day.

As the predominant Western world view shifted slowly from a belief in religious truths to a belief in scientific explanations, developments in science and technology influenced artists heavily. In the nineteenth century, the development of the camera freed the painter from the role of visual historian, and research on the nature of perception prompted Impressionist painters to undertake pictorial explorations of how and what we see.

In the twentieth century, scientific discoveries and technological developments proliferated at an unprecedented rate. The scientist became absorbed with the ultrafast, the ultrasmall, the ultraslow, the infrared, and the ultraviolet; all were invisible, to be dealt with as conceptual abstractions that could be experienced only by inference and calculation. Without becoming a scientist or technologist, the artist could no longer keep abreast of all the new events. Although perhaps related at a philosophical level, the artistic and scientific communities became increasingly alienated.

During the past two decades, there have been developments that herald the return of a relationship among science, technology, and art; for example, the efforts of scientists to represent abstract concepts visually, of technologists to increase the possibilities of telecommunication and simulated experience, and of artists to utilize today's most potent means of communication—video and the computer.

Developments in Science

Considerable effort in the scientific world is being directed at developing richer interactive systems. Whether the intent is communication or simulation, there is a common goal of creating more convincing representations of reality or of hypothetical structures. This scientific focus presages an interest on the part of our entire culture. The pseudoexperience systems that are evolving will be applied to education, psychology, art, and telecommunication.

Conception Becomes Perception

Lately, there has been a renewed appreciation of our intuitive intellect—the intellect with which we apprehend the everyday world of physical objects. Scientists recognize that they can better understand concepts if these concepts can be visualized and can be manipulated as objects. In other words, concepts that can be physically experienced are more easily understood than are those that can only be thought about. To this end, chemists and technologists have developed techniques for displaying complex chemical models in three dimensions using interactive computer displays that permit scientists to manipulate the computer model just as they used to twist and turn the old physical models made from sticks and balls [1]. On a larger scale, computer animation is giving astronomers the chance to study the dynamics of galaxies over billions of years.

Understanding the value of complete interactive representations of reality has led to the development of three-dimensional graphic systems that allow the user to explore a three-dimensional design space visually. Mathematical functions are commonly shown as three-dimensional surfaces. Even abstract mathematicians, such as topologists, find that visualization can spur conceptual thinking. Our representations of the unseeable and the conceptual are evolving to the point where we can not only see them, but also hear, feel, and walk around in them.

Super Senses

We are no longer creatures of five senses: technology has given us hundreds of senses. We can see the universe throughout the electromagnetic spectrum. We can hear vibrations, from the infrasound of the seismologist to the ultrasonics used in destructive testing. We can feel molecular forces. We can stand outside the universe to get the big picture. We can sniff the stars through spectral analysis. We can sense the age of ancient objects. But, in every case, we must convert the data from these new senses into a form that our original five senses can understand.

The field of medicine has made some startling contributions in this area. Physicians have always longed to see inside the body without doing injury to it. A number of such noninvasive techniques have been developed; in each case, however, this complex data must be presented in a form that can be grasped intuitively by the radiologist.

There are thermographic video cameras that show a color-coded heat map of a person's body [2]. Ultrasound imaging, initially devised for radar and sonar, is now used to explore within the human body without ill effects. In obstetrics, ultrasound has virtually replaced other methods of visualizing a developing fetus; it is also widely used in cardiology [3]. Computed axial tomography (CAT) scans provide another view inside the body [4]. Magnetic resonance imaging (MRI) allows a doctor to view the chemical processes in the body [5]. Positron emission tomography (PET) gives an animated view of the brain in action, a means of visualizing thought [6]. There are also radiation treatments that allow the physician to act inside the body, to perform surgery without breaking the skin [7].

Simulation Is Artificial Experience

As the tools of science become more expensive and the tasks to which they are set more ambitious, there is increasing pressure to minimize the risks of operator error and to anticipate effects of bad design by rehearsing the situation as fully as possible through simulation.

Electronic circuits, mechanical systems, chemical factories, and military strategies are all tested first in computer-based simulations. Medical and business students can see the effect of their decisions on simulated cases. Flight simulators that are used by military and commercial pilots provide not only isolated skills, but a representation of the whole experience [8]. Simulation is becoming a common form of training for tank crews, tanker captains, police officers, and salespeople.

These simulations must sense the actions of the trainees and respond appropriately. As these simulations become more realistic, their perception of human behavior will become more complete. By having the computer perceive our actions in the everyday environment, we can make it a simulation of what we would like the world to be.

Intelligent Objects and Agents

Systems that can sense our actions will also be able to anticipate our wants, and to act for us. Simple examples of such environmental systems that the layperson encounters today are the thermostat in the home and the automatic door at the grocery store. The minimal requirement for this type of system is a sensor that determines when the system's function should be performed. Not only can we expect to find automatic sensing systems in more of the technology we encounter, but already we have traffic sensors that merge one line of traffic with another, ultrasonic burglar alarms, and automated battlefields. It is easy to anticipate devices that sense our presence, recognize us on sight, and engage us in conversation.

As these isolated devices become more sophisticated and are integrated to form systems that have the ability to move and speak, we will be faced with the presence of the computer in our lives as an apparently living force. What we are now witnessing is a birth process— the birth of the artificial entity as an integrated, perceiving, behaving system. Whether or not these entities will evince intelligence is a separate issue; the artificial entity is inevitable. The early forms are already here.

Communication or Coincidence

An interesting aspect of communication that is seldom noted can be illustrated as follows. A number of years ago, whenever one of my son's friends called on the telephone, he would ask, "Is Mikey here?" Being in command of the facts of geography, adults usually think of communication as the transmission of information from one point to another. Children, on the other hand, believe that, if they can talk to someone, they must be in the same place. In other words, our concept of place is based on the ability to communicate. The place created by the act of communication is not necessarily the same as that at either end of the communication link, for there is information at each end that is not transmitted. The place is defined by the information that is available simultaneously to both people.

There is a definite trend toward expanding the sense of being in the same place. We can see this trend in the development of transmission systems from Morse code to the telephone, to radio, to black-and-white television, and finally to color television. Each of these broadcast and dissemination systems allows us to perceive events from afar more completely than does its predecessor. Systems that are now being developed will allow us not only to perceive distant events, but also to act at a distance. For example, ground-based fighter pilots can fly airplanes that are faster and more maneuverable than they would be if a pilot were aboard; and Russian scientists sitting on earth explored the moon via their remotely-controlled lunar vehicle [9].

Expanding Art

The development of new technologies has been paralleled by the invention of new aesthetic concepts. Beginning with the Dada movement in the early twentieth century, the traditional assumptions about what art is have been challenged continuously. New ideas and new forms have been tried and discarded or filed away for future reference. However, artists have been more interested in exploring immediate possibilities than in laying the groundwork for a new medium. Their lack of technological skills and, more significant, their lack of empathy with technology itself have often prevented them from seeing that their early insights contained the basis for a new aesthetic tradition.

Surrendering Control

As artists have discarded traditional forms, new attitudes have begun to appear. Most important is a feeling among artists that they need not be the creators of objects. They are no longer to be judged exclusively by their command of a medium. In fact, in many cases, it is the artist's willingness to forego control that constitutes a contribution. The theme of surrendering control to influences within or beyond the artist recurs in recent theorizing motivated by a desire both to discover new kinds of order and to involve an audience.

The composer John Cage was an early influence on this school of thought. He advocated a search for new sound patterns based on the translation of all sorts of relationships drawn from other areas. Where other people use the word *randomness* when describing his method, Cage himself spoke of *unintended sound* [10].

Happenings

Cage's ideas influenced the Happenings of Allan Kaprow in the 1960s [11]. A Happening was theater without an audience. Nothing was conceived with the passive spectator in mind. A loose series of possibilities was planned; the participants were the ones who actually gave the work its final form. Here, as in Cage's work, the artist surrendered immediate control, stepped back to a higher level, and gave the actors and the audience a level of control heretofore unknown.

Artificial realities also require the artist to accept reduced control, to think in terms of a structure of possibilities that leaves the final realization of the piece in the hands of each participant.

Conceptual Art

We usually think of an artwork as a physical object that we perceive directly through our senses. In conceptual art, although there may be objects or events that are the physical manifestations of a piece, these have little aesthetic significance in themselves. The art lies in the concepts that are suggested by these outward signs or are explained by written or graphic documentation. The perception that is evoked is a product not of our senses, but rather of our intellect. Thus, conceptual art emphasizes the appreciation of ideas as a source of aesthetic experience [12].

Process Versus Object Art

Perhaps one reason that process as art has gained favor is that craftsmanship has been devalued by machines that can produce slick objects in a fraction of the time it would take an artist. When objects are part of today's artistic process at all, they are often intended only as clues to an intelligent process of aesthetic exploration.

This attitude is appropriate. The artist's objective today should be experimentation with new modes of thought and new technology. When a degree of mastery is achieved, the results can be tested against whatever criteria still seem relevant.

Art and Technology

In recent years, artists and technologists have embraced new tools and sought to create a new type of imagery. Computers, video, film, and electronic music have been wedded in a variety of experimental forms.

Video art has broken with television's traditional role as a broadcast medium, and has exploited its techniques to create a new art form. Video technology provides a variety of new image-processing techniques. It also allows the recall of images, both for instant replay and for long-term storage. Whereas commercial television usually uses video as though the latter were film, video art attempts to exploit the medium's unique characteristics.

Early computer art was based on a batch-processing, rather than on an interactive, model of programming. The task was specified and programmed, and the output was the composition. More recent systems allow an artist to explore a line of development, to intervene at every step, to judge the outcome, and then to use or discard that outcome. The computer can increase the artist's ability to experiment, so that the final compositions are based on a rich experience with the medium and the full expression of the artist's ideas.

Interactive Computer Art
Much of the art that has been produced with the computer could have been produced by other means, albeit tediously. True computer art would be impossible without a computer. One essential aspect of the computer is that it can assimilate information and make decisions in real time. In the past 20 years, artists have attempted to create an art form dependent on this computer capability. Although there are only a few such works, they point to a major new thrust in both technology and art.

These steps toward a collaboration between art and technology are a positive trend. An artist who is alienated from technology cannot speak for a technological culture, any more than a technologist who disdains aesthetics can design a humane technology. The artificial reality has its roots in this confluence of science, technology, and art.

Conclusion

Human–machine interaction has progressed a long way since the LINC Trainer in World War II and O.K. Moore's 1950s experiments using humans to simulate machines for learning environments [13]. Human–computer interaction started with punched cards, progressed to text-based dialogs, and currently employs graphics and sound. We are now proceeding toward immersion in a world created by the computer. Interaction is not only the dominant mode of using computers—it is gradually becoming the dominant mode of working in general. The human–computer interface is no longer a component of a computer system; it is now the primary function of the computer. Today, the human controls the machine. Tomorrow, the human and machine will function together as a unit, each performing the tasks suited to its abilities. It is the definition of that relationship in which both art and science are interested, and for which the aesthetic approach is more scientific. The scientific method works best when objects and forces can be isolated and studied one at a time. An aesthetic approach can be used to address complex problems with many influences, ill-defined criteria, and diffuse goals.

References

1. J.S. Lipscomb, "Three-Dimensional Cues for a Molecular Computer Graphics System," doctoral dissertation, University of North Carolina at Chapel Hill, NC, 1979.

2. Thermovision, AGA Corp., Secaucus, NJ.

3. G.B. Devey & P. N. Wells, "Ultrasound in Medical Diagnosis," *Scientific American*, 238 (May 1978), pp. 98–104.

4. W. Swindell & H.H. Barrett, "Computerized Tomography: Taking Sectional X Rays," *Physics Today*, 30 (December 1977), pp. 32–41.

5. "Imaging Unveils Medical Mysteries," *INSIGHT*, (16 October 1989), pp. 8–16.

6. Ibid.

7. "Head Surgeon," *Popular Science*, (December 1988), p. 71.

8. "NOW, 'Artificial Reality'," *Newsweek*, (8 February 1987), pp. 56–57.

9. B. Miller, "Remotely Piloted Aircraft Studied," *Aviation Week and Space Technology*, 92, No. 22 (1 June 1970), pp. 14–15.

10. J. Cage, *Silence*, (MIT Press, 1967), pp. 8–11.

11. H. Geldzahler, "Happenings: Theater by Painters," *Hudson Review*, 18, No. 4 (Winter 1965–66), pp. 65–66.

12. L. Lippard, Six Years: The Dematerialization of the Art Object, from 1966–1972 (Praeger, 1973).

13. O.K. Moore, "O.K.'s Children," *Time*, 76 (7 November 1960), p. 103.

2

Early Work: GLOWFLOW, METAPLAY, and PSYCHIC SPACE

Introduction

In the late 1960s and early 1970s, I worked on human–computer interaction at the University of Wisconsin. Although I started looking at practical problems, my approach was always driven by aesthetic—as distinct from artistic—concerns. My interests led me to participate in, and then to lead, a series of rather romantic experiments. The insights gained during this period have informed all subsequent work.

GLOWFLOW: An Environmental Art Form

In early 1969, I became involved in the development of GLOWFLOW, a computer art project conceived by Dan Sandin, well known as the inventor of a widely-used video image processor; Jerry Erdman, a minimalist sculptor; and Richard Venezsky, a computer scientist. GLOWFLOW was exhibited at the Memorial Union Gallery of the University of Wisconsin in April 1969.

GLOWFLOW was a computer-controlled light–sound environment that had limited provision for responding to the people within it. Although the original plan was conceived by a group, the visual and musical designs were developed separately. Jerry Erdman designed a darkened room in which a visual display created a perceived space that was only partially faithful to the actual physical space. Changes in the display were indirectly contingent on the actions of participants. This part of the design was deliberate; the designers believed that direct responses would become a focal point reinforcing noise in what was intended to be a quiet, contemplative environment.

The physical space was an empty rectangular room constructed within the gallery (Fig. 2.1). The display consisted of a suspension of phosphorescent particles in water, pumped through four transparent tubes attached to the gallery walls. Each tube contained a different colored pigment. Since the room was dark, the lighted tubes provided the only visual reference and were arranged to distort the viewer's perception of the room, causing the room to appear wider in the center than at each end (Fig. 2.2). The disorienting darkness also caused viewers to assume that the bottom tube was level with the floor. Thus, as they walked the

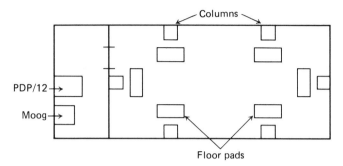

Figure 2.1
The Gallery Floorplan for GLOWFLOW.

length of the room and found the floor rising with respect to their own position, participants thought they were going downhill. This illusion was so strong that people actually leaned backward as they moved.

The tubes were run through opaque columns along the walls, each of which contained four lights, one for each tube passing through it (Fig.

Figure 2.2
GLOWFLOW Tubes on a Gallery Wall.

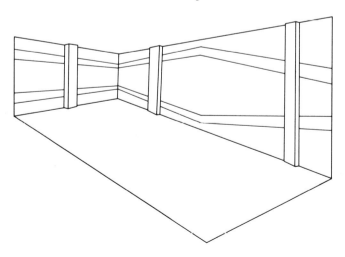

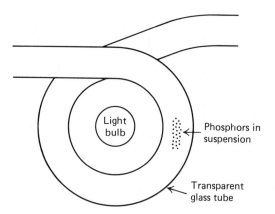

Light bulb

Phosphors in suspension

Transparent glass tube

Figure 2.3
The System for Activating Phosphors.

2.3). When a light was turned on, the phosphorescent substance flowing through the corresponding tube glowed as it emerged from the column. The glow's intensity decreased as the phosphorescent fluid moved along the wall, until the light finally decayed approximately 20 feet from the originating column.

There were six columns, two along each of the side walls and one on each end wall. With four lights per column, there were a total of 24 lights that could be turned on or off in any combination by the computer. Thus, it was possible to light all the tubes coming out of a single column, a single tube as it came out of every column, or a random combination of tubes and columns.

Electronics

The environment was controlled by a PDP-12 minicomputer manufactured by Digital Equipment Corporation (DEC). The PDP-12 controlled the lights, the speakers, and a Moog synthesizer via an interface. The computer could direct the Moog output through any combination of the six speakers. Sounds could rotate around the room or bounce from one wall to the other. The only sensing devices were pressure-sensitive pads in front of each of the six columns; these pads could sense a person standing on them.

The GLOWFLOW Experience

Between 15 and 20 people were in the darkened room at any one time. New people were allowed in as others left. There tended to be several stages in each person's experience of the environment. First, there was a disorientation due to the darkness. During this period, people stayed near the entrance. As their eyes grew accustomed to the low light level, they would explore the room, discovering the illusory nature of the perceived space. Later, they might sit or lie down on the floor, interacting with other people or contemplating the experience quietly. As long as there was some turnover of people, no one was pressured to leave the room.

People had amazing reactions to the environment. Communities would form among strangers. Games, clapping, and chanting would arise spontaneously. The room seemed to have moods, sometimes being deathly silent, sometimes raucous and boisterous. Individuals would invent roles for themselves. One woman stood by the entrance and kissed each man who came in, while he was still disoriented by the darkness. Other people acted as guides, explaining what phosphors were and what the computer was doing. In many ways, the participants in the room seemed like a primitive people, exploring an environment they did not understand, trying to fit it into what they knew and expected.

Since the GLOWFLOW publicity mentioned that the environment could respond to the viewers, many people assumed that every visual pattern they saw and every sound they heard was in response to what they personally were doing the moment before, and they would leave convinced that the room had responded to them in ways that it simply had not. For instance, if a tube started glowing after they spoke, they would assume that their speech had turned it on. If a sound occurred after they hit the wall, they would assume that striking the wall would elicit more sounds. Often, they would persist in the behavior long after the results should have convinced them that their hypotheses were incorrect. The birth of such superstitions was continually observed in a sophisticated university public.

Interactive Dilemma

The artists' attitude toward interaction between the environment and the participants was ambivalent. Responsive relationships were seen as conceptually interesting, but the artists did not believe that it was important for the audience to be aware of those relationships. The idea of direct response to movement and voices was discarded. The designers feared that, if immediate responses were provided, the participants would become excited and would think only of eliciting more responses. This active involvement would conflict with the quieter mood established by the softly glowing walls. The artists recognized the power of responsiveness, but chose to subordinate it to a predominantly visual conception.

The environment responded to people in various ways. For instance, a sound might rotate around the room or the pattern of lights might change, when a person stood or sat on a certain pad. However, people had little sensation of interaction, for several reasons. First, there were programmed delays between action and response. This time lapse blocked people's awareness of the causal relationships. Second, the large number of people in the room meant that any response could have been elicited by someone else's action. Finally, the medium of glowing and flowing was itself slow to respond; it required seconds for a glowing line to appear and decay. Thus, if a person did cause a response, he could not immediately repeat it to verify its cause. With such intermittent responsiveness, the participants could not establish the relation between action and display.

Although GLOWFLOW was successful visually, it was precisely the visual conception that limited its interactive potential. The arrangement of the tubes on the wall was guided by Erdman's minimalist aesthetic, which had no concern for the variety of responsive relationships. Also, since the environment was seen as a sculpture that could be admired by a number of people simultaneously, the need for each person to have a distinct effect on the environment was not considered. Even if the participants are to be kept in the dark about the interactivity, it is desirable for the artists to be able to understand the relationships to see whether those relationships are working.

Lessons From GLOWFLOW

GLOWFLOW succeeded as a kinetic environmental sculpture, rather than as a responsive environment. However, the GLOWFLOW experience led me to draw the following conclusions:

1. Interactive art is a potentially rich medium in its own right. Since it is new, interactivity should be the focus of the work, rather than a peripheral concern;

2. So that it can respond intelligently, the computer should perceive as much as possible about the participants' behavior;

3. Only a small number of people should be involved at a time, so that the experience can highlight the relationships between the environment and the participants, rather than those among participants;

4. Participants should be aware of how the environment is responding to them. Just as we do not ask people to admire invisible paintings or to listen to inaudible music, interactive art is pointless if the audience is not cued in to it. Computer technologists have provided us with many inexplicable computer experiences. We do not need artists to contribute to our frustration;

5. The choice of sound and visual response systems should be dictated by the system's ability to convey a wide variety of conceptual relationships. The tubes of GLOWFLOW did not have a sufficient variety of responses; they made a single visual statement, rather than providing a medium of expression;

6. The visual responses should not be judged as separate art works; nor should the sounds be judged as music. The only aesthetic concern should be the quality of the interaction, which may be judged by general criteria: the ability to interest, involve, and move people, to alter perception, and to define a new category of beauty.

When I came to these conclusions, I was surprised that I had such strong ideas about what computer art should be. Art had never been important to me. It had a musty feeling about it. It was safely locked away in museums in the same way that disease was segregated in hospitals. When I thought about the visual impact of the Sistine Chapel in the Rennaissance or that of the Impressionists' paintings in the late 1800s, I realized that there was no contemporary art that had such force. Part of the problem was that Rennaissance media were still considered the proper vehicles for aesthetic statement. When I imagined an art form based on interactivity, I was confident that it would speak with great authority. I was surprised when none of the artists to whom I offered these ideas had any interest in them at all. Perhaps, if C.P. Snow was correct that there are two cultures (humanist and technological), it is also true that every culture has its art and that the technological culture would have to produce its own artists. If I wanted to see art that was important to me, I would have to create it. I would have to become an artist.

METAPLAY: Computer-Facilitated Interaction

Following the GLOWFLOW experience, I conceived and directed METAPLAY, which was exhibited at the Memorial Union Gallery in May 1970. METAPLAY was a radical departure from GLOWFLOW; it integrated visual, sound, and responsive techniques into a single framework. I set aside traditional criteria for judging art. I rejected any thoughts about responsive subtlety so that I could focus on interactivity. My goal was to discover an interactive medium. If the result was art, fine. If not, that was OK too, because I was sure that an interactive medium would have value, however it was classified.

I knew that a responsive art form should perceive as much as possible about the participants' behavior and should respond through richly expressive displays. I elected to simulate an interface, which was far beyond the technology of the day, in order to discover how people would react to it. By employing human perception and human decision making where I hoped to use computer intelligence in the future, I was able to investigate the expectations of human participants. By standing in for future computers ten hours per day, six days per week, for six weeks, we were forced to make far better observations and to develop far more powerful intuitions than we could have had we created an automated experience.

The computer was used to create a unique real-time relationship between the participants in the gallery and the artist, who was in another building. The live video image of the participant and a computer graphic image drawn by the artist were superimposed and rear-projected on the screen at the end of the gallery space. The viewer and artist both responded to what they saw on the screen.

I needed a commanding real-time display to express the interactive relationships. The most versatile existing real-time displays were the graphic display computer and closed-circuit video. The problem with both of these media was one of scale; the standard 25-inch monitor was too small to be an environmental display because we are conditioned to sit in front of it and to watch it, rather than to interact with it physically. The solution was to convert the computer image to video and to rear-project it on the eight-foot by ten-foot screen using a video projector. The computer image was superimposed on the live video image. METAPLAY may well have been the first project in which these two media were combined.

Computer-Facilitated Human Interaction

My approach was to use my own perception and intelligence to simulate the interface I hoped to create later with the computer. This strategy itself created a new category of interactive system in which I could use the computer to enhance my ability to interact with another person. Participants walked into the METAPLAY environment and saw their live video images projected life size in front of them (Fig. 2.4). Then, they saw line drawings appear on the projection screen, superimposed on

Figure 2.4
The METAPLAY Floorplan.

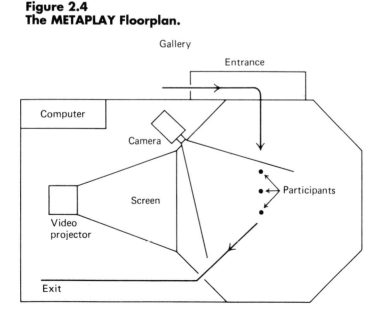

their images. From the participants' point of view, the interaction was between their images and the computer graphic drawing.

Hardware

The computer image generation began with a data tablet, an instrument that enabled the artist to draw or write on the computer screen (Fig. 2.5). I use the term *artist* although the person at the data tablet did

Figure 2.5
METAPLAY Communications System.

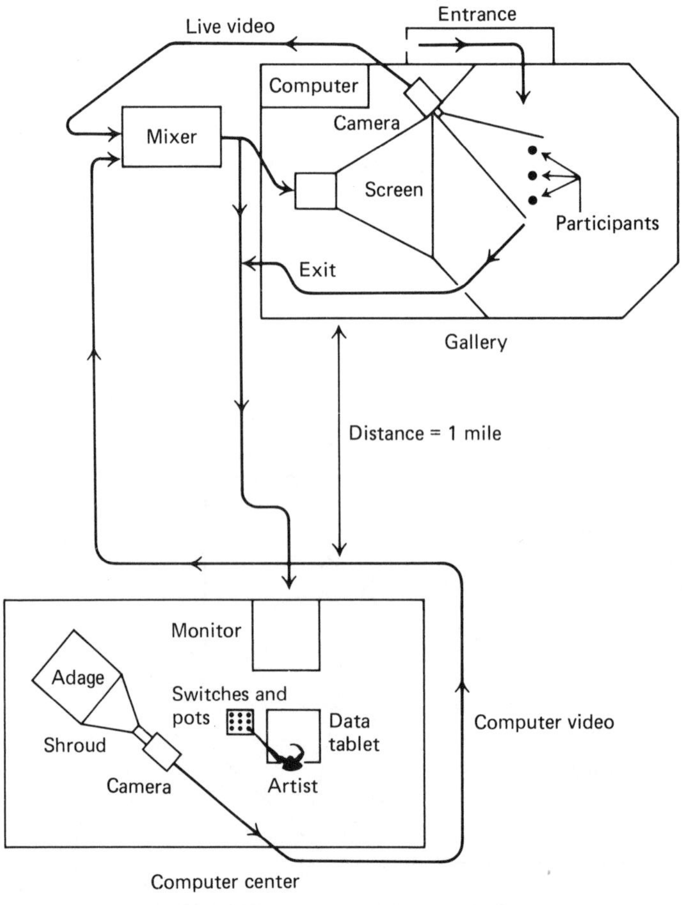

not necessarily possess recognized artistic skills. One video camera, in the university's computer center, was aimed at the display screen of a graphic display computer (manufactured by Adage Corporation). A second camera, one mile away, picked up the live image of people in the gallery. A television cable transmitted the video computer image from the computer center, where it was displayed on a video monitor to provide feedback for the artist, who could speak to the cameraman in the gallery through the audio channel associated with the video signal. She could draw on the display screen by moving the pen on the data tablet. By using buttons, switches, knobs, and a keyboard, the artist could rapidly modify the pictures generated or alter the mode of drawing itself.

The software provided a variety of techniques for defining and manipulating picture elements. Any object could be moved about the screen and changed in size. The horizontal and vertical dimensions of an object could be scaled independently of each other. One visual effect of this manipulation was an apparent rotation of the object in three dimensions. A simple set of transformations controlled by knobs yielded apparent animation of people's outlines. Finally, previously defined images could be recalled or exploded.

Although, in theory, this drawing could be done without a computer, the ability to erase, recall, transform, and animate images rapidly required considerable processing and created a far more novel means of expression than a pencil and paper could have provided.

These facilities offered a rich repertoire for an odd kind of dialogue. We tried many approaches, and new ideas cropped up throughout the duration of the show. The artist could draw on a participant's image, or could draw around it so that the participant appeared to be standing in a shower stall (Fig. 2.6). Or, she could draw a graphic door that opened when a participant touched it. Alternatively, the artist could communicate directly by writing words, or could attempt to induce the participants to play a game, such as tic-tac-toe. Finally, she could play with the act of drawing itself, as she transformed one kind of picture into another.

Live Graffiti

One type of interaction derived from the artist's ability to draw graffiti on the participant's image. In another interaction, an outline could be drawn around a person and animated so that it appeared to

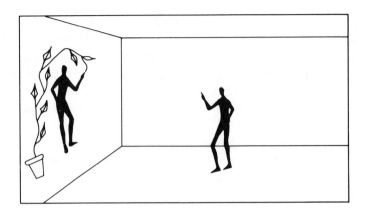

**Figure 2.6
A METAPLAY Drawing.**

dance to the music in the gallery. The drawing process proceeded with the artist trying one idea after another in an effort to involve a particular participant. If that person could not be induced to play, the artist directed the cameraman in the gallery to focus on a different person. The artist thus had control not only of the drawing, but of the camera as well.

One of the most interesting relationships came from our desire to create a way for the people in the environment to draw. An electronic wand designed for this purpose was not completed in time for the exhibit. The following serendipitous solution was perhaps preferable. On one of the first days of the show, I attempted to draw on someone's hand. He did not understand what was happening, and he moved his hand. I erased what I had drawn and started over where his hand had moved. Again, he moved. This became a game, with him moving his hand just before I finished my drawing. The game degenerated to the point where I was simply tracking the path of his hand with the computer line. Thus, by moving his hand, he could draw on the screen. This idea became the basis for many interactions.

We tried to preserve the pleasure of our original discovery for each of the people we wanted to involve in this way. After we had played some of the graffiti games with each group, we would focus on a single person. We would busily draw around the image of his hand. The reaction was usually bewilderment. After a minute or so, the increasingly self-conscious person would make a nervous gesture, such as scratching his nose. Another minute would pass with the person's hand frozen, while he pondered. Then a tentative movement of the hand. The line followed. It worked! And he was off, trying to draw. Then, other people would want to play. Using a finger, the first person would pass the line to someone else's finger, which would carry it to the next. Literally hundreds of interactive vignettes developed within this narrow communication channel.

Drawing by this method was a rough process. Pictures of any but the simplest shapes were unattainable, mainly because of the difficulty of tracking a person's finger as it moved. If it moved slowly, there was a chance that something recognizable could be drawn—otherwise, there was none. The data tablet used to put the drawing into the computer was also a low-resolution device, further frustrating real drawing. But neither the artist nor the audience was ever concerned by these limitations. What excited people was interacting in this peculiar way through a video–human–computer–video communication link spanning one mile.

The Experience

The sequence of events started with a group of six to eight people entering the darkened environment. The lights were brought up and their projected video images became visible. The typical audience reaction at this point was surprising. Often, faced by the large screen where the only active element was their own image, people would sit down and watch. Large-screen video projection was apparently undreamed of by many of the participants. We therefore allowed at least one minute for them just to appreciate the phenomenon. After they overcame their initial awe, one of the interactions would ensue. These interactions were terminated by the lights dimming and the artist writing "Good-bye" or the equivalent.

PSYCHIC SPACE: Human–Machine Interaction

PSYCHIC SPACE was exhibited in the Memorial Union Gallery during May 1971. This environment provided both a richly composed interactive vignette and an instrument for musical and visual expression. Computer-facilitated interaction among people was temporarily set aside so that I could focus on automated human–machine experiences.

PSYCHIC SPACE provided an experience quite different from that of either GLOWFLOW or METAPLAY. GLOWFLOW was a group event, and METAPLAY included the obtrusive intervention of an artist. PSYCHIC SPACE, on the other hand, was the experience of just one person with the responsive environment.

Since the reactions were private, the environment was quieter than it had been in the previous exhibits. Its moods clearly reflected the personality of the individual, rather than the spirit of a group. Since the experiences were automated, I observed less of the participants' behavior. Only one attendant stayed with the exhibit, and the attendant's role was minimal—showing people where to go, answering a few questions, and restarting the computer from time to time. I often left one of my children— they were five and six years old at the time—in charge. These tots, lurking in the dark of the gallery and apparently competent with computers, set an eerie tone for visitors and became a part of the piece. Computers truly were child's play. I often overheard people in the student union talking about "these incredible kids who were running a computer show in the gallery."

The environment constructed within the gallery was larger than the space used for METAPLAY. It was large enough to run in, yet still small enough to provide intimacy with all displays (Fig. 2.7). The floor, walls, and ceiling were covered with black polyethylene. One end of the room was dominated by a rear-projection screen; the other was painted with a phosphorescent pigment. The floor was divided into a sensing grid of six

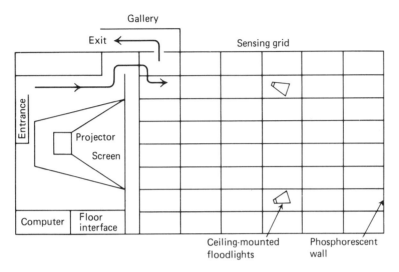

Figure 2.7
The PSYCHIC SPACE Floorplan.

rows of eight two-foot by four-foot modules. Each module was covered with black plastic. Visually, this arrangement was very effective, with its suggestion of function and the repetition of modular design (Fig. 2.8). These modules contained pressure sensors that detected participants'

Figure 2.8
Floor Sensing Modules in PSYCHIC SPACE.

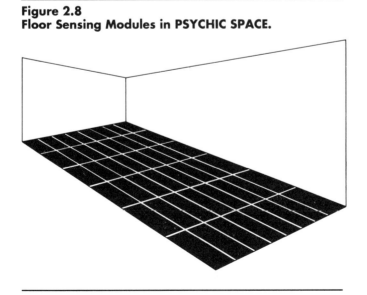

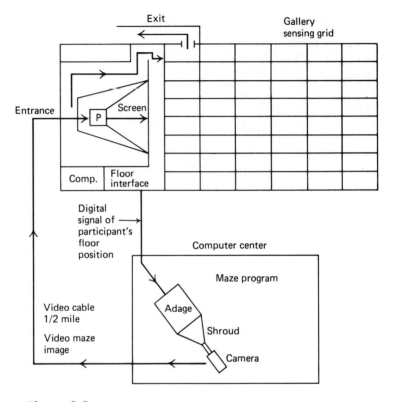

Figure 2.9
The Data and Video Communications System for PSYCHIC SPACE.

footsteps as they moved around the room. The sensing grid comprised 24 rows by 16 switches. Position information from the floor was the basis for all the interactions.

A PDP-11 in the gallery scanned the floor, transmitted the participants' position to the Adage graphic display computer in the computer center, and used a Moog synthesizer to generate audio responses to the participant's movements. The graphic image created by the Adage was again transmitted to the gallery and was rear-projected into the responsive environment (Fig. 2.9).

Interactive Composition—The MAZE Experience

The MAZE experience was a highly variable interactive vignette shown in the PSYCHIC SPACE installation. Its purpose was to demonstrate a carefully composed sequence of relations that would result in a coherent experience. It was a finished piece in the artistic sense. It focused completely on one person's interaction with the environment. The experience consisted of navigating a maze (projected on the screen) by moving around the room. A participant's interest was piqued by the computer's responses to her efforts to walk through the maze.

During the MAZE experience, the PSYCHIC SPACE environment was totally dark, with the exception of a rear-projected graphic symbol that moved when the participant moved. People noticed this relationship quickly, as there was nothing else happening. If you moved to the left, it moved to the left. If you moved right, so did your symbol. If you walked toward the screen, it moved down; if you walked away from the screen, it moved up.

This initial exploration was a training period during which participants learned the relationship between their movements and the movements of their symbol. After a couple of minutes, a square appeared on the screen. Virtually everyone wondered about the function of this new symbol and walked over to get acquainted.

When the person's symbol reached the square, the square disappeared and a maze appeared; the participant's symbol was at the maze's entrance. In fact, the purpose of the square was to induce the participant to move to the starting point of the maze. This expedient allowed us to avoid writing a more complicated program that could have generated a maze with an entrance wherever the participant happened to be (Fig. 2.10).

Confronted with the MAZE, no one questioned the inevitability of walking through it. (An observation that undoubtedly reflects on our educational system.) Because the corridors of the MAZE were small relative to the size of the room, the participant had to take very small steps to navigate them. Participants minced up and down and across the room, intent on their efforts to solve the puzzle. Then, after a few minutes of taking tiny steps, participants would realize that there were no physical constraints in the room. In fact, there was nothing to prevent cheating. So, most people began to cheat. Often with great ceremony, they would lift

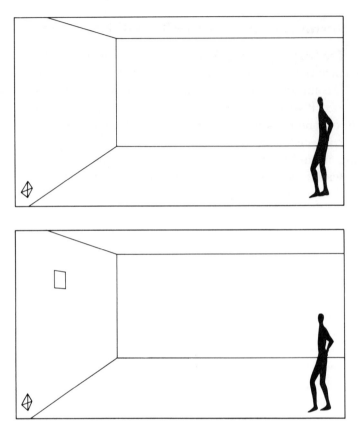

Figure 2.10
The MAZE Experience in PSYCHIC SPACE.

a foot and place it on the other side of a boundary. At this moment, the real MAZE experience began. We had anticipated the cheating response and had composed numerous gambits to thwart it.

The first time a participant tried to cross a boundary line, it would stretch elastically, keeping the participant's symbol enclosed. Later, the line would disappear, removing a barrier, but the rest of the MAZE would change simultaneously, eliminating the apparent advantage. Next, the person's symbol would split in half at the violated boundary, with one half remaining stationary while the other half, the alter ego, continued to follow movement. However, no progress could be made until the halves of the symbol were reunited at the violated

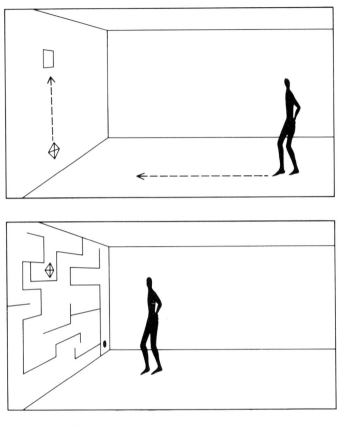

Figure 2.10
continued

boundary. At another point, the whole MAZE would move so that the participant's symbol appeared to push it off the screen. In all, there were about 20 different moves the computer would use to retaliate if the participant cheated.

Even when the participant was moving legally, changes were made in the program contingent on her position in the MAZE. Several times, as the goal was approached, the MAZE changed to prevent immediate success. Or, the relationship between the floor and the MAZE was altered, so that movements that once resulted in vertical motion now resulted in horizontal motion. Alternatively, the MAZE could be moved while the symbol representing the participant was kept stationary.

Ultimately, success was prohibited. When the participant finally seemed about to reach the goal, additional boundaries appeared in front of and behind the symbol, boxing it in. At this point, the MAZE slowly shrank to nothing. Although the goal could not be reached, the composed frustration made the route interesting. (Allowing the participant to succeed seemed anticlimactic and out of keeping with the perverse humor behind the piece.)

The MAZE experience induced a unique set of feelings. The video display created a sense of detachment enhanced by the displaced feedback; movement on the horizontal plane of the floor translated onto the vertical plane of the screen. The popular stereotype of dehumanizing technology seemed fulfilled. However, the MAZE idea was engaging, and people became involved willingly. The lack of any other sensation focused their attention completely on this interaction. As the experience progressed, their perception of the MAZE changed. From the initial impression that it was a problem to solve, they moved to the realization that the MAZE was a vehicle for whimsy, playing with the concept of a maze and poking fun at their compulsion to walk through it.

The Environment as a Musical Instrument

The floor in PSYCHIC SPACE had a dual role. In addition to reporting the location of a person walking the MAZE, it also was used as the keyboard of a musical instrument that the participants could play by moving around the room.

When a person entered the room, the computer automatically responded to his footsteps with electronic sound. We experimented with a number of different schemes for generating the sounds based on an analysis of people's footsteps. In studying the floor data, we discovered that a single footstep consisted of as may as four discrete events: lifting the heel, lifting the toe, putting down the heel, and putting down the ball of the foot. We called the first two the *unfootstep*. We could respond to each footstep or unfootstep as it occurred, or we could respond to the person's average position. We tried a number of response schemes; the most pleasing was to start each tone only at the beginning of a footstep, and then to terminate it on the next unfootstep. Thus, it was possible to cause silence by jumping, or by lifting one foot, or by putting both feet down together.

A participant's typical reaction to the sounds was instant under-standing, followed by a rapid-fire sequence of steps, jumps, and rolls. This phase was followed by a slower and more thoughtful exploration of the environment, in which more subtle and interesting relationships could be developed. In the second phase, the participant discovered that the room was organized with high notes at one end and low notes at the other. After a while, the keyboard was abruptly rotated 90 degrees, challenging what the participant had learned.

Although the sounds generated by the participants' footsteps were not complex, we observed a variety of styles. The differences in the sounds reflected the differing natures of the participants. Some people seemed to want to cause as many different sounds as possible. Other people would tire audibly and then rest silently. Others would try to pick out a tune, which was difficult. Occasionally, quite distinctive sounds would emerge, prompting me to investigate their source. A few times, very monotonous sequences of tones signalled someone who was totally unimpressed by the sound responses, or perhaps was deaf to them. These people just walked as they would anywhere else. Thus, there was no intelligent relationship between one sound and the next. One time, I heard an extremely atypical pattern of single notes, separated by long pauses. I found an Asian monk. He would take a step, stop to ponder its consequences and, only after some delay, take another. He professed to be quite moved by his experience.

On another occasion, pleasant bubbling sounds greeted me as I returned to the gallery. I learned from the people who had been looking after the exhibit that an attractive couple was dancing together. When they came out, we asked for an encore.

Conclusion

During the PSYCHIC SPACE exhibit, we gained a better feeling for the mechanics of putting on an automated show, of getting people in and out of it, and of minimizing the amount of verbal instruction required. At the same time, we had some misgivings about the workability of this type of exhibit, which inevitably attracted more people than it could handle. Even without any publicity, METAPLAY and PSYCHIC SPACE always had long lines of people waiting to participate. As a result, we had to gear the experience to handle the crowds, making it shorter and allowing more people in at one time. Since the MAZE experience lasted about 15 minutes, we had to use it sparingly. But this restriction compromised the whole point of the work: personal interaction with an environment. So, I became interested in creating an ongoing facility in which the conceptual, compositional, and technical aspects of responsive environments could evolve.

3

VIDEOPLACE

Introduction

VIDEOPLACE had its origin in an incident that occurred during METAPLAY. Digital signals from the computer in the gallery were being transmitted to the graphics display in the computer center. Since both machines had a graphics capability, one displayed the wave-form being sent, and the other displayed the information being received.

At first, I talked over the telephone with a colleague in the gallery about the displays we each had in front of us. However, after a few minutes of frustrating discussion, I realized that we had a far more powerful means of communication available. Using the two-way video link, we turned the gallery camera on the computer screen there. The computer-center camera was already aimed at the graphics machine. Both of us could now see a composite image juxtaposing the information being sent with that being received (Fig. 3.1). We discussed the two signals and speculated about the source of our transmission errors. As we did this, it was natural to use our hands to point to various features on the composite display. The resulting conversation was exactly the same as it would have been had we been sitting together at a table with a piece of paper between us.

After a while, I realized that I was seeing more than an illusion. As I moved my finger to point to the data my colleague had just sent, the image of my hand briefly overlapped the image of his. He moved his hand. Although I noticed this phenomenon, its significance did not register immediately. When it happened again, however, I was struck with the thought that he was uncomfortable about our images touching. Without saying anything, I subtely tested my hypothesis. Sure enough, as I moved the image of my hand toward his, he repeatedly, but unconsciously, moved his hand to avoid contact. I even felt a phantom sensation when we touched. Although his reactions were exaggerated and even bizarre, he never noticed my actions or his. The inescapable conclusion was that the etiquette of maintaining personal distance and avoiding touching that exists in the real world was operating at that moment in this purely visual experience.

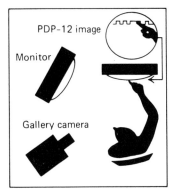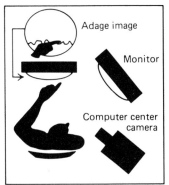

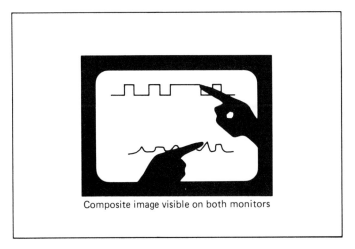

Composite image visible on both monitors

Figure 3.1
Video Communications Link.

VIDEOTOUCH

We experimented after exhibit hours with what I dubbed VIDEOTOUCH, and confirmed that indeed there was a powerful effect operating. In 1972, I submitted a proposal for a two-way installation titled "VIDEOTOUCH" to the National Endowment for the Arts. The piece was to consist of two environments, each containing a rear-screen video projection of a composite image of two participants. A single participant would

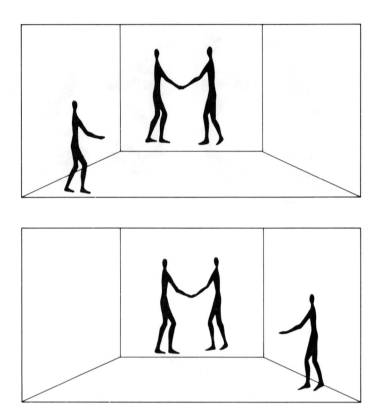

Figure 3.2
The Computer Detects Contact Between the Video Images of Two Participants.

enter each of the separate environments, and each screen would display both of the people's video images (Fig. 3.2). If their images chanced to touch, sound would be generated. The nature of the sounds was to depend on where the images touched. Thus, two strangers would be placed in a situation where their normal embarrassment about touching would be in conflict with their desire to explore this unexpected way of interacting.

VIDEOPLACE: The Concept

The experience during METAPLAY had demonstrated that two people who saw their images juxtaposed would interact as though they were actually together. We also observed that people feel at least some of the same self-consciousness about their images that they feel about their bodies. Later experimentation convinced me that people have a proprietary feeling about their image. What happens to it, happens to them. What touches it, they feel. When another person's image encounters theirs, a new kind of social situation is created.

Over the next two years, the concept of VIDEOTOUCH matured as I realized its broader implications. Whereas we usually think of telecommunication as being between two points, a new premise evolved: Two-way telecommunication between two places creates a third place consisting of the information that is available to both communicating parties simultaneously (Fig. 3.3). When two-way video is used, a shared visual environment that we call VIDEOPLACE is created.

The idea of a video "place" led me to consider the characteristics of a real place and how they could be reproduced or replaced by alternatives in a video environment. If two people are together, they can see, hear, and touch each other. They can move about the same visual environment, seeing the same objects. They can manipulate objects and hand them to each other. Finally, they can share an activity, such as dining together.

We can embellish the sense of place by providing a graphic setting furnished with graphic objects and inhabited by graphic creatures (PLATE B). The ultimate consequence is an artificial reality experienced through the participation of one's video image in the portrayed world. Although it was conceived in the context of two-way communication, VIDEOPLACE can also be used to stage interactions involving a single participant. By suggesting, but not duplicating, familiar reality, this new graphic

**Figure 3.3
The VIDEOPLACE Concept.**

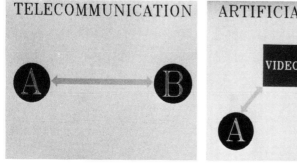

experience can highlight assumptions and expectations of which we are never aware, because it does not occur to us that our world could be other than it is.

The computer has complete control over the relationship between the participant's image and the objects in the graphic scene (Fig. 3.4). It can also tell when images and objects make contact, and can coordinate the movement of a graphic object with a participant's actions (Fig 3.5). Thus, the participant's video alter ego is able to lift, push, or throw an

---

Figure 3.4
Occlusion by a Graphic Object.

Figure 3.5
The Computer Detects Contact Between the Participant's
Image and a Generated Object.

object or creature across the screen (Fig. 3.6). One person can lift another's image. He can press down on the image of another person's head and make that person's image shrink under the pressure. A participant in New York could toss a ball to a Californian (Fig. 3.7). The moment an object responds to a participant's touch, both the object and the experience become real.

The world VIDEOPLACE simulates need not be a real one. Unlike the real world, VIDEOPLACE is not governed by immutable physical laws. Gravity may control your physical body, but it need not confine your image, which can float freely about the screen (PLATE A). You can use special gestures simulating flying, swimming, or climbing to maneuver your image around the displayed world (Fig. 3.8). The consequence of any action is programmable. When you push against a graphic object, the

Figure 3.6
Picking Up a Graphic Object.

computer can choose to move the object or to move you. Stamping your feet can cause flowers to grow or volcanoes to erupt.

Although VIDEOPLACE cannot literally duplicate the fullness of the real world, it invents a new model of reality with methods of interacting

Figure 3.7
Three-Way Catch in VIDEOPLACE.

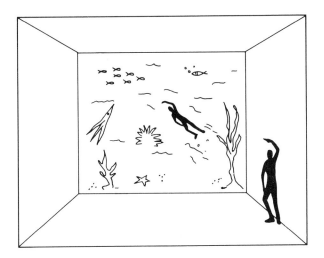

Figure 3.8
Swimming in VIDEOPLACE.

that are equally compelling. Thus, although some aspects of reality are abridged in VIDEOPLACE, others are enhanced, since many of the constraints and limitations of reality can be overcome. Interactions within the environment are based on a quest to understand the rules that govern this new universe. A person's expectations can be teased, leading to a startled awareness of previously unquestioned assumptions, much like the experience one has when viewing a Magritte painting.

VIDEOPLACE: The Bicentennial Experience

Starting in July 1974, VIDEOPLACE was proposed as the theme of the United States Bicentennial celebration, updating the Centennial project that had introduced the telephone to the public.

People would enter VIDEOPLACE from installations distributed around the world. Each participant would see her image join a group of other participants' images to form a single composite image (Fig. 3.9), or she might see part of a much larger graphic space in which she could move around, encountering other people from other locations. The natural greeting was expected to be, "Hello, where are you?"

Figure 3.9
The Bicentennial Mosaic.

In addition, VIDEOPLACE was to be used to hold panel discussions among participants in different states. I planned dance pieces with dancers thousands of miles apart, the choreography for which existed only on the video screen. Note that such a performance would be pure video; there would be no physical place a person could go to "really" see it. In addition to these more contrived and formal events, the VIDEOPLACE was also to provide a facility for ongoing exploration of a new kind of play by serious artists and serious children of all ages.

In July 1974, I traveled to Washington to seek support for the Bicentennial project. High-level administrators at the National Science Foundation (NSF) expressed considerable appreciation for the ideas; however, as I descended to the lower-level offices from which specific projects were funded, I encountered a different reaction. The people in computer science turned up their noses and said, "that sounds like engineering." They cited automata theory as an example of a viable research area. Another person in NSF, who thought the ideas were important, told me point blank but with great sympathy that NSF would never fund VIDEOPLACE because the idea was "creative." This was the first of many exposures to that word as a pejorative term. At the Defense

Advanced Research Projects Agency (DARPA), I was told that human–machine interaction "had been done." NASA told me that their satellite was beaming birth-control messages down to India, but there was another satellite that I could use—if I could get it launched.

My last stop in Washington was the one place I was absolutely certain would react enthusiastically—the Japanese Embassy. (I was proposing that VIDEOPLACE include an installation in Japan and one in Europe.) The Embassy representative was sure that, if I could get the United States committed, Japan would want to be involved. Other stops on that trip included Bell Laboratories, RCA Laboratories, and IBM. The result of this trip was a clear indication that there would be no ambitious projects inspired by the Bicentennial.

Although VIDEOPLACE was not implemented on an international scale, an exhibit introducing the VIDEOPLACE concept was shown at the Milwaukee Art Museum in 1975. Two environments with rear-screen video projections were placed 300 feet apart. A person entering either environment saw his own image combined with the image of the people in the other environment. Strangers finding their images together often invented pantomime interactions. Mock battles were staged, backs were scratched, and remote partners danced.

For the next four years, I worked under an arrangement with the University of Wisconsin Space Science and Engineering Center by which I did computer graphics research for them and was provided laboratory and office space to work on VIDEOPLACE and to seek funding for it. As a result, I received grants from the National Endowment for the Arts and the Wisconsin Arts Board. I worked on VIDEOPLACE nights and weekends for the next four years; by 1976, I had a primitive working prototype with enough real-time perception to demonstrate a few simple visual interactions.

In 1978, I joined the Computer Science Department at the University of Connecticut. I brought the working VIDEOPLACE system with me from Wisconsin. At Connecticut, I improved the graphics and composed a number of interactions. In 1985, I left the university; I have been independent since.

Installation

In the VIDEOPLACE installation, the participant faces a video-projection screen that displays his live image combined with computer graphics. A large sheet of translucent plastic behind the participant is backlit by

Figure 3.10
The VIDEOPLACE Installation.

fluorescent tubes, producing a high-contrast image that enables the computer to distinguish the participant from the background. The projection screen is about 20 feet away from the participant. The projector is driven by separate red, green, and blue (RGB) signals, instead of by a single composite signal, which means that it displays much sharper colors than those seen on a home television, which uses NTSC encoding (see Glossary). A black-and-white surveillance camera looks at the participant from beneath the projection screen (Fig 3.10).

The VIDEOPLACE System

Each participant's video image is digitized and is fed to a series of specialized processors that analyzes the resulting silhouettes. These processors analyze each image in isolation (e.g., posture, rate of movement) and with respect to graphic objects and live images on the screen. (For example, is the participant touching the graphic light switch? Has her image reached a graphic door?)

When the participant's actions are understood by the specialized processors, they are reported to the executive processor that decides what the responses should be. Depending on the participant's behavior, it can move an object, change that object's color, move the participant's image, or make a sound. Another set of specialized processors is then directed to generate visual and auditory responses.

Two or more environments can be linked, with the addition of a little extra hardware. Each participant's image must be analyzed separately and then compared to the other graphic objects and human images on the screen. In addition, each input image requires a separate transformation processor to shrink or rotate it. Two environments demand that more complex decisions be made, but the basic operation of the system is unaffected.

VIDEOPLACE Art

Many interactions have been created in the VIDEOPLACE framework. Since this is a new medium, it should be explored and its essence sought. Indeed, the goal should be to express the medium itself.

To communicate the wealth of opportunity that interactivity provides, we have always presented VIDEOPLACE as a medium within which interactions have been composed in a variety of styles, rather than as a single piece. Although the result may seem disjointed visually, the interactions are connected conceptually. Some of them are studies. Whereas in the past artists did studies for their own consumption, in an interactive art form it is necessary to exhibit studies as well as finished pieces in order to observe how people react to them.

Since there are many interactions and the exhibit is usually unattended, a rationale is needed for switching from one interaction to another. The computer could switch interactions arbitrarily, but this technique would not be in keeping with my notion that nothing should happen in an interactive medium unless it is a response to some action by the participant. Instead, the current interaction continues until the participant leaves. A new interaction is selected when the next person enters. This principle is discoverable, and often one person will step off the screen and reenter over and over to experience a number of interactions. However, it is not necessary or even desirable for every person to see all the interactions. Indeed, as we near 50 compositions, it is becoming impossible. The enlarging repertoire is an intentional statement about the rich potential of the medium.

Interactions

The current interactions are based on a variety of themes and motivations. Some are visually beautiful and provide a link to traditional aesthetics. Other interactions introduce the ingredients of artificial realities one at a time, to see how people relate each one. A final category of interaction involves a real-time dialog between two people in different environments.

CRITTER

One of the most popular interactions traces its origins back to METAPLAY. As I moved the cursor around the screen, I noticed that people reacted to it as though it were alive, batting it away when it approached them. This observation led to the creation of the CRITTER, a playful sprite with an artificial personality.

CRITTER's general behaviour is to cavort with you, chasing your image around the screen (Fig. 3.11; PLATE 3). If you hold out a hand, CRITTER will float down and land on it. If you stand still, CRITTER's ambition is to climb up your silhouette until it reaches the top of your head, where it does a jig in celebration. At other moments, CRITTER chases an open hand or dangles from an outstretched finger. After seeing thousands of people try to capture CRITTER with their hands, we made it sense when it is surrounded, search pathetically for an exit, and explode if there is no escape. Happily, reincarnation is instantaneous. The current CRITTER interaction was completed in 1984, but CRITTER's evolution is resuming to take advantage of new animation techniques we have developed that will, in turn, require high-resolution graphics.

The original CRITTER had already evolved over a period of years. Thousands of hours of work went into its creation and behaviour. John Rinaldi, Bruce Shay, Thomas Gionfriddo, and Katrin Hinrichsen did their masters' theses on problems surrounding its implementation. Many boards were built to provide the information needed for CRITTER to behave in real time. An elaborate software system was developed to permit rules of behaviour to be described in Conceptual Dependency Notation, a knowledge representation developed by Roger Schank at Yale to understand English. Thus, although CRITTER is not yet intelligent, its implementation employs artificial-intelligence techniques.

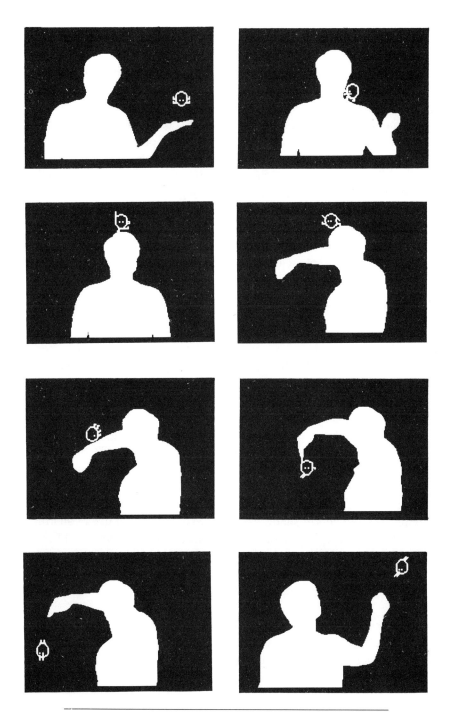

Figure 3.11
A CRITTER Sequence.

INDIVIDUAL MEDLEY

The next class of interactions is purely visual. Each is a restricted aesthetic medium that can be composed through body movements. In fact, your body becomes a means of creating art. The goal of these interactions is to communicate the pleasure of aesthetic creation. Since these media are unfamiliar, dwelling as they do on dynamic images controlled by movements of the viewers' bodies, artists trained in traditional static media have no automatic advantage in creating pleasing results.

Each of the INDIVIDUAL MEDLEY interactions captures your eight most recent silhouettes and colors them according to how they overlap on the screen (PLATE E). Each method of assigning color constitutes a distinct interaction and leads to different behavior by the participants. If each new silhouette is placed on top of the others, the result suggests a political poster. If one silhouette is used as a matte, succeeding silhouettes break the person's image into a jigsaw-puzzle pattern.

Each of these interactions has its own idiom. A person's work changes over time as she sees the effect of her actions on the visual patterns. I can often tell how long a participant has been in the environment, whether he will stay in long, and whether it matters how long he stays. Some people do not listen to what their experience is telling them. They move their arms in a herky-jerky manner, rather than synchronizing their movements with the rhythm of the current feedback relationship. Since the visual results are dynamic, a participant creates feedback for himself only as long as he keeps moving. The moment he stops, his past catches up with him. If he does nothing, he sees nothing.

BODY SURFACING

In the BODY SURFACING interactions, the participant's image paints continuously as it moves about the screen. The colors that are applied by the participant's body shade from one to another. The use of shading provides a sense of depth, defining beautiful metallic surfaces (PLATE 9). As these surfaces are defined, colors flow along them in the direction of the participant's movement. This interaction is so peaceful that it suggests an active form of meditation.

REPLAY

Another visual interaction stems from the image-capture capability used in the INDIVIDUAL MEDLEY interactions. When a stationary participant starts moving, the system captures a sequence of 16 silhouettes, and then plays them back. The instant REPLAY is continuous. If you have watched sequences of satellite images repeated several times on television, you may have noticed a lurch when the last image of the sequence is followed by the first image. To avoid this problem, the sequences are played forward, then back, then forward, and so on. The result is smoothly continuous motion. No one ever notices that the sequence reverses.

One typical response to this interaction is that a person enters, sees her silhouette mirroring her actions, and assumes that nothing else is going to happen. When her entrance is repeated, she pauses, confused. When she realizes what is happening, she does a doubletake. This action triggers another capture. The doubletake is repeated endlessly. There is something about a single gesture being repeated over and over that makes the gesture seem absurd.

FRACTAL

One day the system started making complex geometric patterns that changed as the participant moved (PLATE H). There was clearly some sort of hardware problem. Rather than fix it, I spent several weeks understanding why a loose wire created a dynamic fractal pattern. The colored silhouettes of the participant were mapped into the patterns in complex ways. Once I understood the process, I realized that this occurrence was just one instance of a whole family of fractal patterns. The simplest of these were incorporated into a special board devoted to the FRACTAL interaction. As movements of the body control elements of the visual FRACTAL pattern, we have also defined pleasing sounds that are controlled by the participant's hands to enhance the experience.

This interaction is not one I would have created on purpose, since abstract geometric patterns are not as involving as your own image. However, when the medium spoke so directly, I thought that it would be ungrateful not to listen.

Minimedia Family of Interactions

Each member of another family of interactions creates images that suggest a familiar style of art. In the BROADWAY BOOGIE WOOGIE interaction, the participant creates images reminiscent of Mondrian's work. Dynamic rectangular shapes are arranged around the participant's invisible silhouette. In a related interaction, the participant's movements create circles, triangles, rectangles, and polygons that are superimposed over the participant's body. Each area where the shapes overlap the participant's image or each other is colored in a way that is also controlled by the person's movements. The visual results are often stylish high-tech designs.

GAME OF LIFE
The GAME OF LIFE is an interaction featuring audio as well as visual effects. Your image is filled with little cells that divide, move around, and die helter skelter. This animated pattern is a bit of technological culture. The pattern is a simple mathematical game developed by British mathematician John Conway years ago. Every point on the screen looks at its immediately adjacent neighbors to see whether they are dead or alive. If exactly two of them are alive, the cell remains in its current state. If exactly three neighbors are alive, the cell comes to life regardless of its previous state. In all other cases, the cell dies.

This game is known to most technophiles. It is not the Bible or Shakespeare, but it is a bond of shared understanding within this community. Many students were given the GAME OF LIFE as an early programming assignment. A conventional computer can generate a new generation about once per second. Computers are faster than humans at many tasks, but when there are 64,000 points on the screen and the rules described must be applied to every one of them, the typical personal computer is overwhelmed by the sheer number of points. A technical person, knowing this, is knocked out when he sees this algorithm being applied at 60 generations per second. We have had it running at 357 generations per second! However, at that rate, the patterns looked more like a flickering flame than like discrete particles, so we slowed it down.

DIGITAL DRAWING
The next family of interactions give the participant explicit control over a simple medium. In DIGITAL DRAWING, a participant can draw on the video screen using the image of her finger (PLATE 4). This interaction is the automated version of the drawing process that was discovered in METAPLAY in 1970. If several people are in the environment, each is assigned a different color. Early in the evolution of this interaction, we noticed that people waved their hands over their drawings when they wanted to

erase them. Since we made this observation, VIDEOPLACE has interpreted an open hand as a command to erase the screen. To participants, it is a delightful affirmation of humanity to find that a bit of magic that they wanted was anticipated and made part of this new universe. Participants can erase selectively by "rubbing" two fingers held close together over a part of the image.

DIGITAL DRAWING is an extremely successful interaction. It is somehow liberating to be able to draw on a screen across the room without holding anything. It is a pleasure to be able to erase the screen so totally, so immaculately. That the experience has scale is also important. Drawing on a wall-sized screen is very different from drawing on a piece of paper or a monitor.

FINGER PAINTING

FINGER PAINTING is a variation on the drawing interaction (PLATE F). The image of each finger creates a stream of flowing paint. As in FRACTAL, the participant's image is not shown on the screen in this interaction. The painted image looks more attractive without the intrusion of the silhouette. However, the participant's control of the painting process suffers when he cannot see his image.

VIDEOSYNCRASY

VIDEOSYNCRASY is another variation on the drawing theme. Your finger traces an invisible path traveled by pulses of light that have a decaying tail. Particles follow the path, accelerating and decelerating along its length. Since new particles start the path at fixed intervals, there is a tendency to synchronize the current drawing process with the particles that are visible. By timing the act of drawing appropriately, you can create a unified rhythmic pattern. To accomplish this effect, you consciously rock back and forth as you draw, synchronizing your movements with the pattern you have drawn so far.

VIDIOCY

Another playful interaction that provides direct control is VIDIOCY. Each finger can be used to fire a graphic bullet that travels across the screen and explodes when it hits another person (Fig. 3.12). The visual effect is quite comic. We always show this interaction when people ask about military applications.

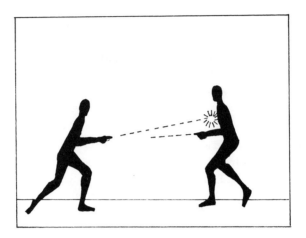

Figure 3.12
A VIDIOCY Interaction.

CAT'S CRADLE

CAT'S CRADLE lets you play with graphic string. A graphic curve appears on the screen, attracted by your fingertips in the image (Fig. 3.13). The curve adapts to the movements of the fingers, no matter how fast the fingers appear and disappear. The effect is exactly the same as it would

Figure 3.13
A CAT'S CRADLE Interaction.

 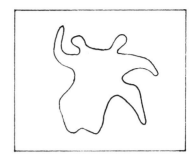

Figure 3.14
One and Two Person SPLINEMAN Configurations.

be were you playing with graphic string—except that there is nothing there. Three or four people will often cooperate to control the curve. More fingers create more complex shapes.

SPLINEMAN

SPLINEMAN gives you a new graphic body. A graphic curve is loosely fitted to the outline of your silhouette (Fig 3.14). That curve then becomes your body. As you move, you discover the possible shapes this form can attain. The result is like shadow play. Your new body is essentially a puppet. If two people are in the environment and their images overlap, both of them are wrapped in a single curve. The resulting shape loses its human origins. The effect is much like two children playing under a blanket.

One day, during an exhibit at the Computer–Human Interaction Conference, I came into VIDEOPLACE to find two researchers lying on the floor with their feet up in the air. They were making a W. As I watched, they performed X, Y, and Z. I had missed the rest of the alphabet. I then recognized one of them as Scott Kim, known for his creative calligraphy and word play, author of *Inversions* [1].

Transformations of Human Images

The next class of interactions frees your image from the constraint of gravity. As noted earlier, your image can be moved, scaled, and rotated in real time. If your image fills the screen, there is a limited number of relationships that you can enter into with graphic objects or graphic creatures. On the other hand, if your image is small, you are free to move around the screen. You can hide under graphic objects, float over them, or play with CRITTER on equal terms.

HUMAN CRITTER

The oldest interaction in this genre is HUMAN CRITTER. Your image is reduced to one-tenth of its normal size. You fly your image about the screen by pointing your hand in the direction you want to go.

After one minute of erratic flight, a box appears at the bottom of the screen. The intent of the box, like the second symbol that appeared during the MAZE interaction in PSYCHIC SPACE, is to lure you into landing on it. Although the attraction is not as strong, participants usually land on the box in a short time.

When you alight, your image starts to grow. Your new body consists of your original image and its mirror image reflected downward (Fig. 3.15). After spending a few moments exploring the behavior of your new body, you discover that you can use the hands of the reflected image like feet. If you raise your hands, the image of your reflected arms lengthens and pushes against the graphic platform, elevating your body.

After further experimentation, you discover that raising your hands rapidly propels your body off the box. You can jump in the air and

Figure 3.15
A HUMAN CRITTER Interaction.

Figure 3.16
The Rockettes.

descend back to the box under simulated moon gravity. During the slow descent, you can twist and turn, posing your vertically reflected body.

On your fifth jump, the launching pad disappears, and a new platform appears on your left. When you reach this new stage, a host of new images joins you. They hold hands with one another to form a chorus line—the Rockettes. Each of these silhouettes is from an earlier moment in time. Your movements ripple down the line in true Busby Berkeley fashion (Fig. 3.16).

MANDALA

In MANDALA, seven copies of your silhouette are arranged in a circular pattern on the screen. The left edge of one silhouette is joined to the right edge of the adjacent one, creating a pattern that initially appears to be abstract (Fig 3.17). Movements of your limbs are repeated simultaneously all around the pattern. Raising an arm causes a concentric movement from the outside to the inside of the MANDALA. The size of the circular pattern changes as you move. The resulting kaleidoscopic medium can captivate people for an hour. Participants often move smoothly in and out of awkward postures that suggest they are doing Tai Chi in free-fall.

Skiing

By shrinking your image, we can place you in a graphic scene. Although it would be trivial to create an elaborate setting in which interactions can

**Figure 3.17
MANDALA.**

occur, our informal rule has been to put nothing on the screen with which participants cannot interact. Creating a truly interactive setting is a more difficult problem. One simple example that has been implemented in VIDEOPLACE places your silhouette on graphic skis at the top of a graphic mountain (Fig. 3.18). To maintain your equilibrium, you must bend your knees and control your center of gravity. If you do this when you hit the jump, you take off and land smoothly. If you fail to bend your knees, you wipe out, and end up rolling down the hill.

VIDEODESK ↔ VIDEOPLACE Teleconference
One fundamental ingredient in the original METAPLAY exhibit and in the Bicentennial Proposal was telecommunication. In 1987, I became nostalgic for the personal contact between the artist and audience that METAPLAY had required. There was a nice amateur feeling about METAPLAY. Much of what happened was unexpected, discovered jointly by the artist and participants.

In METAPLAY, human intelligence stood in for future computer intelligence. It seemed time to use human intelligence again, to control the sophisticated computer reflexes that were now part of VIDEOPLACE.

A second VIDEOPLACE environment had been created so that we could continue development while the first system was being exhibited. Since we had only one video projector, this second environment was

Figure 3.18
To Ski or Not To Ski.

limited. It consisted of a light table with a camera mounted above and aimed down at the table's surface (Fig 3.19). If you rested your hands on the table, their image appeared on a monitor in front of you.

When the exhibit system returned, it was natural to connect the two systems together so that the giant image of one person's hands was juxtaposed with the image of the other person's body, which could be full screen or scaled down in size. By itself, this visual effect was interesting. Many of the VIDEOPLACE interactions can be shared by the people in the two environments. They can play with CRITTER or CAT'S CRADLE. They can cooperate on a drawing. Without instruction, people pick up tricks that they see the other person use.

Figure 3.19
The VIDEODESK Installation.

To date, the person at the VIDEODESK has been an informed participant who understands the system. There is a menu of interactions from which to choose, operated by VIDEOTOUCH. The person at the VIDEODESK plays hostess to the participants in the VIDEOPLACE environment.

Our purpose in putting human intelligence in control of the computer reflexes was to force ourselves to focus on issues such as choosing new interactions intelligently, timing novel responses, teaching the other participant about the interactions, and seeing whether a vaudevillian sense of humor could be conveyed interactively. Just as we later automated the decisions we made during METAPLAY, we plan to use this experience to improve the intelligence of the system.

TICKLE

TICKLE dates back to the 1972 "VIDEOTOUCH" proposal submitted to the National Endowment for the Arts. If a person in one environment touches the person in the other environment with a finger, the computer responds with a sound—the more fingers, the more sounds. Each person sounds different when touched. This interaction often becomes quite comical as people realize what is happening.

MAN-IPULATE and TELECISION

In MAN-IPULATE, the giant hand of the VIDEODESK operator reaches in and pushes the VIDEOPLACE participant's image across the screen. After a moment, the participant typically resists, pushing back and then punching. A full-scale battle often ensues. At some point, the hand pokes the participant in the face. The participant's image tips over and pops up again. This punch line gets a genuine laugh, suggesting a whole new avenue of VIDEOPLACE interaction and performance (Fig. 3.20).

Figure 3.20
A MAN-IPULATE Interaction.

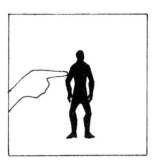

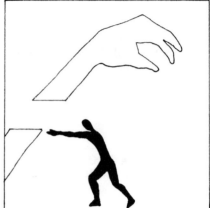

Figure 3.21
A TELECISION Interaction.

A moment later, the situation is repeated, but this time, when the participant touches the giant hand, he lops it off, sending it spinning off the screen. This interaction was put in to maintain the balance of power between the two environments (Fig 3.21).

BALLOONACY
Another series of interactions revolves around the idea of throwing and catching. In BALLOONACY, every motion of the participant's hands causes a ball to appear and travel in the direction of that motion. If the participant tries to throw to a particular location, one of the balls will go there. The purpose of this phase of the interaction is to introduce the idea of throwing. Gradually, fewer balls are created, until only a single ball appears with each throwing motion.

At this point, the giant hand appears. The participant throws a ball toward it. The hand extends a finger. The ball orbits around it and proceeds back to the thrower, who discovers that he also can attract the ball with his hand and accelerate it smoothly back toward the hand. After a few minutes of this play, the VIDEODESK hand positions itself with four fingers extended vertically so that they appear as one in silhouette (Fig. 3.22). The thumb is opened to the left, making a basket and inviting the participant to shoot. When thrown, the ball hits the upright fingers and bounces off the backboard they form. It then bounces on the thumb and back to the backboard before sinking in between thumb and forefinger

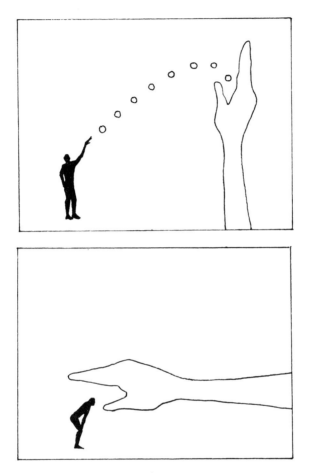

Figure 3.22
A BALLOONACY Interaction.

for a score. Actually, no points are awarded. Instead, the giant hand reaches over and pats the tiny participant on the head.

ARTWHEELS
In ARTWHEELS, your image rolls down a graphic string extended between the upright forefingers of the desk operator's two hands (PLATE 6). If you are in VIDEOPLACE, you can change your shape by raising and lowering

your arms and kicking your legs. This motion influences your movement down the string. It is also possible to do cartwheels along the contour of the VIDEODESK operator's hands. By shifting your center of gravity, you can control the direction in which you roll. If the second giant hand is nearby, you can decide whether you want to reach for and swing to that hand. It will soon be possible to leap from one hand to the other and to do gymnastics by swinging from finger to finger.

HANGING-BY-A-THREAD
The final two way interaction is one of my favorites, both for its simplicity and for its wordless communication of a subtle opportunity that is usually grasped instantly by the participant. In HANGING-BY-A-THREAD, the VIDEODESK hand appears with a string hanging down from the extended forefinger. The image of the VIDEOPLACE participant is dangling at the end of the string (PLATE 5).

After a moment's investigation, the participant wonders whether it is possible to swing on the string. He shifts his weight from side to side, and his image shakes a bit. Then, he moves more obviously from side to side, and his image starts to swing. By synchronizing his movements with the swinging on the screen, he can pump for greater elevation.

Everyone wonders, is it possible to do a 360? By running back and forth frantically, the participant can make his image swing over the top. The crowd cheers. Then, the giant finger twitches, sending his image flying. The VIDEODESK participant demonstrates her superior power by effortlessly twirling the participant around and around. This scenario is not hypothetical or even unusual—it has been repeated many times.

VIDEOPLACE Plans

I would like to tie together many VIDEOPLACE environments across a great distance. Each participant would enter a large and complex graphic world from a different physical location. Each would see only a small portion of that world, including her own image and those of other participants who are also in that part of the graphic world. The participant could interact with the others or could leave the current location and travel to a different part of the graphic world. Along the way, she would encounter other participants from other real locations. Such a megaenvironment could include hundreds of participants (Fig. 3.23).

Figure 3.23
The Megaenvironment.

Now that the medium has been created, we must balance its various components so that all are equally mature. In particular, auditory responses have thus far received less emphasis than have visual ones. We have been working to improve the sound responses, and to include an auditory component in all interactions. In addition, many of the current interactions define a single relationship for the participant to explore. In the future, interactions will unfold, creating plausible sequences with smooth transitions that fit together like the scenes in a well-edited movie.

Simultaneously, we will upgrade all aspects of the medium. High-resolution graphics will permit smooth animation and three-dimensional graphic scenes. High-resolution cameras will allow the computer to watch the participant's whole body and yet still to discriminate small features, such as the fingers. With a higher video sampling rate, the system will be able to track rapid movements more accurately. By using several cameras, the system will perceive the partipants' movements in three dimensions. As always, the purpose of these improvements will be to produce more sophisticated, more interesting, and more compelling interactive compositions.

Conclusion

I always saw VIDEOPLACE as closely related to a technology that had been invented earlier by Ivan Sutherland and that we shall discuss in the next chapter. I saw my work on unencumbered full-body participation and telecommunication as complementing his. Both technologies were instances of a larger concept that I called *artificial reality*. An artificial reality is a graphic fantasy world in which a person uses her whole body to participate in an experience created by the computer. I realized that this was more than a technology—it was a culture-defining concept. From the beginning, I wanted to establish an interdisciplinary facility in which to develop the medium, and to ensure that it was applied to aesthetic, scientific, and practical ends simultaneously.

References

1. S. Kim, *Inversions*, W.H. Freeman, 1989.

4

Goggles and Gloves

Introduction

VIDEOPLACE represents one ideal in that it is unencumbering. There is nothing to hold, nothing to wear, no wires. In another approach, you immerse yourself in a three-dimensional world by wearing special goggles, to act in that world with special gloves and clothing, and in some cases to feel the graphic objects in your grasp. In this chapter, the development of that technology will be summarized. This discussion does not purport to be exhaustive or definitive. It highlights the efforts of researchers to create physically involving artificial realities and overlooks important contributions—most notably the extensive history of flight simulation and heads-up displays.

Before the Beginning

Computer technologists were not the first people to think of providing realistic artificial experiences. In the mid-1950s, the movie industry went through a period of experimentation that introduced Cinerama and Cinemascope. In 1956, Morton Heilig invented an arcade-style attraction called *Sensorama*, which still exists (Fig. 4.1). You sit on a seat, grasp motorcycle handlebars, and hold your head up to two stereo-mounted lenses. The seat and handlebars vibrate as you look at a three-dimensional movie taken at eye level in Manhattan traffic. Wind blows in your face at a velocity corresponding to your movement in the scene. As you travel, the smell of exhaust fumes and the aroma of pizza are presented at the visually appropriate moments. *Sensorama* was conceived as the ultimate film experience and, since it did not contemplate interactivity, was not an artificial reality as that term is currently understood. However, *Sensorama* was prophetic in its developer's desire to immerse the viewer completely in a synthetic experience, and, had it succeeded commercially, artificial realities might have been attempted in video games from the latter's beginnings.

Figure 4.1
The *Sensorama* Machine, Invented by Morton Heilig.
Photo courtesy of Morton Heilig.

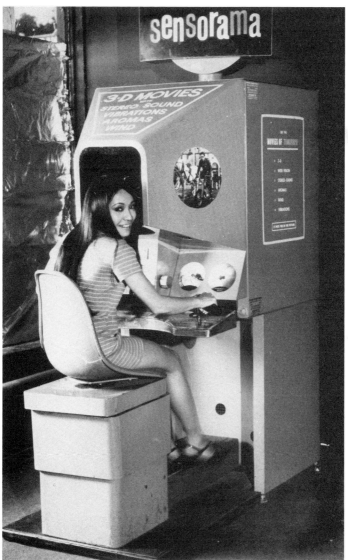

The Beginning

Running parallel to the development of VIDEOPLACE was an oft-broken thread of research within the scientific community. In 1969, at the University of Utah, Ivan Sutherland, the father of computer graphics, implemented a head-mounted display that generated two stereoscopic images of a three-dimensional scene [1]. These images were displayed on two tiny monitors, one for each eye. These monitors were mounted on an apparatus suspended from the ceiling and strapped to the viewer's head.

As the viewer turned his head, he could look around a three-dimensional graphic room. The movements of his head were detected by the apparatus and were relayed to the computer, which generated the appropriate view—that is, the view that the person would see if he were in the room, looking in that direction.

In 1976, P.J. Kilpatrick, working under Fred Brooks at the University of North Carolina, connected a radioisotope manipulator to a simple graphic world (Fig. 4.2) [2]. These manipulators have been used since the 1950s to handle radioactive materials. As an operator in a safe room maneuvers one manipulator, a similar unit in the next room performs identical actions and actually handles the hazardous materials. The operator observes the second manipulator through a protective glass.

Figure 4.2
The Grope System.

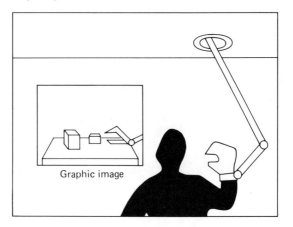

Graphic image

Kilpatrick's system, GROPE-II, used a mechanical arm to operate a graphic manipulator in a graphic world viewed through a stereo display. If the user tried to move the graphic manipulator through the graphic table, she felt the physical arm resist the motion. Similarly, if the user picked up a graphic block, she felt the weight of the block as she raised her hand. The manipulator also prevented her fingers from closing, just as the block would if it were actually in her hand. The concept of a reality glove with force feedback had been fully realized when I visited North Carolina in 1978.

In the late 1970s, a series of related DARPA-sponsored projects was undertaken at the Massachusetts Institute of Technology (MIT). *Put-That-There* used a three-dimensional pointing device in conjunction with limited speech understanding to suggest an alternative human interface [3]. The user sat in a chair facing a large projection screen. As he pointed at the screen, the computer could tell where he was pointing because of a magnetic transducer that he wore on his hand. The user pointed to the graphic object as he said "Put that" and then pointed to a destination as he said "there."

Movie-Map used three video disks to store thousands of still frames recorded in Aspen, Colorado [4]. The screen displayed a road scene depicting what you would see if you were traveling down a particular street in Aspen. By touching different points on the screen, you could move forward or turn left or right. Thus, you could navigate the streets of Aspen, using the same visual cues that you would have if you were there.

Starting in 1966, Tom Furness worked at Wright Patterson Air Force Base, guiding an incredible variety of experiments investigating how information could be presented to a pilot in combat conditions, and how the pilot could operate his weapons when subjected to high G-forces. In particular, Furness continued the development of heads-up displays that allowed pilots to see graphic instruments on the inside of their helmet visors. Traditional cockpit displays are mounted below eye level, so the pilot must constantly decide whether to look down at the gauges or out of the cockpit. Obviously, this head bobbing could be dangerous in combat. With a heads-up display, the pilot could always keep his head in the upright position, deciding whether to look at the display reflected in front of his eyes or to look through that image at the world outside the cockpit.

It occurred to Furness that he could display computer graphic representations of information outside the cockpit in the same way [5]. The technology required to implement this "virtual cockpit" was developed through the 1970s, and was turned on in 1981. Using this technology, Furness depicted the three-dimensional graphic space through which the pilot was flying. This display depicted as graphic objects the enemy missiles and the airspace controlled by enemy radar. Pilots could look around in this space by turning their heads. On a graphic wing, they would see graphic missiles, reminding them of their unexpended weapons. Pilots found this system effective because the visualization of the three-dimensional combat environment, previously gained only through long experience, was now portrayed in a concrete way that they could understand much more quickly.

Since this work was classified, it was unknown to the world at large until 1983. Even then, the technology was specialized to the cockpit environment and was far too expensive for general applications.

The second wave of participants in the development of artificial realities differed from the first in that they were specifically interested in artificial reality as a general concept and were eager to find a way to implement it. Even when their work was tied to particular applications, artificial reality itself was the goal. They wanted to make it happen.

In 1984, Michael McGreevy at NASA became interested in following up Furness's work [6]. He was informed by the Air Force that the helmet for the "virtual cockpit" had cost $1 million. He and contractor Jim Humpries observed that flat panel displays in hand-held televisions would be suitable [KRUEGER83]. With only a modest budget ($20,000), they built an affordable helmet that used two liquid-crystal displays to provide stereo images, special optics to make the eyes think the images were more than 1 inch away, and a magnetic position and orientation sensor to determine where the user was looking. As the user turned his head, the magnetic sensor detected his movements and the computer displayed the appropriate view of a three-dimensional world depicted with line graphics.

Scott Fisher, who had worked on Put-That-There at MIT and later on heads-up displays at Atari, joined NASA to continue the work started by McGreevy. Under Fisher's direction, the helmet display was reduced in size to become what I call *reality goggles* (PLATE C). Fisher contracted VPL Research of Redwood City, California to build a high-resolution

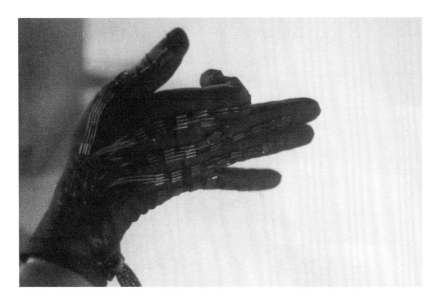

Figure 4.3
The DataGlove.
Courtesy of VPL Research.

version of that company's existing bend-sensing glove to NASA specifications. (A *bend-sensing glove* measures the bending of the wearer's fingers (Fig. 4.3) [7]. The VPL glove derived from a design developed by Tom Zimmerman in 1980 [8]. An earlier bend-sensing glove was invented by Dan Sandin and Richard Sayre in Chicago in 1977, under a grant from the National Endowment for the Arts (Fig. 4.4) [9]. Another glove was patented by Gary Grimes at Bell Laboratories [10].)

NASA then added the Polhemus magnetic position and orientation sensor, which allowed the flexing of the hand to be referenced accurately to a point in three dimensions [11]. I will refer to the combination of the bend-sensing glove and an absolute position sensor as a *reality glove*. This additional capability allowed the glove to be used for pointing and manipulating objects in a three-dimensional artificial reality. The image of the gloved hand in front of the graphic hand displayed on a computer screen succinctly communicated the essence of the artificial-reality concept to the media and the public.

Figure 4.4
The Sayre Glove.
A piece of sensitive clothing developed at the University of Illinois at Chicago by Daniel J. Sandin, Thomas A. Defanti, and Rich Sayre in 1976.

The NASA laboratory developed many ideas using this system. Several of the early demonstrations were implemented by Warren Robinett, who established the conventions for using the glove that are employed today. One of these allows you to ride an escalator and to look around as you ascend. In others, you can use your index finger to draw in three dimensions or to shoot a bullet. You navigate the graphic world by pointing your finger in the direction you want to move. In what NASA calls the virtual workstation, a special hand gesture causes a graphic control console to appear floating in the air. The user can then touch graphic buttons to issue commands. When he is done with the menu, he performs another special gesture and the menu disappears. Controls can be placed wherever the user wants them, regardless of where he happens to be in the artificial reality.

One of NASA's plans for this technology is to control the manipulator on the space shuttle that is used for unloading the cargo bay in orbit. Given the difficulty and expense of extravehicular activity (EVA) in space, another thought is to have operators inside the space station control robots that work outside. Similarly, an operator in the space station could control a robot that has been sent to repair a satellite in its orbit. The operator then could skip the trip. This technique would also be desirable in dangerous situations, including meltdowns in nuclear power plants, handling of radioactive materials, maintenance of undersea oil platforms, and many military operations.

NASA's work first became widely visible in 1985 through an article in *Scientific American* [12]. Since April 1989, there has been a tremendous surge of interest in the topic, including front-page headlines in the *New York Times* and the *Wall Street Journal*, "Artificial Reality" [13,14].

In parallel with NASA's activity and spurred on by it, a new industry has been aborning. The most visible player in this arena has been Jaron Lanier, the founder of VPL, whose company was the first to go beyond the original NASA demonstrations by using powerful Silicon Graphics workstations that greatly simplify the display of full-color, three-dimensional scenes in real time. The VPL DataGlove and EyePhones are now widely used in the research community.

Although a number of VPL's demonstrations have been very playful, the intent has been to provide research tools for industry—a single system costs over $200,000. One product, called RB2 (Reality Built for Two), observes that an artificial reality is fundamentally a telecommunication concept (PLATE 16). Two people wearing reality goggles and reality gloves are able to interact with each other in a graphic world. Typically, each participant sees two disembodied hands, one that appears to be her own and another that belongs to the other person. Thus, they are able to commune physically in a common world. One reality portrayed in RB2 was a day-care center. The participant could choose to experience the room either from an adult height or from the perspective of a small child. In a more recent demonstration, a Mad Hatter's birthday party was simulated, and the participants were served graphic tea [15]. Also recently, RB2 has been used by Matsushita Electric to sell kitchen interiors in a retail showroom in Tokyo.

VPL, Abrams/Gentile Entertainment Incorporated (AGE) of New York, and Mattel were involved in a redesign of the DataGlove using conductive inks to measure finger flexing and ultrasonics to determine position. The advantage of conductive ink sensors is that they can be fabricated inexpensively. When the surface on which the ink traces are printed is flexed, less current is transmitted and four levels of bending can be discriminated. The product based on this design, the Power Glove, is being marketed by Mattel. Broderbund has introduced an infrared sensor called U-Force. So far, these products are sold as inputs for video games.

Autodesk—a software company known for its CAD tools, specifically AutoCAD—has demonstrated a prototype system that was developed under the direction of Bill Bricken [16]. Since this system is less expensive than is VPL's, the graphic speed and the quality of the rendering are more limited. It was conceived as a starter system for people who want to explore the technology. The demonstrations provide a simple graphic world that you can navigate with a variety of controls, such as a reality glove, a steering wheel, and a joystick. Although it would be natural for Autodesk to focus on applications related to CAD, the company's vision is to provide the very general software tools needed to create a broad-based artificial-reality industry. Thus, Randal Walser, who is currently directing the Autodesk development, has a strong interest in educational and athletic applications (PLATE D).

The flurry of industrial activity has been accompanied by renewed work at the University of North Carolina, as is appropriate given the pioneering efforts of Fred Brooks. One of that team's novel projects is a treadmill that is used to walk through graphic spaces. They refer to this technique as the *shopping-cart metaphor*. In addition, Brooks has renewed his long-term interest in force feedback in support of pharmaceutical research.

Another program has been started at the University of Washington under the leadership of Tom Furness, who is trying to transfer to the private sector the virtual-cockpit technology that he developed for the military. In addition to the raw hardware, the Air Force has assembled a wealth of information about the human-factors issues surrounding this technology.

Finally, Dave Zeltzer's graphics group at the MIT Media Laboratory has recently produced films in which animated creatures move around a simple graphics world. In much computer animation, graphic characters know nothing about their environment. Instead, their walking movements are independent of the terrain on which they are placed. As they perform these movements, the program moves them around the scene. In Zeltzer's work, the creatures perceive their environment, and their walking movements are motivated and planned with respect to this perception [17]. Since the original goal of this work was to produce films, the system operated off-line. The researchers have more recently been redirecting their work toward real-time interactions.

After there being almost no academic research on it during the last 20 years, artificial reality has become legitimate as a research topic at the moment that its technology is being employed in toys. This timing points out a bizarre irony: The economics of toy manufacture are more favorable than are the economics of research. Although it would seem preferable for research to have preceded application, as long as academic research is done in the spirit of invention and application—as is possible at the institutions mentioned—there is a useful role for universities to play. They can identify opportunities, demonstrate feasibility, and invent techniques, as well as training practitioners. On the other hand, to the extent that publishable research in the form of mathematical theories and solutions to "hard problems" is emphasized, university efforts are likely to be irrelevant. Whatever principles are needed will be invented by the engineers who build the products. The chips are already on the table.

Acceptability of Current Technology

There is no denying that stereoscopic three-dimensional displays that put you in a graphic world offer incredible promise for creating compelling experiences. In the past, however, people have shown a resistance to using stereo glasses. Three-dimensional television has been possible for decades, but there has been no great desire to commercialize it. If people have been unwilling to wear lightweight glasses for entertainment, it seems likely that a technology that asks people in everyday situations to don goggles, gloves, and wired suits to do their jobs will meet resistance. Greatly improved goggles may be acceptable, but the reality glove and reality suit are likely to be too uncomfortable for long-term use.

Certainly, children will use these devices for games. Adults who have to wear goggles and gloves anyway—such as astronauts and pilots—may not mind. There is also a host of activities for which people cheerfully put on special clothing: skiing, scuba diving, football, and dancing, for example. There will almost certainly be a community of artificial-reality hackers who will be happy to spend much of their time submerged in artificial worlds, no matter how uncomfortable the technology. The question is whether this technology will enter the mainstream as an entertainment medium and a means of performing routine tasks. Since the technology is expensive as well as encumbering, we need to look at how future trends will alter current technology to make it more acceptable and more affordable.

Future Forces

Artificial reality will continue to be propelled by a number of technology trends. One of today's most explosive technologies is computer graphics. It is one of the few areas where American industry operates aggressively. Although three-dimensional graphics has been seen as a luxury item in the past, it will become standard in the near future. As one who has worked in three-dimensional graphics for years, I can say that the opportunity for this technology is enormous, particularly for consumer applications. People's homes and yards are three-dimensional, as are most of the products they buy. Humans evolved to understand a three-dimensional world. Two-dimensional communication is a recent invention, the province of abstract symbols and schematics.

Another driving force will be the resurgence of video games, dominated by Nintendo; there is likely to be a flurry of "me too" business activity in this country. (To put things in perspective, consider that Nintendo is larger than the entire robotics industry.)

There is another powerful trend underway in the home. Because of the remote-control television-channel selector, it is common for people watching television to switch channels every few seconds. The ultimate passive medium is being made interactive by its audience. Although the remote control gives new power to the viewer who holds it, the experience of having channels flick by is excruciating for other viewers, who are wrenched capriciously from one program to another. An alternative would be for each person to wear headphones and to watch television through reality goggles.

The reality goggles are a direct result of a long-term Japanese commitment to the development of flat-panel displays for calculators, portable computers, and hand-held televisions. In fact, the single enabling event for NASA's research was a portable television display. (In a new research paradigm, American researchers disassemble toys and use the Japanese components to create new research tools.)

At the moment, the LCDs used in reality goggles limit the technology because they are low-resolution devices, whereas the graphics processors driving them are high resolution. It is not clear whether the markets perceived for artificial realities are large enough to drive the color LCD technology, especially since display manufacturers operate in markets where millions of units are the norm.

High-resolution monochrome displays already exist. The most impressive of these is a one-inch cathode-ray tube (CRT), about 1/4-inch thick, developed for the Air Force for the virtual cockpit system. These displays have greater than 2000-line resolution, with 1000 gray levels; this resolution is equal to that of the best graphic workstations [18]. Since these devices were developed for the military, they are doubtless expensive, because both engineering and manufacturing costs must be borne by small production runs.

Another display technology with implications for artificial realities is based on light-emitting diodes (LEDs). Reflection Technology of Cambridge, Massachusetts, uses a linear array of LEDs reflected in a vibrating mirror to create a single eye display with resolution comparable to that of an IBM PC display. The problem with LEDs is that full color is difficult to obtain at the moment. In particular, blue LEDs are not yet available in linear arrays. It will probably be several years before this technology is available in full color. By then, new technologies are likely to have appeared.

Ultimately, if reality goggles are to be successful, they must be made to be less cumbersome. The current goggles are clumsy because they use heavy lenses that trick your eye into thinking that the display is more than one inch away. One possible alternative is to use a laser-scanning system that paints the image directly on the retina. According to Tom Furness, this technology requires no optics and could be made to fit in standard-sized eyeglasses [19].

One well-known principle that is seldom invoked in discussions of reality goggles is that, in general, smaller electronic devices are less expensive to fabricate than are larger ones. The larger the device, the more it is subject to random errors during the manufacturing process and to reduced yields. Therefore, it is likely that a high-resolution display goggle can be made less expensive than can a high-resolution video monitor. This observation is important given that the video monitor is an expensive component of a high-end graphic display system. If this logic is correct, then goggles offer a new option to the computer graphic, computer terminal, and high-definition television (HDTV) markets. Since no massive vacuum tube is required, graphic systems using reality goggles could take up far less space in the home or office than do current systems.

As reality goggles continue their evolution, they must be made to be visually indistinguishable from eyeglasses. These *reality glasses* should not alter the appearance of a person who normally wears glasses. You should be able to look through them into the real world or at them to view a graphic world, choosing moment by moment to which world you want to attend. Alternatively, graphic objects and creatures could be displayed as though they existed in the real world. With such a technology, a group of city planners could sit around a bare conference table and look at a three-dimensional graphic model of an urban-renewal project floating above the table.

Thus, reality goggles should benefit from a number of technology trends that will reduce their cost, increase their performance, and improve their acceptability. If these trends contribute the technologies, widespread use of artificial realities will be inevitable because there will be so little financial risk in implementing them. Traditional applications will be experienced as artificial realities because the displays are cheaper, not because the viewing technique is superior. If this scenario is played out, specialized hardware and software will be created because the technical community wants to create artificial realities and will do so on its own time, if necessary.

The Glove as a Gesture Technology

The virtue of the reality glove is that it provides a quick way of suggesting three-dimensional interaction with artificial objects. However, the reality glove, like VIDEOPLACE, is currently a *gesture technology*. You can move your hands as though to perform an action, but you do not receive the tactile and force feedback required to actually do that action.

For instance, imagine you were wearing a reality glove and wanted to reach around a graphic object and insert a bolt on the far side. This task would be impossible, because you could feel neither the bolt in your hand nor the moment when the bolt contacts the other side of the object. In fact, nothing would prevent you from putting your hand and the bolt through the object.

In the real world, the bolt does much of the work. In a manner of speaking, it knows that it has been picked up. It reports the fact to you by resisting the pressure of your fingers and providing additional mass that you feel as you move your hand. In an artificial reality, the bolt tells you nothing, because there is no bolt. The system must calculate the relationship between your fingers and the imaginary bolt. These calculations are time consuming, and they must be repeated many times per second.

What the glove can do is point in three-dimensional space and be used to make simple hand gestures. Because its shape is perceived in three dimensions, it has a larger vocabulary of gestures than does VIDEOPLACE. Gestures include pointing and opening or closing your hand in the vicinity of a graphic object. The limited use of a small number of natural gestures as commands is comfortable. Intensive use of awkward symbolic gesture commands is likely not to be. Thus, in the long run, a combination of speech and simple gestures will probably prove preferable to an elaborate gesture language.

Synthesis

Since VIDEOPLACE and the reality glove are both gesture technologies, it is reasonable to ask whether VIDEOPLACE could be used to substitute for a reality glove. VIDEOPLACE technology can track a single finger in three-dimensional space with little difficulty. Multiple cameras and gray-scale processing can be used to track two hands with straightforward, but computationally intensive, techniques. Therefore, some of the functions of the reality glove could be realized with video input, albeit more expensively. My assumption is that wearing a glove will be unwelcome in many situations. In these cases, we can imagine unencumbered VIDEOPLACE gesture input operating with slightly encumbering reality glasses.

Three-Dimensional Human Images

When artificial realities are used for teleconferencing, the appearance of the teleparticipants is critical to the communication. Although the reality suit can locate the major joints of the participant's body, it provides no information about facial expressions. If we acknowledge that the most straightforward way to do face detection would be to use video cameras, we should consider having video cameras to do the job of the reality suit as well.

The system would possess a model of the participant's body. The purpose of its perception of the participant would be to determine the state of that model. The computer then could use that model to generate a graphic representation of that person in that exact posture, as seen from any point in the artificial reality. The model would include information about what the participant is wearing, what the tone of his skin is, and what the length and characteristics of his hair are. It would also focus much of its perceptual resolution, mathematical modeling, and graphic rendering on the expression on his face.

The images of participants in other locations could be inserted into your visual environment. These other people, in turn, could see an appropriate view of you in their surroundings. People in and out of the artificial world would look natural to one another. Eye contact would be possible. We have no difficulty imagining people using such a technology. We have no difficulty in guaranteeing the technology's feasibility. Only the economics and the time table are open to question.

Tactile and Force Feedback

The most compelling reason for making wearable devices is to provide tactile and force feedback so that the participant can feel objects in the graphic world. Although goggles and gloves are potentially inexpensive, devices that apply mechanical force are not yet subject to the enormous cost reductions associated with computers and electronics. At the moment, the consumer enjoys only a few machines that have mechanical power: the car, the dishwasher, the washing machine, and the lawn mower. Obviously, these mechanisms are neither highly sophisticated nor subtle. Japanese dominance of video cassette recorders (VCRs), floppy disks, and robotic actuators is largely due to the Japanese superiority in what they call *mechatronics*, the intersection of electronic and mechanical technologies. Mechatronics is exactly the kind of interdisciplinary and practical work with which the United States has difficulty. The subject is barely mentioned at many universities. Even more important, the total lack of human-portable power storage means that force-feedback systems either will be tethered to a power source or will provide only weak feedback.

Tactile and force feedback are essential to the "ultimate" artificial reality. However, if we think of how we live our lives, there is a great deal of experience that does not depend on tactile or force feedback. Except for shaking hands, the typical businessperson depends on touch very little. Therefore, there is much that can be done without touch, and we should not consider the lack of force feedback an impediment to applying the technology in hand.

Conclusion

With the advent of VIDEOPLACE and systems based on goggles and gloves, the basic artificial-reality technology is available in a form that can be applied in many domains. Many other approaches will be taken. Many new devices will be tried. Refinements will continue for decades. Better goggles, better head tracking, better VIDEOPLACE perception, and devices to provide tactile feedback will be added. Although much of the discussion of this technology focuses on the creation of practical tools, whether artificial realities are used for practical, playful, or aesthetic purposes, they offer a medium as powerful as the printed word or television.

References

1. I. E. Sutherland, "A Head-Mounted Three-Dimensional Display," *Proceedings of the Fall Joint Computer Conference (AFIPS)*, 33-1 (1968), pp. 757–764.

2. P. J. Kilpatrick, "The Use of a Kinematic Supplement in an Interactive Graphics System," doctoral dissertation, University of North Carolina, 1976.

3. R. Bolt, "Put-That-There: Voice and Gesture at the Graphics Interface." *SIGGRAPH '80 Proceedings*, published as *Computer Graphics*, 14, No. 3 (July 1980), pp. 262–270.

4. A. Lippman, "Movie-Maps: An Application of the Optical Videodisc to Computer Graphics," *Computer Graphics*, 14, No. 3 (1980).

5. T. Furness, personal communication.

6. M. McGreevy, "The Exploration Metaphor," *Human–Machine Interfaces for Teleoperators & Virtual Environments*, Santa Barbara, CA March 4, 1990.

7. S. Fisher, M. McGreevy, J. Humpries, & W. Robinett, "Virtual Interface Environment for Telepresence Applications," *Proceedings of ANS International Topical Meeting on Remote Systems and Robotics in Hostile Environments*, J.D. Berger, ed. (1987), pp. x–y.

8. T. Zimmerman, J. Lanier, C. Blanchard, & S. Bryson, "A Hand Gesture Interface Device." *CHI '87 Conference Proceedings* (April 1987), pp. 189–192.

9. T. DeFanti & D. Sandin, US NEA R60-34-163 Final Project Report, 1977.

10. G. Grimes, "Digital Data Entry Glove Interface Device," US Patent 4414537, 8 November 1983.

11. F.H. Raab, E.B. Blood, T.O. Steiner, & R.J. Jones, "Magnetic Position and Orientation Tracking System (Polhemus Device)," *IEEE Transactions on Aerospace and Electronic Systems*, AES-15, No. 5 (September 1979), pp. 709–718.

12. J.D. Foley, "Interfaces for Advanced Computing," *Scientific American*, pp. 126–135.

13. A. Pollack, "What is Artificial Reality?," *New York Times*, Vol. CXXXVIII #47,836, 10 April 1989, p. 1.

14. G.P. Zachery, "Artificial Reality," *Wall Street Journal*, 23 January 1990, p. 1.

15. P. Elmer-Dewitt, "(MIS)Adventures in Cyberspace," *Time*, 3 September 1990, pp. 74–75.

16. D. Churbuck, "The Ultimate Computer Game," *Forbes*, 5 February 1990, p. 154.

17. M. McKenna, S. Pieper, & D. Zeltzer, "Control of a Virtual Actor: The Roach," *Proceedings of 1990 Symposium of Interactive 3D Graphics*, Snowbird, Utah, SIGGRAPH (March 1990), pp.165–174.

18. T.A. Furness, "Experiences in Virtual Space," *Human–Machine Interfaces for Teleoperators & Virtual Environments*, Santa Barbara, CA, 4 March 1990.

19. T.A. Furness, "Experiences in Virtual Space," *Human–Machine Interfaces for Teleoperators & Virtual Environments*, Santa Barbara, CA, 4 March 1990.

5

Artificial Reality:
A New Aesthetic
Medium

Introduction

Artificial reality is better understood as an aesthetic medium like film than as a technology like computers. As a new medium, artificial realities are particularly timely in light of the current state of the arts. For some time, artists have lamented the diminishing effectiveness of their traditional tools. People often say that painting is dead. In his book, *Beyond Modern Sculpture*, art historian Jack Burnham suggested that art itself is dead [1]. To these obituaries, I would like to add my own hyperbolic statement, and then to examine the extent to which it is true.

The static image is dead! We are constantly bombarded with static images in magazines and dynamic images on television and in the movies. Most of the images we see are carefully crafted for maximum effect, and many are beautiful. The result is that we cannot take in all that we see. Numbed by the onslaught of visual information, insulated by categories and filters, vision, our most heavily trafficked sense, is no longer capable of reacting to paintings or graphics as art. Sending a static message through vision alone is like sending it through channels; you can be sure that it will be processed correctly, but also that it will be treated as routine. To touch people today, you have to slip past their defenses and involve them in an unfamiliar way.

Beyond Interpretation

Oddly, art history, art criticism, and art appreciation are among the deterrents to experiencing art. Repeatedly, people leaving GLOWFLOW, METAPLAY, and PSYCHIC SPACE said "I really liked it, but what did it mean?" For some reason, they thought that what had happened should be reduced immediately to words. In fact, people have a tendency to accept events in terms of the words that they will use to describe them. Therefore, there is a place for a medium that can resist interpretation. An artificial reality can take steps to individualize responses and to thwart analysis. If each person has a different experience, each will experience less pressure to arrive at the "right" interpretation. Since each person moves about the space differently, each will receive different feedback, even if the controlling program is exactly the same. If there are many programs alternating control of the environments, each participant's adventure will be unique. Thus, two people can exchange experiences, but since they have had no common experience, they cannot analyze what happened to death.

Another reason for emphasizing variety is to resist the pressure on artists to find a single, saleable style. Once she discovers that style, the artist simply repeats it, afraid that, if she tries anything new, it will not be as successful. There is no need to sign the work—it is identifiable at a hundred paces. The work itself is a signature, the aesthetic equivalent of a corporate logo. Joan and Russell Kirsch developed a computer program that creates new works in the style of painter Richard Diebenkorn [2]. They argue that, if a computer can duplicate the style of an artist and use that style to create original work, then artistic skills are not of any higher order than are more prosaic skills, such as writing a program. However, Diebenkorn's achievement was to invent the style. Only if an artist continues to quote himself after developing a distinctive style are the Kirsches correct.

Active Versus Passive Art

All our traditional art forms have one thing in common: They assume a passive audience. Passivity was appropriate when most humans toiled physically. After centuries of effort, however, we have all but eliminated the necessity for physical exertion. Ironically, since our bodies require a certain amount of exercise for health, we face a new problem—how to make our lives more active. Sports fulfill this need for some people, but there is a place for new forms of art and entertainment that involve our bodies rather than deny them.

Response Is the Medium!

Artificial realities suggest a new art medium based on a commitment to real-time interaction between people and machines. The medium comprises perception, display, and control systems. It accepts inputs from or about participants, and then responds in ways those people can recognize as corresponding to their behavior. The relationship between inputs and outputs is variable, allowing the artist to intervene between the participants' actions and the results perceived. Thus, for example, participants' physical movements can cause sounds, or their voices can be used to navigate a computer-defined visual space. It is the composition of the relationships between action and response that is important. The beauty of the visual and aural response is secondary. Response is the medium!

In principle, the perceptual system could allow the system to respond to your voice, location, posture, movement, or gestures. It could respond to the time elapsed since the last movement, the time since you entered the environment, or your general rate of movement. It could respond to your height, clothing, hair color, or facial expression. If there were several people in an artificial reality, it could respond to them individually or to some relationship among them. It could also respond to relationships between an individual's image and objects in the graphic world. The perceptual system defines the limits of meaningful interaction; the exhibit cannot respond to what it cannot perceive.

The purpose of the displays is to provide a context within which the interaction occurs and to define relationships between the participants' actions and their perceived consequences. This context is an artificial reality in which the laws of cause and effect are composed by the artist. The beauty of the displays is not as important in this medium as it would be if the form were conceived as solely visual or auditory. Artists are fully capable of producing effective displays in a number of media. This fact is well known, and to duplicate that feat produces nothing new. What is unknown and remains to be tested is the validity of a responsive aesthetic.

The control system determines the appropriate response to the participant's action and initiates the generation of that response. While the simplest responses are little more than direct feedback of a participant's behavior, allowing the system to show off its perpetual ability, far more sophisticated results are possible. In fact, a given aggregation of hardware sensors, displays, and processors can be viewed as an instrument that can be programmed by artists with differing sensitivities to create completely different kinds of experiences. These artists must balance their desire for interesting relationships against the commitment to respond in real time.

We can think of an artificial reality in the following ways:

1. It is an entity that engages participants in dialog. An artificial reality expresses itself through light and sound, whereas the

participant communicates with physical action. Since the experience is an encounter between individuals (human and machine), it might legitimately include greetings, introductions, and farewells—all abstract, rather than literal. The artist's task, in this case, is to imbue reality itself with a distinctive personality. This idea is not an obscure one; simply imagine the feedback relationships that you might employ to create a haunted house or an enchanted garden;

2. It is a personal amplifier. In Dorothy's initial encounter with the Wizard of Oz, the Wizard uses technology to enhance his ability to interact with those around him. An artificial reality can be used in the same way. Currently, the person at the VIDEODESK is the Wizard in the two-way exhibit between the VIDEODESK and VIDEOPLACE;

3. It is a space that the participant can explore, where he can interact with graphic creatures or become involved in a graphic adventure;

4. It is a setting for human-to-human interaction. Two or more people can interact with one another in the interactive medium. Since the computer defines and can change the relationships that exist between participants, it is a third party in the dialog;

5. It is an instrument that participants play by moving about the space. In PSYCHIC SPACE, the floor was used as the keyboard of a simple musical instrument. In an artificial reality, musical objects and creatures can respond to a participant's touch;

6. It is a means of turning the participant's body into an instrument. An individual's limbs and fingers can be used to control images and sounds;

7. It is a game between the computer and the participant. This variation is an extension of the pinball machine or the video game, the most commercially successful interactive environments;

8. It is an experiential parable in which the theme is illustrated by the events that happen to the protagonist—you. Viewed from this perspective, the MAZE in PSYCHIC SPACE became pregnant with meaning. It was impossible to succeed, to solve the MAZE. The MAZE

could be a frustrating experience if you were trying to reach that goal. If, on the other hand, you maintained an active curiosity about how the MAZE would thwart you next, the experience proved amusing and thought provoking. Such poetic composition of experience is one of the most promising lines of development to be pursued within artificial realities.

Implications of the Art Form

An interactive exhibit augurs new relationships for artists with their audience and with their art. The artist operates at a metalevel. The participant provides the direct performance of the experience. The artificial reality hardware is the instrument. The computer acts much as an orchestra conductor, controlling broad relationships, whereas the artist provides the score to which both performer and conductor are bound. This relationship might be a familiar one for musical composers, although even they are accustomed to being able to recognize one of their pieces, no matter who is interpreting it. But here the artist's responsibilities become even broader than those of a composer, who typically defines a detailed sequence of events. The interactive artist is composing a network of possibilities, most of which will not be realized by a given participant.

Since the artist is not dedicated to the idea that the entire piece be experienced each time by each participant, the concept of a *piece* is no longer appropriate. The artist can deal with contingencies that arise during an interaction. She can take into account the differences among people. Her job is to define a rich context within which interesting momentary interactions can be defined and altered in compelling ways. At the least, this context will include a visual setting and causal laws.

In the past, art has often been a one-shot, hit-or-miss proposition. Paintings, hanging in rows in galleries or museums, have the same problem as do boxes of detergent at the supermarket: somehow, each work must distinguish itself from its competitors. (In fact, people often consume art in what I think of as "supermarket" mode. They typically intend to see 100 works of art per hour.)

My preference for exhibiting a large variety of interactions is partly based on this issue. If "shoppers" glance in and see one interaction and leave, they will be surprised if they compare notes with someone else who saw the exhibit. They will discover that they saw different work, and they may return for the purpose of really seeing the piece. This is my "second-strike" capability. It has been a conscious strategy since METAPLAY, and it has worked. People often tell me that they have returned for this reason.

An interactive exhibit can deal in novel ways with the problem of attracting and maintaining attention. It can perceive and respond to people who are not within its confines, attempting to lure them in. Or, it can refuse to compete with other pieces by offering nothing to the casual observer, demanding a commitment from the viewer by responding only when its space has been entered. Note that this issue is different for artificial realities created with data goggles, which cannot entice you to put them on. It is less clear whether the greater commitment you must have to enter such a reality makes it less likely that you will leave prematurely.

With both technologies, once you enter, the exhibit can judge your level of involvement, and can modify its behavior if your interest begins to wane. It can learn to improve its performance, responding not only to the moment, but also to the entire history of its experience with other participants. The piece becomes an aesthetic entity whose behavior matures through experience. It may take paths unanticipated by the artist. Indeed, one of the strong motivations guiding this work is the desire to compose works that surprise their creator.

In VIDEOPLACE, you are confronted with a completely new kind of experience, stripped of informed expectations and forced to deal with the moment on its own terms. You are actively involved, discovering that your limbs have been given new meaning and that they can express themselves in new ways. Your experience will be unique to your movements and may go beyond the intentions of the artist, or beyond what the artist had thought were the possibilities of the piece.

McLuhan called attention to the medium's effect on the message; in that vein, we can ask what is communicated by artificial realities and what they can be used to communicate [3]. First, the medium presents some unavoidable facts about current technology. For better or worse, our technology will perceive us. It will communicate with us. Our relationship with it will become cozier and more intimate as time passes. The artificial reality introduces some of the most up-to-date technology in a way that makes the technology's implications palpable. The experience can serve as an early-warning system for people who seek to know what they may be called on to adapt to.

Technology for Fun

More important than the specific knowledge a person may gain about technology is the attitude toward technology that is conveyed by an artificial-reality exhibit. The interactive exhibit is technology for fun. Americans are incredibly attuned to the idea that the sole purpose of technology is to solve problems. We seem unable to grasp that only by completely integrating our technology with the whole of our lives can we understand its implications sufficiently to use it with confidence. In 1982, well before the collapse of the video-game industry or its resurgence led by Nintendo, I wrote "Consequently, with the recent and probably temporary exception of video games, we buy entertainment equipment almost exclusively from other countries which are better able to see the implications of our inventions in terms of day-to-day life." [4] This sentence reflected my awareness that American businesspeople have a distaste for technology products that are used by individuals, as opposed to those used by organizations.

Artificial realities also illustrate ways that technology can be personalized and humanized. It is possible to program an interactive environment so that each person has a dramatically different experience, not only because each acts differently, but also because the relationships that govern the interaction are different.

Finally, in an exciting and frightening way, interactive exhibits dramatize the extent to which we are savages in the world that our technology creates. Contemporary laypeople are probably more ignorant of their culture's technology than have been any people in human history. The layperson has extremely little ability to define the limits of what is possible with current technology, and so will accept all sorts of cues as representing relationships that do not in fact exist. The constant birth of such superstitions indicates how much we have already accomplished in mastering our natural environment, and how difficult the initial discoveries must have been.

Interactive art also stands as a serious indictment of our cultural style. It offers nothing to the passive audience. A passive individual can enter and—ignoring the invitation to become involved—leave, having experienced nothing. Although some interactions may cajole the participant into a conversation, others might not bother. The way the exhibit treats its participants will reflect the attitudes of the artist.

Aesthetic Issues

Is the interactive exhibit art, or is it just a passing social statement—an aesthetic one-liner? Or, does it contain the seeds of a new branch of aesthetic endeavor? If it does, which dimensions of the interactive medium have the greatest aesthetic potential?

Interactive art shares concerns with existing art forms. VIDEOPLACE is about the human image, one of the most consistent features of Western art. The focus of most of the interactions is how the participant's image is displayed and what happens to the image. People have always been fascinated with their own images. An art form that challenges a person's self-perceptions will continue to be of interest.

Artificial realities are fundamentally conceptual. Since the system's response to an action need not be the expected result of that action, participants are forced to think. They must constantly conceptualize theories that explain the experiences that they are having. As the relationships change, participants must update their theories or create metatheories that tie together the patterns of change.

An artist's actions have also become an accepted subject of art. Willem de Kooning painted in a way that reveals the physical act of painting. Jackson Pollock made his physical acts the subject of his painting. In an artificial reality, the artist is again observing and commenting on movement. In this case, however, the action of the participant, rather than that of the artist, is the subject of the work.

Active Participation

Making movement a subject of the artificial reality relates the latter to traditional art. Switching the focus from artist to participant, however, constitutes a radical departure. True, we can move about and admire a sculpture and, to a minimal degree, we can interact physically with a painting. However, in its attempt to involve the audience, the artificial reality has closer ties with the Happenings of the early 1960s than it does with these more conventional modes of art. When participation becomes the subject of the aesthetic work, the viewer's critical faculties are given new responsibilities. The viewers are no longer judging the finished work of the artist. Their own actions complete the piece. Thus, within the framework of the artist's exhibit, the participants also become creators.

From this perspective, participation must be seen in a different light. Usually, artists are allowed to act, and the audience is not. Dancers are strenuously involved in their work and feel aesthetic pleasure from their own performance. Indeed, one can argue that the passive appreciation of any art form is enhanced by having once created within it. The graceful movements of a dancer take on new meaning to a member of the audience who has learned to dance, just as a painter can identify with the sensuality of another artist's painting experience as revealed by the brushstrokes.

This proprioceptive sense can be addressed directly in an artificial reality. Awareness of your body is a vital part of experiencing the medium. When you find that bending an elbow has one effect and tilting your head has another, you discover a new way of relating to your body. Your body becomes a set of transformations that operate on reality. Although this model is always valid, changing the consequences of mundane actions drives home the point. Similarly, as the relationship between your actions and their effect on your perception changes, you are led to ponder your relationship to reality itself. In the real world, the relationship between immediate cause and effect is usually predictable. A consistent set of physical laws mediates our everyday experience. Our feet are held to the ground by gravity. An object that is released above the ground will fall. Bricks are heavy and feathers are light. We do experience surprises—when we trip over a rug or when an apple falls on our head—but these usually occur because we are unaware of the presence of particular objects, persons, or forces, not because the laws governing their behavior are unexpected. Thus, by creating an interaction in which the laws controlling the relationship between action and response are composed rather than immutable, an artificial reality offers a way to comment on experience itself at a philosophical level.

Just as music addresses the intellectual machinery with which we understand sounds—particularly speech sounds—artificial realities can touch the primitive mechanisms through which we apprehend physical reality. The environmental experience can be composed in terms of our abstract sense of spaces and objects and the expectations we have for the effects of our actions on the world. If the pattern of confirmed and broken expectations has a coherent and satisfying structure, the result should be an aesthetic experience. As the innate and culturally learned rules of human expectation are understood, artists will be able to create a great variety of compositions that explore this part of our makeup.

Artificial realities have another aspect that distances them from the traditional museum arts. A painting or a sculpture defines a single set of perceptions that are bounded in space and time. On the other hand, artificial realities are not static works to be admired by a passive observer. Artificial realities are experiential—a radical departure from the traditional museum arts. By providing experience, they may be closer to literature, theater, or film—all of which relate a sequence of events that are experienced by a cast of characters. However, the narrative art forms define a linear sequence of events with a beginning, middle, and end that are presented identically to all members of the audience. Artificial realities, on the other hand, allow the artist to define a universe of possible experiences, so each participant can create a unique experience. Thus, an interactive composition defines a new category that demands its own criteria.

Traditional art is created by an artist and appreciated by a viewer. In an artificial reality, the relationship between the artist and the viewer is only one of several possible relationships. The relationship of one viewer to another can also be the explicit subject of the work. Thus, for the first time, the artist can compose relationships between friends and strangers where the very nature of the interaction can be changed as casually as we change the subject in a conversation. The importance of this opportunity is one lesson I have learned from my work. For most people, interacting with computers is a distinct activity, whereas interacting with other people is life itself. Rather than isolating people further from one another, the challenge for artificial realities is inventing new ways to bring people together.

The interactive exhibit has the potential to endure as an art form. It shares traditional art's concerns about perception, the human image, and the representation of human experience. However, the interactive version of beauty will stimulate conceptual insight as well as perceptual pleasure. The intellectual opportunity to discover an entirely new aesthetic makes traditional media, which have been explored for centuries, seem impoverished by comparison.

Design Considerations

In designing these experiences, we have a host of concerns. Some of these concerns relate to interactivity itself; others are related to production values.

Clarity

One of the key design issues is the clarity of the participant's experience. It is important that participants perceive that the environment is responding to them. Various issues bear on that certainty.

The first of these is the sense of awareness that the environment projects. If the environment can correctly perceive every action you perform, it can respond in appropriate ways and make you feel connected to what is going on. If you move your hand and CRITTER chases it instantly, you feel that the creature is responding to your behavior. If you jump and the system is unable to perceive that behavior, you will feel some dissatisfaction every time that jumping fails to elicit a response. It is not necessary that the system's perception be perfect, as long as interactions are designed with the perceptual limitations in mind.

In VIDEOPLACE, the environment's awareness can be affected by the number of people present. It is more difficult to perceive the actions of several individuals, because the people's silhouettes may overlap. In addition, when several people are present, the system should consider the relationships among them. These relationships start competing with those between each individual and the environment. We have said that response is the medium—and response is clearest when one person is alone with the exhibit. If there are numerous people in the space, there must be a way for each to associate his actions with a corresponding response; otherwise, the responsiveness becomes meaningless.

Clarity also requires consistency of response. If each response is unique, the participant will not see a connection between his actions and the environment's responses. Thus, feedback relationships have to be repeated long enough to establish a pattern. Unique responses can occur, but they are events, deviations from the pattern. Similarly, it is acceptable to change the pattern, but the change itself should occur in a way that seems appropriate, rather than arbitrary. For instance, there are interactive systems now that have several feedback modes, and that switch from one mode to another with no regard for what the participant is doing. I prefer to have people leave the environment to quit one interaction, and to reenter to start the next.

In longer interactive compositions, there are moments that can be established as punctuation marks, separating one part of an interaction from what preceded it. These are moments when the participant expects something to happen. In PSYCHIC SPACE, events such as moving your symbol to the new symbol or crossing a MAZE boundary were used to trigger transitions. Today, when people capture CRITTER, it explodes. But, if it were captured a second time and a new interaction ensued after the explosion, participants would not be offended, because change is a believable consequence of a dramatic event. Similarly, if you are flying around an artificial reality and see a graphic doorway, you expect to be in a different environment after you have gone through it. The artful composition of such transitions will be an important aspect of the medium in the future.

Control

Control is another important design issue. Most of the time, the participant is in direct control of the interaction. However, there are occasions when the artist wants to make something happen to the participant. For instance, in MAN-IPULATE, the operator at the VIDEODESK uses the image of her hands to push the participant's image. For that moment, the participant is not in control of the image of his own body and this lack of control is amusing. If the participant loses control for too long, however, he becomes frustrated. It is important that these moments be brief, and be justified dramatically.

This concern is particularly important when there are two participants. Currently, the person at the desk is knowledgeable about the system and she is carefully coached in her role, which is to facilitate the experience of the other participant. If there were two unprepared participants, the problem of control would be challenging. There have to be moments when one participant can affect the other. However, these moments—during which a participant loses control—have to be budgeted. They have to be divided fairly and, like wild cards, they have to be played at the most opportune moments.

Self-Explanatory Experience

It is important that participants understand the experience. They must know or be able to figure out how they are influencing events in the artificial reality. Times when they are confused about how they are participating or what they must do to proceed should be minimized, for such moments are never pleasant. Nevertheless, I think it is desirable to avoid giving explicit instructions. New relationships should be introduced by discovery, rather than through explanation. Since the discovery process must proceed at its own pace, this requirement is not always consistent with the needs of galleries that must allow large numbers of people to pass through an exhibit. However, reliance on explicit explanation is not worth the time saved; unexpectedly, the most obtrusive presence is that of an authoritative human.

One situation where explanation is difficult to avoid is at the end of an experience. The problem of ending a piece exists in any temporal medium. The ending should be self-explanatory, and should be consistent with the rest of the piece. One elegant solution used in PSYCHIC SPACE was to respond only to movements toward the exit. This strategy invariably resulted in people moving in the desired direction. The experience was over when the person found that he was no longer in the gallery.

Another strategy was used in an early CRITTER interaction. Each time CRITTER reached the top of the participant's head, a new set of relationships was introduced. After several such transitions, participants came to expect them. On what was to be the last time, when CRITTER reached the top of the participant's head, it jumped up and down, causing the participant's image to disappear. CRITTER then floated gently down to the bottom of the screen. You could see people look down to see whether their real bodies were still there.

Although these techniques work, it seems a little arrogant for the exhibit to dispatch the participant. My model of a personal encounter does not really require a fixed endpoint. However, there are occasions when one participant thoughtlessly occupies the environment for a long time when other people are waiting to enter. A discreet means of asking him to leave would be appropriate.

Randomness

Random processes have often been used in computer art to create complexity. This use of randomness has been necessary because it is difficult to create complex stimuli with computer programming alone. In an interactive medium, the participants are a source of unpredictability. Furthermore, perception is uncertain and the idea of physical interactivity is unfamiliar, so complexity is inherent in the medium and no random processes are needed to make the experiences interesting. On the other hand, with both sound and graphic patterns, it is possible for the artist to describe the general texture desired, and then to use random functions to generate low-level details. The advantage of this approach is that it is easy to create a large number of variations around a single theme.

The Space

The environments that I have implemented so far have been housed in darkened, empty, rectangular rooms. If a shaped space were substituted, the compositions would reflect ideas suggested by the shape. Shape would determine content. The empty rectangle has the advantage of being so familiar that physical space is eliminated as a concern and response is the only focus. The walled space is much like a frame for a picture or a pedestal for a sculpture; it separates the composition from the rest of the world. By blocking all distraction, it allows the artist to control the experience. In a darkened space, the participant can perceive only what the artist chooses to show. The darkness also helps to free people from inhibitions, making them less self-conscious and more playful. Turning down the lights in theaters similarly separates people from the real world and focuses their attention on the performance.

Location

There are situations where it would be desirable to bring responsiveness into the everyday environment, such as a shopping mall, to create a Happening or an active space that is delineated only by its effects.

Such responsive interactions would be most effective if done for short periods or only at particular times in special places. Two or three people walking down a street late at night would notice if each person's footsteps were accompanied by a distinctive sound. On the other hand, when hordes of preoccupied people walk through an environment, there would be no way for it to respond meaningfully to them as individuals or as a group. In general, this new medium requires people's focused attention, so that it cannot be relegated to the status of responsive muzak.

Production Values

In addition to the issues that are unique to responsive media, the fact that the latter are experiential means that their creators may ultimately share some of the same design concerns as film directors. Production values such as the quality of the graphic scenery, the smoothness of the animation, the credibility of the physics, the depth of characterization of the synthetic creatures, the pacing of the interaction, and the tightness of the writing will all become more important as artificial reality becomes an established medium.

Interactivity

An artificial reality is created for participants. Therefore, any aspect of the exhibit that is designed for passive spectators at the expense of the active participants is a violation of the medium. Likewise, any documentation of interactive capabilities that the exhibit does not have or that would be absolutely meaningless to a participant is a misrepresentation. This issue is significant because far more people will experience the medium passively through magazine pictures, videotape broadcasts, and presentations than will interact with it first hand. Since there is a tradeoff between the static visual quality and the dynamic quality of the interaction, there is a temptation to focus on documentation rather than interaction, on the passive audience rather than the participants. The Disney films "Song of the South" and "Who Framed Roger Rabbit" demonstrated that animated characters could be made to interact with human actors in any way imaginable. Now, we must show that what is mere illusion to the the passive observer can be compelling experience to the participant.

Conclusion

Artificial reality opens a new dimension for the arts just at the moment when the power of existing forms seems to be on the decline. The focus on live interaction allows the artist to compose a rich variety of alternatives, rather than a set of final decisions. The freedom from finality allows a piece to grow and the computer to learn. The artist starts the process and each participant may contribute. The interactions take participants into an exploration of their own senses and of their own mental processes. Ultimately, however, the artificial realities are more than an art medium; they constitute a whole new realm of human experience.

References

1. J. Burnham, *Beyond Modern Sculpture*, George Braziller, New York, 1968.

2. J. Kirsch & R. Kirsch, "Computer Grammars for the Syntactical Analysis of Paintings," *Proceedings of the Twenty-Sixth International Congress of the History of Art*, Washington, D.C. (1986).

3. H.M. McLuhan, *The Medium Is the Massage*, Random House, 1967.

4. M. Krueger, *Artificial Reality*, Addison-Wesley Publishing Company, Reading, MA, 1982.

6

Perception

Introduction

A traditional computer system receives input from a *user*. An artificial reality perceives the behavior of a *participant* in the context of a graphic world. This change in vocabulary redefines the human–computer interface. The computer's ability to respond appropriately depends on the quality of the perceptual system and the computer's ability to interpret what it perceives. Information about the participant's behavior can be obtained from passive sensors, such as video cameras, or from devices worn by the participant that track the major joints of the body. These sensors, their associated circuitry, and the interpreting software constitute the perceptual system.

The perceptual system may yield either static or dynamic information about participants. Static information—such as height, weight, or the color of clothing—does not change during the experience. It can be useful for distinguishing individuals when several are present. In addition, knowledge of a participant's height allows the computer to scale an interaction, so that a small person is able to reach all interesting objects in a graphic scene. However, in general, a computer response to a static attribute is unlikely to be meaningful to the participant, who cannot identify the cause or control the effect. Dynamic information—including posture, rate and direction of movement, and pitch or volume of voice—can be controlled by a participant and is more useful as the basis for interactions.

The perceptual system determines what the computer knows and thus to what it can respond. If the computer is aware of only the participant's arms and hands, small movements of the fingers will be invisible and thus will be irrelevant to the interaction. Behavior that evokes no response is less likely to recur. After the first few minutes, a participant will subconsciously adapt and will typically behave only in ways that the computer can perceive.

What the Computer Should Perceive

Since the goal of an artificial reality is to involve participants physically in a relationship that they can understand, it should be possible for them to recognize which aspects of their behavior are eliciting responses. A person's first experience with this kind of feedback usually leads him to focus on large movements of his body—for example, arm waving in VIDEOPLACE or turning the head to look around the graphic world with reality goggles. Only after a participant has spent some time in an artificial reality is it possible to involve him in more subtle relationships based on small movements, such as nods or shrugs.

The design of a perceptual system requires a tradeoff between the need for the computer to know as much as possible about a participant's behavior and its commitment to respond in real time. To respond intelligently, the computer must have a wealth of information. It must be sensitive to small movements, be able to identify individuals if several are present, and be capable of keeping track of those individuals as they move around.

On the other hand, the perceptual system must not provide too much information. Unneeded detail will require extra processing, which might be better used interpreting more limited input or enriching the output responses. When there is more perceptual information than the computer can handle, the processing must focus on a small subset of it so that the amount of data being considered is consistent with the real-time nature of the medium.

What to Wear to an Artificial Reality

The most significant difference between the two artificial-reality technologies discussed in this book lies in their answers to the question of what the the participant should wear when using them. VIDEOPLACE is "come as you are." With NASA's technology, you must wear "whatever is necessary." The choice makes the task of perception much more difficult in one case, but makes the technology less friendly in the other.

Video Perception

The VIDEOPLACE concept assumes high-speed computer vision. Creating true real-time vision has never been a fashionable research problem because of an orthodoxy in the research community that finds off-line, highly mathematical approaches more intellectually satisfying than it does the high-speed techniques that must necessarily involve ad hoc short cuts. However, there are advantages to real-time approaches. Thirty frames arrive every second, 100,000 per hour. Because results are acquired so quickly, we gain much more experience with our problem. Consequently, our algorithms become more robust.

For VIDEOPLACE, computer vision has been a means to an end. To create unencumbered, interactive experiences, we had to enable the computer to see people. We chose to create a minimal perceiving and behaving real-time system right from the start, and to improve its performance gradually. Thus, in VIDEOPLACE,

> 1. The subject of recognition is the human body. The computer must be able to identify parts of the body, including the head, arms, legs, trunk, hands, and fingers;

> 2. The system is interested in dynamic as well as static analysis of the human form. Human movements are understood in terms of actions such as touching, hitting, throwing, kicking, and jumping;

> 3. The need to discriminate the human form from the background is finessed by providing a neutral background;

> 4. Color and gray-scale information are ignored. The computer perceives the human silhouette;

> 5. Perception is accomplished in real time. No more than 1/30 second elapses between a participant's action and the system's response. If a participant is moving quickly, pattern recognition is necessarily rough. When the participant moves slowly, perception can be more sophisticated;

> 6. At any instant, perception is not fully general. The system interprets its input in terms of the current interaction and of its knowledge of the moment immediately before. Its attention may be focused on a small part of the screen to see whether a particular event is about to happen. It may completely miss events that occur elsewhere;

> 7. The behavior of the human participant is to be understood in the context of the graphic scene into which the person's image has been inserted. Since the computer has defined the graphic objects,

it has no problem recognizing them. Therefore, it is free to focus on structural relationships between the participant and the microworld.

The task of understanding the body is intuitively simple; the difficulty stems from the fact that, even with a low-resolution camera, a single frame contains 256 x 256 = 64,000 pixels. Just counting all these pixels can take a significant fraction of a second. Obviously, recognition of specific two-dimensional shapes in the image will take much longer. Noting that there are 30 frames per second makes the problem seem hopeless. It would literally take all day for the best computer-vision program to find a person dressed in checks or plaid standing against a complex background.

To simplify the problem, the VIDEOPLACE participant stands against a brightly backlit sheet of translucent plastic. This setup produces a high-contrast image in which any bright spot can be assumed to be the background and any darker spot is the participant. Thresholding hardware, followed by nearest-neighbor filtering to eliminate isolated noise pixels, produces a binary image in which each pixel is either a 0 or a 1 (Fig. 6.1).

The simplest approach to locating a participant is to monitor specific points on the screen to see whether the participant is touching them. If the pixel is a 1, it is being touched; if it is 0, it is not being touched. Thus, you can think of the point as a switch. If the participant touches it, the computer can initiate a response. The problem with this technique is that you do not know what part of the body is touching the point; a simple function such as drawing is impossible, because the computer cannot identify a finger. We used this technique in VIDEOPLACE in the mid-1970s, but abandoned it because too little could be recognized in real time.

Instead, in 1976, we started developing an elaborate processing system for VIDEOPLACE that seeks to understand human movements in the same way that people do—a system that can *see*. Since normal computers are too slow to perform this task, the binary image is passed to a number of specialized processors that operate in parallel. (A *specialized processor* is designed to execute just one program or a small family of programs.) Although there is a prejudice against specialized computers in the computer-science community, some of these processors execute 10,000

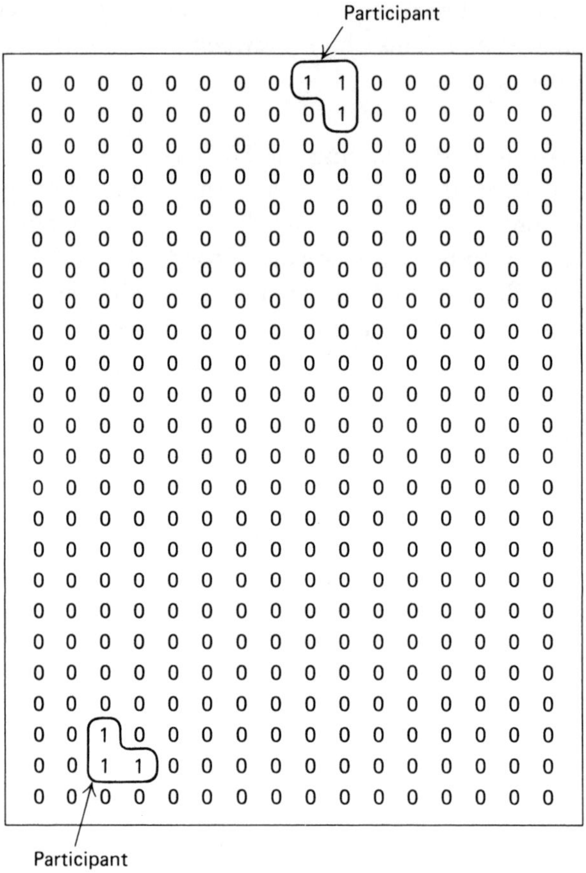

Participant

Figure 6.1
VIDEOPLACE Binary Image.
Participants' feet are seen by the computer as 1s in a field of 0s.

times faster than a personal computer, making them irresistible for our purposes.

Although these specialized processors are very fast, they are not very smart; therefore, many of the features they find have to be culled by more sophisticated testing. For instance, spurious fingers caused by stray noise pixels, a wisp of hair on the head, or a wrinkle in a sleeve have to be recognized as errors and eliminated from consideration.

Ambiguities also arise because VIDEOPLACE uses only one camera. If you hold a hand out by your side, it is easily detected by the computer. However, if you point at the screen, your hand cannot be seen (Fig. 6.2). If you hold your hand out by your side and move it forward, it appears to get shorter. By using a model of the human body to guide its perception, VIDEOPLACE makes the most of the information it receives. First, it looks for the features that are most unambiguous. For instance, when it has found one hand, it knows that it has to look for at most one

Figure 6.2
What Has Happened to the Arm?
A problem in software understanding of human movement.

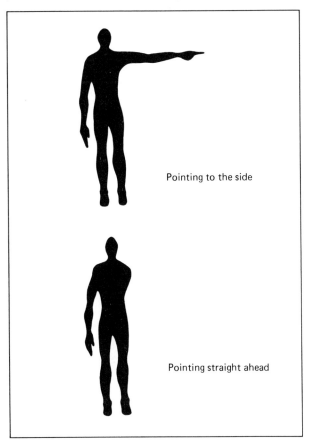

Pointing to the side

Pointing straight ahead

more if there is only one participant. It also uses the state of the model from the previous frame to help understand what it is seeing in the current frame. If there appears to be a finger coming out of a person's head, it can decide that it is indeed a finger and not a wisp of hair if there was a finger near the head in the previous frame and this person's hair did not stick out in the past.

At the VIDEODESK, a second camera, mounted beside the first, has been used to provide stereoscopic information to track a single finger in three dimensions. Alternatively, a second camera viewing the participant's hand from the side can provide similar information. Locating 10 fingers on two hands in three dimensions would require more cameras and more elaborate processing. Additional cameras can be used to track the person's body in three dimensions in the VIDEOPLACE environment. Cameras can be mounted all around the participant as well as overhead, looking down. Each of these cameras will be used to locate his extremities. The cameras with the most unambiguous views of each limb will be used to constrain the model of the participant's body. Only when these high-confidence images are analyzed will more detailed processing of the other views be performed, and then only if there are features not yet accounted for.

Gray-Scale Processing

If, instead of analyzing silhouette images, the VIDEOPLACE system were to use gray-scale and color information, more sophisticated edge processing would permit us to dispense with backlighting and ultimately to permit complex backgrounds. In addition, gray-scale processing could be used to locate your face, to identify your facial features, to determine which way you were looking, and to interpret your expression.

Tracking facial features is a difficult but tractable problem. In 1986, we submitted a proposal to the National Institute of Mental Health (NIMH) to do research on this problem. (In 1990, RCA announced a method of identifying individuals watching television in the home for the Nielsen television rating service [1].) Although *interpreting* facial expressions would be difficult at first, it would be possible to place cartoon features on a participant's face and to control them with his actual expressions.

There is another level of awareness that would be desirable for the VIDEOPLACE system to have. Often, people interacting with VIDEOPLACE are simultaneously interacting with people off-screen. It would be useful for the system to perceive these other people as well, in order to understand the social context of the interaction. The concept of a sensory floor, as used in PSYCHIC SPACE, has been resurrected for this purpose. The sensory floor would also aid the computer in tracking the movements of a participant in environments with complex backgrounds. The position and orientation of the feet could be easily determined and provide starting points for the vision processing. If the floor is capable of measuring degrees of pressure as well as presence, that information can be used to predict when the participant is about to jump.

The discussion of environmental technologies has emphasized the use of video cameras because we have taken that approach and because the video image is used to represent the participant in the artificial reality. In the long run, any environmental means of perceiving the participant's movements is of interest. For instance, Cyberware Laboratory of Pacific Grove, California, mechanically rotates a digitizing camera around a person's head while scanning the head with a laser beam to create a three-dimensional model of the person's face [2]. It requires 15 seconds to digitize the subject, which is 450 times longer than the time required for a video camera to capture an image. In the future, a system that does not involve mechanical scanning should be able to digitize a person's full body in real time.

Wearable Technologies

An alternative to VIDEOPLACE's video perceptual system is to have the participant wear sensors or transducers on each major joint of his body. (See the EXOS Dextrous Hand Master in Figure 6.3.) Obviously, a deliberate act such as putting on this equipment changes the character of the ensuing experience. It puts you on notice that you are entering another space. It is like an airlock. You cannot just happen on it.

In principle, wearable technology should trivialize the problem of locating the participant's head and hand in space. The computer does not have to identify body parts, since it knows that the goggles are on the participant's head, the glove is on her hand, and a dedicated sensor is attached to each joint of the arms and legs. If the sensors were perfect, the computer could read them to obtain three-dimensional coordinates for

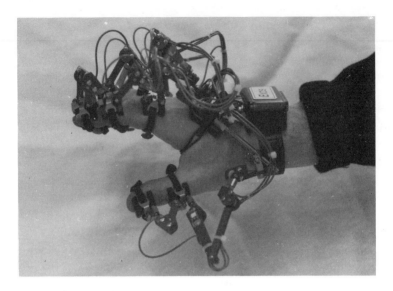

Figure 6.3
The EXOS Dextrous Hand Master.
Courtesy of EXOS, Inc.

every part of her body. Unfortunately, locating the participant is not that simple. Inaccuracies in finding reference points occur because the Polhemus device averages three readings for each coordinate in turn, which means that the x, y, and z positions are not taken at the same point in time. In fact, the point reported may be a location never occupied. In addition, the mathematical calculations needed to interpret the raw sensor signals require significant processing time. The sensor delays are added to delays attributable to the operating system and the graphic rendering so that the position reported by this device may be 1/4 to 1/3 second old before the system can respond to it. Thus, when you turn your head, there is a noticeable lag before the graphic world catches up to you.

It is surprising that people working with this technology are not more offended by this lag. A number of alternative approaches are being developed. At North Carolina, three head-mounted cameras detect patterns of LEDs on the ceiling, and the resulting video images are analyzed to determine the participant's position in the room [3]. Kicha Ganapathy at Bell Laboratories has demonstrated a related system in

Plate 1
PAINTING THE TOWN.
Katrin Hinrichsen interacts with the New York skyline, turning on the lights in the buildings with her fingertips. *Courtesy of Hank Morgan.*

Plate 2
A VIDEODESK Application.
The image of the user's hands is used to position a rectangle in a diagram. *Courtesy of Hank Morgan.*

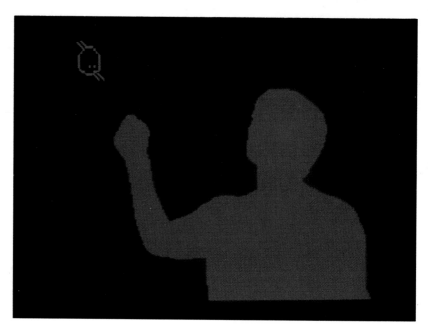

Plate 3
CRITTER Interaction.
CRITTER is a playful artificial entity that cavorts with a VIDEOPLACE participant. Its rules of behavior are described in Conceptual Dependency Notation and are controlled by a real-time expert system.

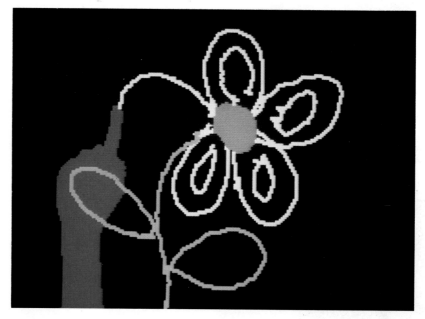

Plate 4
DIGITAL DRAWING Interaction.
In DIGITAL DRAWING, the VIDEOPLACE participant uses her finger to draw; opening her hand erases the drawing.

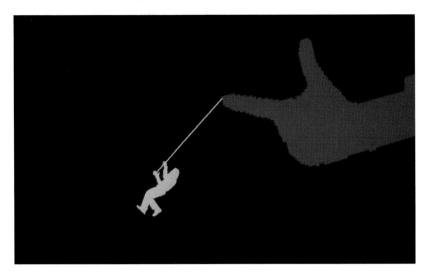

Plate 5
HANGING BY A THREAD.

The VIDEOPLACE participant's image dangles from a graphic string suspended from the VIDEODESK participant's finger. By moving from side to side, the VIDEOPLACE participant can cause his image to swing. Since the two people can be a distance apart, this two-way interaction is really a playful teleconference.

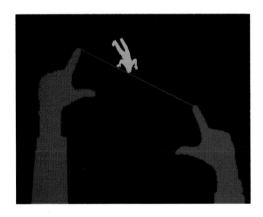

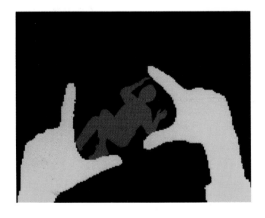

Plate 6
ARTWHEELS Interaction.

In this two-way interaction, a VIDEOPLACE participant rolls down a graphic string held by a VIDEODESK participant.

Plate 7
A VIDEODESK Participant Lifts the Image of a VIDEOPLACE Participant.

Plate 8
A VIDEODESK Participant Captures the Image of a VIDEOPLACE Participant.

When released, the VIDEOPLACE participant can perform gymnastics on the other person's fingers.

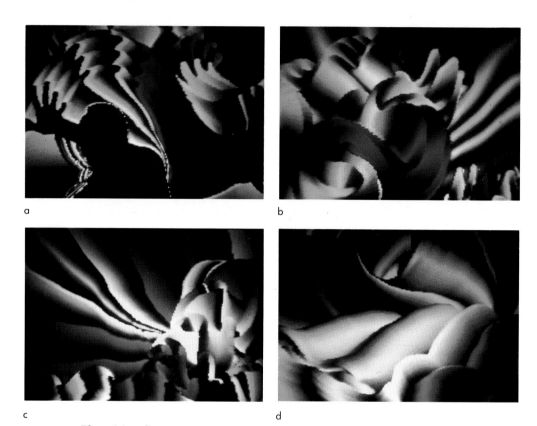

a

b

c

d

Plate 9 (a–d)
Images From BODY SURFACING Interaction.
During this interaction, the VIDEOPLACE participant's body is used to create flowing patterns on the screen.

Plate 10
An Image Generated by Harold Cohen's Simulated
Artist Program, Aaron.
After the image was generated, it was hand painted by Cohen.
Courtesy of Harold Cohen.

Plate 11
The Pseudopod from *The Abyss*.
The pseudopod suggests a liquid body that might be inhabited by a human dancer. *Copyright*
© 1989 Twentieth Century Fox. All rights reserved. *Courtesy of Industrial Light and Magic, a division of LucasArts Entertainment Company.*

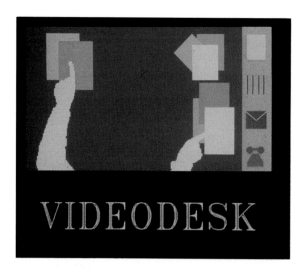

Plate 12
Graphic Paper on the VIDEODESK.
Graphic paper can be moved around the VIDEODESK with your hands, just like the real thing.

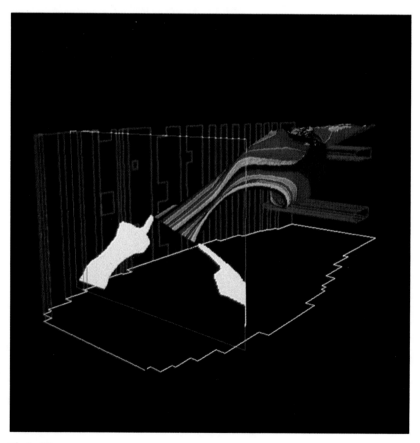

Plate 13
A Three-Dimensional VIDEODESK Application.
The user's hands appear on a sample plane in the combustion chamber of a jet engine. The fingertips define a line. The gas that flows through that line creates a surface that is deformed as it flows through the space.

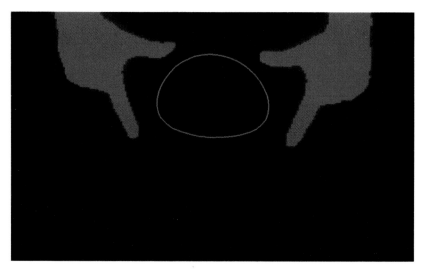

Plate 14
The EXTRUSION ILLUSION.
The VIDEODESK user's fingertips are used as control points of a spline curve that in turn
will be used as the aperture in an extruding device.

Plate 15
The EXTRUSION ILLUSION.
As graphic material is extruded through the aperture defined by the spline curve, the
aperture's shape is changed by moving the fingers, creating a complex graphic structure in a few moments.

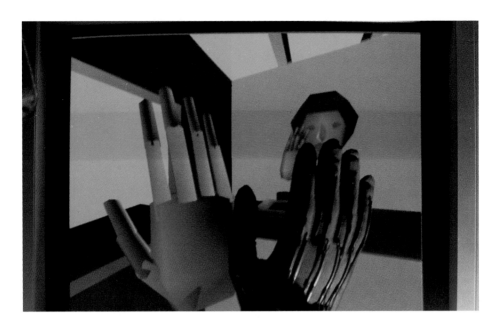

Plate 16
A DataGlove™ (right) and Computer Image of the Glove.
The DataGlove measures finger movements and hand orientation and position. The computer image of the hand tracks the changes. *Courtesy of VPL Research, Inc.*

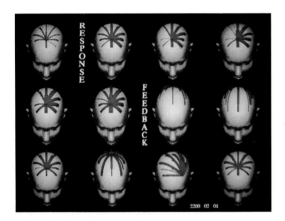

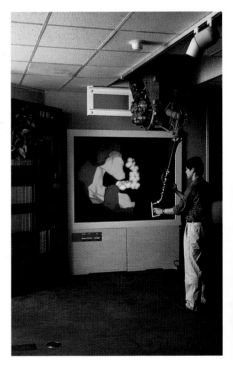

Plate 17
Computer-Animated EEG Data.
A sequence of brain activity states is detected by a 124-channel EEG during performance of a decision task. *Courtesy of Alan Gevins, EEG Systems Laboratory, San Francisco.*

Plate 18
The GROPE III Haptic Display System in Use.
Courtesy of the Department of Computer Science, University of North Carolina at Chapel Hill.

Figure 6.4
A Costume to Aid Computer Pattern Recognition.

which a single camera views a circle of LEDs mounted on a plane [4]. The camera could be mounted on the ceiling and the LEDs worn on the head. Obviously, if video cameras turn out to be the best device to track head movements, we can make an argument for using video techniques throughout. Specially marked costumes and gloves could facilitate three-dimensional tracking without wires (Fig. 6.4).

For sensing the movements of the limbs, a reality suit is used (Fig. 6.5). This device senses the orientation of the participant's arms and legs in three-dimensional space. Ivan Sutherland had people wear LEDs on their joints to aid tracking [5]. VPL's current design is similar to that of the DataGlove. One problem with this device is that it must be tightly fitted or the sensors will slip relative to the points on the body that they are supposed to be tracking. Although stretch fabrics could minimize this effect, the suit cannot yet be manufactured in quantity and would not be appropriate apparel in most situations. In fact, the reality suit's appearance may be as important as its function. At the moment, the reality suit is not the focus of attention—only a few have been fabricated and there is a sense that even these are not used heavily.

Figure 6.5
The DataSuit.
Courtesy of VPL Research.

It is worth noting that a high-resolution sensory floor could locate the participant's feet with great precision, determine which way the participant was facing, and provide a reference point to be used with the bend measurements provided by the reality suit to locate the other parts of the body. Thomas Speeter at Bell Laboratories is working on such a high-resolution floor [6].

Another limitation of current wearable technology is the inability to detect facial expressions, which will limit our ability to communicate with other people in an artificial reality. Jaron Lanier has postulated the need for smile detectors to remedy this shortcoming. However, if we acknowledge that people may resist wearing reality goggles, gloves, and suits, then we must assume that they will object even more vigorously if they have to wear smile detectors. Although it is possible that sensors away from the face could detect the muscle potentials that control the facial expressions, the obvious way to detect facial expressions is with video cameras.

At the moment, perhaps the greatest problem with the wearable technologies is not that the participant has to wear something, but rather that he is tethered to the electronics and thus is unable to move around freely. This problem is a simple one; thus, we can hope that it will soon cease to be a concern.

Advantages

Use of wearable technology eliminates many of the difficult issues that VIDEOPLACE faces. Certain problems do not exist at all. Since there is only one person in the reality glove, goggles, or suit, it is not necessary to distinguish one person from another. Fractional images of people, who are only half-visible on the screen, never occur. Perspective does not change the apparent size of participants. There is no need to distinguish between adults and children (except when they are being "fitted" for a reality suit). In addition, body parts do not appear and disappear. Finally, the analog characteristics of video cameras are of no concern. Clearly, there are benefits to putting on all this paraphernalia, and there will be applications for which people will be willing to do so.

Issues Common to Both Technologies

There are a number of issues related to interpreting the behavior of the participant's body that must be addressed, regardless of how it is perceived. There is also a higher level of perceptual processing that must be performed once the location of the participant's body is known. This processing is independent of how the positions were determined.

Motion Analysis

In an artificial reality, the computer must interpret participants' motions in terms of their implied effect on the graphic world. If there is an object in view and the participant moves a hand toward it, the system must decide not only whether, but also how, the person touches it. Is the participant hitting the object, tapping it, or trying to pick it up? How does the system distinguish between carrying the object, dropping it, and throwing it? Is the object animate or inanimate? It is important for the system to understand the semantics of objects and actions in its microworld; if it does not understand, then it cannot maintain a convincing version of reality.

Accuracy

Both artificial-reality technologies measure the participant's actions imprecisely. Both will benefit from greater accuracy. However, since the human body itself moves imprecisely, it is likely that both technologies will require special techniques for exact operations, like those typical in mouse-based applications. Although the developers of the reality gloves are not unhappy with these devices' resolution, none of the demonstrations so far show precise manipulations being performed. Indeed, precise operations are difficult without a rapid system response.

Sample Rate

In an artificial reality, the only meaningful definition of *sample rate* is the time required for the system to perceive the participant's behavior and to complete a response to that perception. Many workers in the field are confused by the Polhemus device, which claims 60 samples per second, but does not produce a reading for several sample periods because of processing delays in the device. It would probably be preferable to talk in terms of the *response rate*, which would refer to the number of disjoint response cycles (from perception to response) per second.

If you are trying to coordinate a rapid movement, a much higher response rate than that provided by either technology is required. For example, VIDEOPLACE's difficulty in recognizing a throwing gesture and responding with precision occurs because the system samples only 30 times per second. In 1/30 second, the human hand can travel a significant distance. A higher response rate would give the system more information about the trajectory and velocity of the hand, and therefore would permit a more accurate throw. Not only athletic events require rapid response. The fine motor skills of a surgeon are likely to require both rapid response and high resolution.

Sound responses also require high temporal resolution. If perception occurs only 30 times per second, then the participant can initiate sounds only at 1/30 second intervals. Since 1/30 second is the duration of a short note, it is not possible to control the onset of a note with any precision. A pianist can probably time his keystrikes to within a few milliseconds.

Whenever I have used a reality glove, I have been told that it was sampling 10 to 15 times per second, but the rate seemed far slower because I was very aware of the lag between my actions and the system's response. The true system response rate was probably four responses per second, according to the definition. (It is difficult to attribute the delays to specific devices and processing steps without instrumenting the system so that its performance can be monitored with a logic analyzer, as we have done with the VIDEOPLACE system.) I think that 30 responses per second is the minimum rate required to provide a sense of real-time interaction; it is far too slow for many purposes.

Parsing

In both technologies, you have the problem of parsing a gesture. The challenge is similar to recognizing a word. If you hear just one word, you have no problem recognizing when it begins and ends. If you hear a sentence spoken and you listen for the beginning and end of a specific word in the middle of the sentence, you will realize that there are often no hard boundaries between words. Similarly, movements of the body are continuous—one flows into the next. Thus, a throwing gesture must be identified in the context of a great number of other hand movements.

Magic Versus Metaphor

In an artificial reality, an action may be either magic or metaphor [7]. *Metaphor* refers to the actions that are suggested by the juxtaposition of your image with a graphic object. For example, if the image of your hand appears near a graphic beachball, the impression given is that you can pick up the ball, drop it, or throw it. However, if you want to change its color instantaneously, that requires *magic*.

Traditional computer commands are pure magic. While the desktop metaphor added icons and trashcans, in any graphic environment, the number of actions suggested by the physical-participation metaphor is limited. In the real world, there are few tasks that are performed by the body alone; most require us to use tools. But even graphic tools do not solve the problem, since you do not really want to perform tedious or strenuous physical work in an artificial reality. Thus, there are undoubtedly many magical things you would like the computer to do for you.

Also, the physical metaphor is often ambiguous, particularly in a reality where the participants' effects on graphic objects must be inferred from gesture alone. The same physical action may suggest several consequences in a given context. If you reach out and touch a graphic object, the result might be that you can pull it toward you after you make contact, or that it is pushed away by the contact. There is no a priori way for the system to distinguish between the two intentions, or for the participant to predict the likely outcome with a gesture technology.

One of the ways that people have addressed the ambiguity of the physical metaphor has been to use hand gestures. In VIDEOPLACE, you can draw when you extend one finger. When you do not want to draw, you conceal the finger. When you want to erase locally, you use two fingers held close together. When you want to erase the whole screen, you open your hand. The first three commands are metaphor. Although we observed people rubbing their open hands over their drawings to erase them (metaphor), the fact that an open hand erases the whole drawing regardless of where it appears on the screen makes this gesture magic. There are gestures used in NASA's virtual workstation that are definitely magic. Pointing in a direction makes you move in that direction. Twisting your hand makes a menu pop up.

Both technologies have used gestures for commands. Participants receive some satisfaction from a few well-chosen, easy-to-remember gestures. However, I believe that symbolic gestures should be used sparingly, because they conflict with natural behavior; because there are few commonly-used, real-world gestures; and because traditional methods of issuing commands, such as speech and graphic controls, are both more effective and more natural when extensive and explicit communication is required.

Navigation

Navigating in the graphic world presents problems for both technologies. In VIDEOPLACE, you must always be visible to the camera. If you move away from the backlighting assembly, you cannot see the reality on the screen and the camera cannot see you. The reality suit limits your freedom because of the wires that connect the suit, the glove, and the goggles to the computer. Current reference technology does not work over large areas. Also, unless some special navigation convention is used, the artificial reality you are exploring can be no larger than the real room in which you are standing.

To some extent, movement limits can be enforced visually to inhibit you from outrunning your sensor. It is possible to imagine a large floor space with many participants moving around in their own private graphic spaces, each separated from the others by graphic walls. Each person's choices could affect the dimensions of their private space, which in turn would affect the range of movement available to the people around them. The computer would be smart enough to allocate space as needed.

Although walking could be the same action in real and simulated space, if you want to move upstairs or you want to fly, any way you choose to do it will be unrealistic. A simple gesture, like pointing in the direction you want to go, may be workable for the moment, but it is not very exciting. It might be appropriate to hold your arms out to the sides to fly, the way a child might. (Picture Air Force generals maneuvering in this way.) Navigation requires some sort of magic if you want to move around an artificial world in ways you cannot move in your physical surroundings.

We have experimented with different methods of using your body to control the movement of your image around the screen. It is possible to climb a graphic slope with a hand-over-hand motion, or to swim freestyle or breaststroke. You can pivot around the image of one hand so that it looks like you are swinging from it, and then pivot around the other hand. You can hold your hands above your head like Superman

Figure 6.6
The Superman Navigation Interaction.

and steer exactly as you would expect him to (Fig. 6.6). This technique is especially interesting when your image is diving toward the bottom of the screen, since the visual feedback you are using to control your movement is reversed. Tilting your arms to the right causes your inverted image to turn to the left. Such feedback is supposed to be difficult to adapt to, but people adjust to continuous changes in rotated feedback without thinking about it.

Mixed Metaphors

If special gestures are used for navigation, we immediately encounter a conflict. If I point to make myself move, I cannot use the same gesture for another purpose. In fact, I cannot point inadvertently without moving. For example, in VIDEOPLACE, a problem arises if I want to throw a ball while I am flying. Since the angle between my head and arms is used to control the direction of flight, the moment I start to throw, I also change my heading. Although I might be able to adapt to this confusion, it is clearly not ideal. It is preferable to let the participant shoot with a finger instead of throw, because pointing does not conflict with the steering as much as throwing does.

Collision

In video games, the computer must constantly determine whether two objects, such as an alien and a missile, occupy the same place at the same time. Making this determination is the collision problem. The graphic sprites in early video games were treated as points, so you would think that the computer would have no problem in detecting when they collided. But it did. When there were a large number of sprites, each had to be tested with respect to every other sprite. This testing was a time-consuming operation.

If you are dealing with complex shapes, such as the human body, and with complicated objects in three dimensions, rather than with sprites, this problem becomes very difficult for the computer to solve in real time. PLATE 7 shows a VIDEODESK hand correctly picking up a miniature VIDEOPLACE body. If the two bodies were interpenetrating, the computer would have to decide how to respond. If both people are moving rapidly, the video will not reveal exactly what happened since the last sample. We can see where we are now and where we were a moment earlier, but not how we got there. Any response that appears correct in one case will probably not be applicable in another situation that looks the same to the computer. Remember that circumstances change 30 times per second, so if there are cases that your software has not anticipated, they will be encountered during interactions.

Although there are off-the-shelf solutions to this problem for complex fixed shapes, they are computationally expensive and do not consider dynamic shapes such as the human body. I hope that some brute-force method will be found that solves the whole problem in hardware.

Graphic Sensing and Physics

Understanding the participant's actions is only part of the perception problem. Graphic creatures such as CRITTER must also be able to perceive the participant and the objects in the graphic world. The system must also consider the consequences of the actions of these creatures. Even inanimate objects require perception by the system. For instance, if the participant throws a graphic ball at a graphic wall, the system must recognize when the ball hits the wall, and must decide whether the ball should bounce, or knock the wall over. It is easier to think of the ball as a creature with its own kind of perception and its own rules of behavior than it is to create a separate category for inanimate objects. While the local version of the laws of nature need not be realistic or even consistent, it is easier to use simulated physics to create a consistent reality than it is to compose for every eventuality. Note that, as the numbers of participants, creatures, and objects increases, the number of possible interrelationships among these entities undergoes a combinatorial explosion—a familiar hazard in computer systems.

Dramatic Sensing

At a higher level, the system will be asked to recognize increasingly subtle aspects of the unfolding interaction. It must make judgments about the participant's knowledge, expectations, and interest; about opportunities for physical humor as in MAN-IPULATE; and about situations where the current mode of interaction should be changed because the participant has exhausted this mode's possibilities.

Sound Sensing

In the past, VIDEOPLACE has ignored the participant's voice. The idea of the computer responding to human movement was new, and we thought that we should emphasize this modality. If the system understood speech, people might stop acting and start talking. I thought that we talked enough, and that it would be nice to create an activity in which we forgot our verbal selves. In addition, it seemed right to begin by interacting physically because physical acitivity is a universal and childlike

language. My decision was valid at the time, but as the gesture component becomes overloaded, speech input is worth reconsidering.

It may be desirable to be able to talk to CRITTER to change its behavior, to be able to encourage the system when you like the current
interaction and to be able to scold it when you do not. For practical
VIDEODESK applications, "point and talk" has always seemed to be the
obvious interface combination. Current speech-understanding technology requires training. The user has to repeat each word in the system's
vocabulary a number of times before that word can be recognized. In a
public exhibit, such training would be tedious. In the office or home,
information about your speech patterns can be gained over a long period.

Body Signals

People always ask about the possibility of using signals generated
by body functions—such as those shown in electroencephalograms
(EEGs), galvanic skin response (GSR), and electrocardiograms (EKGs)—
as input. These signals are incompatible with the VIDEOPLACE medium
because the participant would have to wear sensors to detect them.
Although such instrumentation is compatible with reality suits, it is not
obvious that these signals report information that is useful during full-
body interactions, because people are not aware of these signals, because
most people cannot control them consciously, and because even those
people who can control these signals cannot do so while they are
physically active.

It is possible, however, to conceive of interactions where the
participant sits or lies down and participates in a visual or auditory world
by controlling her body functions. For example, new technologies are
being developed that appear to show the brain in action. Computer
animations of data from PET scans and multiprobe electroencephalograms
show the different brain centers becoming active or dormant depending
on the mental task the subject is performing (PLATE 16) [8]. If these
technologies meet with continuing success, it would be extremely valuable for an artificial-reality system to be aware of how the participant's
brain was responding to the participant's experience. In a teaching
system, the computer could know whether the student was paying
attention. Alternatively, a participant could watch her own brain think—

an exciting new kind of feedback loop! If a noninvasive sensing cap could be developed that monitored these signals as the participant moved freely, they could provide important clues about the participant's reaction to the experience.

Conclusion

Whether encumbering or unencumbering means are used to perceive the participant's behavior, perception is the most critical function in an artificial-reality system. On the one hand, it is possible to use very simple feedback to define an interesting interaction if the system correctly perceives the detailed movements of a participant's body. On the other hand, if the computer cannot understand the participant's actions, then even the most powerful displays cannot create a meaningful interactive experience.

References

1. W.J. Hawkins, "TV Views Viewers," *Popular Science* (February 1990), p. 74.

2. Cyberware 4020/PS Digitizer, Cyberware Laboratory, Inc., Pacific Grove, CA.

3. J. Wang, V. Chi, & H. Fuchs, "A Real-time Optical 3D Tracker for Head-Mounted Display Systems," *Computer Graphics*, 24, No. 2 (March 1990), pp. 205–215.

4. S.K. Ganapathy, "Machine Perception and Its Role in Virtual Environments," *Human–Machine Interfaces for Teleoperators & Virtual Environments*, Santa Barbara, CA, March 4, 1990.

5. R.P. Burton & I.E. Sutherland, "Twinkle Box—A Three-Dimensional Computer Input Device," *Proceedings of the National Computer Conference and Exhibition, AFIPS*, 43 (1974), pp. 513–520.

6. T. Speeter, personal communication and demonstration.

7. R.B. Smith, "Experiences with an Alternate Reality Kit: An Example of the Tension Between Literalism and Magic," *CHI '87* (April 1987), p. 61.

8. A.S. Givens, N.H. Morgan, S.L. Bressler, B.A. Cutillo, R.M. White, J. Illes, D.S. Greer, J.C. Doyle, & G.M. Zeitlin, "Human Neuroelectric Patterns Predict Performance Accuracy," *Science*, 30 (January 1987), pp. 580–585.

7

Reality Responds

Introduction

An artificial reality must dominate the participant's senses with synthetic stimuli that define a context for an experience that the person will accept as real, even if the world portrayed is not. All of the senses are candidates for illusory input. However, in terms of their importance for creating artificial realities, sight and hearing almost certainly dominate, followed by touch, with smell and taste of lesser significance. Fortunately, there has been a revolution in our ability to produce real-time graphics and computer-controlled sound. These developments, together with the appearance of inexpensive flat panel displays, have made possible the artificial realities that we see today.

Visual Expectations

The most important and best understood sense is vision, which more than any other provides us with our sense of place. When visual cues conflict with data received by the other senses, they usually dominate. This dominance results from expectations based on eons of evolution and a lifetime of experience with physical reality. The following example is taken from personal experience and illustrates the importance of these expectations.

Mystery Ride

Many years ago on the Boardwalk at Ocean City, New Jersey, there was a concession called the Mystery Ride. A group of about ten people entered a very ordinary room, complete with pictures on the walls, a light fixture hanging from the ceiling, and a rug on the floor. We were seated on two benches suspended by heavy beams from either end of the room. When the ride began, it seemed we were being turned upside down. This was alarming as there were no physical restraints to keep us on our benches. After a panicky moment, I reasoned that it was the room that was turning around us, while we remained stationary. Unfortunately, this intelligence was not at all reassuring, for years of experience tell us that ceilings are up and floors are down, and when we find our head by the floor and our feet by the ceiling, we assume that we are upside down (Fig. 7.1).

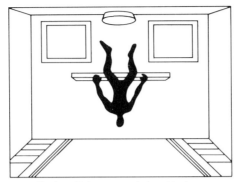

Illusion: Being suspended upside down

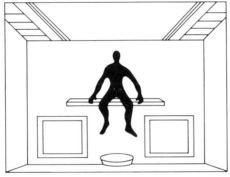

Reality: Room turns upside down

**Figure 7.1
Mystery Ride.**

I closed my eyes to rely on my vestibular sense. The semicircular canals in my inner ear, which are responsible for my sense of balance and had served to make me seasick in the past, were now being asked to offer evidence in support of intellect in its case against untrustworthy vision. Unfortunately, the authority of the visual interpretation made the interior sense unreadable. Although I was familiar with the psychological literature describing visual illusions, I had never guessed how dramatically vision was able to tyrannize the other senses, and to overrule reason as well.

This illusion suggests that there are conventions established by our visual experience that can be exploited for use in an environmental display. More than the other senses, vision defines reality or unreality. We can become disoriented and even unbalanced if the relationships anticipated by our sense of sight are altered. Consider a gymnast standing on a balance beam while wearing reality goggles. It would almost certainly be impossible for her to keep her balance if the computer graphic world was tilted with respect to the real one.

Optical Flow

Some visual expectations are associated with movement in physical space. As we turn our head or move around, we are accustomed to seeing one scene transformed smoothly into the next. Visual feedback could be made to deviate from this expectation. For example, the rate of movement could be exaggerated such that a three-foot stride resulted in an apparent 30-foot change in position on the display, giving the participant the experience of being a 60-foot-tall giant trudging through the graphic world.

Perspective

We expect that, when we approach an object, it will become larger; when we move away from it, we expect that it will become smaller. This relationship could be reversed, so that, as we moved toward a displayed object, it appeared to recede. Or, by moving in a certain direction, people might cause the perceived reality to rotate around them, rather than to approach or recede. These ideas suggest a whole family of translations of physical space into perceptual space.

Connection to the Graphic World

There are several visual issues that connect the participant to the graphic world. When these concerns are observed, the participant feels that he is part of the simulation; when they are omitted, the experience can be uncomfortable.

Self-Image

In any artificial-reality technology, the participant needs to see an image of her hand in order to touch objects in the graphic world. Other participants should be able to see an image of her whole body if they are to interact with her naturally. Since the participant's live video image is integral to the VIDEOPLACE concept, this requirement presents no problem. VIDEOPLACE's simple silhouette image responds instantaneously to participants' actions, making it easy to identify with. This sense of identification will be enhanced somewhat when the participant's real image is shown in full color. In the VIDEODESK system, the image of the participant's hand enters the screen from an edge and includes part of the arm, reinforcing the sense that the hand on the screen belongs to the participant.

In contrast, when you view a three-dimensional world through reality goggles, a disconnected graphic hand is often displayed. This image is disconcerting, as you are accustomed to seeing your hand attached to your arm. In addition, you usually see part of your body and your nose.

Since the developers of reality goggle systems are trying to create a sense of "being" the person or creature inhabiting the artificial reality, they show you only the parts of your body that you would see if you were inside it. The different representations of the participant reflect a conceptual and philosophical difference in our approaches to a common goal.

Both technologies allow the possibility of "being" nonhuman creatures (PLATE 17). VPL has a demonstration in which you are given a lobster's body. Instead of your hands, you see giant claws. The other participants see you as a bipedal lobster. However, "being" an alien creature may not be that satisfying. We have only a limited ability to appreciate our own appearance. That is why we have mirrors. The triptych mirrors in department stores show us how much we miss in flat mirrors. Video tapes show us engaged in activities other than viewing ourselves. If being us is the best way to experience our bodies, why are we so surprised when we see ourselves on video tape? In fact, VPL has mirrors in their spaces precisely for this reason. Note that the experience of using these mirrors is similar to interacting with the VIDEOPLACE screen.

The VIDEOPLACE stance is that it is compelling to see your graphic body from an outsider's perspective and to operate it as though it were a graphic puppet. It may just be more fun to see yourself as a dinosaur than it is to "be" a dinosaur. Your sense of having things happen to you may be stronger when you see them happen to a body with which you have identified than it would be were the same events to happen to a body you could neither see nor feel. There is no right answer. It is like the choice a writer has of using the first person or the third person.

No matter how your body is represented, you have the problem of how to make it move. If you are given four or six legs, how do you control them? Do you know how to trot, canter, or gallop?

One reason reality goggle systems are experimenting with alien bodies may be that it is currently impossible to construct a realistic graphic representation of the participant in real time. Even if the graphics hardware could do the rendering fast enough, these systems have no information about the participants' clothes, hair, and facial expressions.

Lost in Space

When you are navigating a three-dimensional artificial reality, you may find yourself in a corner or turned upside down so that you do not recognize the scene you are looking at. At these moments, you have no way to know where you are. You may be in a book or even in someone else's head. You may have one eye inside and another outside a graphic object. Although a graphic reality is a powerful means of providing an experience, one of the most universal and primordial bad experiences is that of being lost. It is incumbent on the creators of these systems to make this particular experience virtually impossible to have. In particular, it is critical that people's first experiences be positive, so the rules for navigating must be instantly understandable [1]. One step that would be helpful is respecting the integrity of objects so that you cannot walk through walls or put your head in a book—at least not initially.

Motion Sickness

It is possible to get motion sickness from flight simulators. Simulator sickness has not been a problem with the current three-dimensional systems. Perhaps, as the graphics speed is increased, it will cause more discomfort. VIDEOPLACE displays are not authoritative enough that we must worry about this problem; however, if we were to project the same dynamic three-dimensional images that you see through reality goggles on an environmental-scale VIDEOPLACE screen, participants might be disturbed. Intuitively, it seems believable that the visual experience of being on a rocking boat might make us queasy even though we were in a stable environment. It might, however, be surprising that having your viewpoint moved around an artificial reality under someone else's control would make you uneasy. (If you clearly understood exactly how you were being chauffeured around, I think that the experience would be acceptable.)

An approach to minimizing this problem is suggested by a technique that pilots use to combat it. Since the person who has control of the airplane is much less bothered by its motion than the one who does not, the pilot and copilot take turns holding the controls on rough flights. The message is that changes in the participant's perception must be tightly connected to her actions, so each change is the anticipated result of her behavior.

Resolution

For both artificial-reality technologies, display resolution is a concern, both as it affects the experience and as it affects cost. VIDEOPLACE has always used low-resolution graphics. The reason for this was not the technical difficulty of building high-resolution displays, but rather the cost of monitors and projectors, as well as the fact that, for a given computer, having more pixels requires more processing and results in slower interactions.

Temporal resolution—the number of new frames that are generated per second—is as important to the graphics systems as it was to the perceptual system. George Trumbull, inventor of the Showscan film system, argues that a rate of 60 frames per second is required for a passive audience watching a film [2]. I suspect that the fact that the participant is physically involved turning his head and moving his body will require even faster graphics. The precise tracking of moving objects required for artificial-reality athletics may push the update rate even higher still. If a baseball travels at 100 miles per hour, it travels 2.4 feet in 1/60 second ((5280 feet x 100 mph) ÷ (60 min x 60 sec x 60 per sec) = 2.4 feet per frame), which means that you cannot know where it is with enough accuracy to catch it.

If we agree that there has been a revolution in three-dimensional graphics, we may assume that the same has occurred for two-dimensional graphics. Although two-dimensional graphics systems have higher resolution than in the past and can display more colors, the world of two-dimensional graphic animation is not so radically different from what it was eight years ago.

The current VIDEOPLACE graphics system was built in 1985 and has not benefited from the graphics revolution. However, although VIDEOPLACE graphics have low resolution, the architecture is sophisticated. It permits the combination of transformed live images with computer graphics. The graphics can be generated by traditional software or by special-purpose graphics generators that reside on the bus. Since VIDEOPLACE graphics are currently limited, there is much room for the graphics experience to be enhanced by higher resolution, and by new animation hardware. Also, the VIDEOPLACE experience can be projected easily into a three-dimensional graphic world. In fact, VIDEOPLACE is positioned to take advantage of whatever graphics hardware is available.

Environmental Displays

An artificial reality must make the participant feel that he is immersed in the graphic world. One primary difference between VIDEOPLACE and the wearable technologies is in the method of presenting the artificial reality to the participant. VIDEOPLACE currently uses a 6.5-foot-diagonal projection screen. Although people have no problem becoming absorbed in the world it portrays, the experience would be enhanced by a larger screen or by a circular screen that completely surrounded the participant, with images on the floor and ceiling as well.

Although such a display would not duplicate the effect of the reality goggles, it would give the participant a powerful sense of connection to the graphic world. OMNIMAX theaters project a 70-millimeter film on the interior of an egg-shaped viewing surface to produce a high-resolution display of such visual power that you react viscerally to the most subtle movements of the camera [3]. The effectiveness of this display is a visual standard by which the ultimate interactive realities should be judged, however they are implemented. If

VIDEOPLACE could generate and project such imagery in real time, it is not obvious how much stereo display would add to the experience.

Laser Projection

As an alternative means of creating an environmental scale display, we have used VIDEOPLACE perception and laser projection to draw the outline of a participant on a large scale. We will soon enable participants to fly their laser images up and down the building, and to engage in a free-fall choreography with graphic creatures (Fig. 7.2).

Figure 7.2
Laser Projections Cavort on a Building.

This interaction is part of a general theme of redefining our relationship to our larger environment, especially to the impersonal buildings that dominate our cities.

Laser Floor: STEP LIGHTLY

A limited but engaging version of reality can also be created on the floor. In the 1990 SIGGRAPH Art Show, we exhibited an environment entitled STEP LIGHTLY. The idea for this piece dates back to 1969, when I was thinking about a graphic floor constructed with thousands of LEDs. A sensory floor similar to the one used in PSYCHIC SPACE—with three-inch as opposed to one-foot resolution—was designed and implemented by Katrin Hinrichsen. A laser mounted on the ceiling projected computer-generated graphics down on the floor (PLATE G). The most successful interaction depicted a graphic fish that chased the participants as they walked around the room. The exhibit was very funny. People instantly reacted to the fish and ran away. Very young children crawled around the floor and tried to grab the fish. If we made the fish larger, they were frightened. Having the display on the floor instead of the wall gave a very different feeling to the experience. The fish on the floor enters the participant's space and interacts with her real feet, whereas in VIDEOPLACE it would be her image that interacted with CRITTER. With a series of such lasers, it would be possible to create interactions that involved a number of people interacting over a large floor area.

Three-Dimensional Displays

While VIDEOPLACE is currently two-dimensional, there is nothing to prevent it from making use of three-dimensional graphics. Although, initially, three-dimensional scenes will be shown with traditional projectors, it would be desirable to provide stereo depth cues. True three-dimensional displays are starting to appear that do not require the viewer to wear glasses. In one system, two LCD cells are associated with each point in the image [4]. Behind the cells and perpendicular to the screen is an opaque barrier, and behind the barrier is an illuminated pixel. The arrangement of these components is such that the left eye sees the lighted pixel through the left LCD cell, while

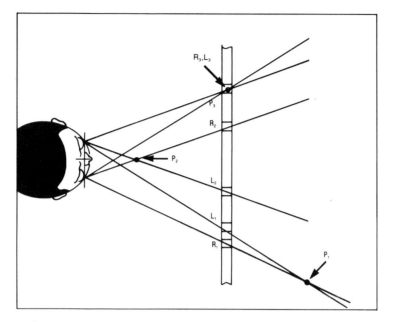

Figure 7.3
Autostereoscopic 3D.
Courtesy of Dimension Technologies, Inc., Rochester, New York.
Reprinted with permission of the publisher from the April 1990 tabloid
edition of Computer Technology Review.

the right eye sees the lighted pixel through the right LCD cell (Fig 7.3). This device displays a single view that does not change as you move your head, but that does provide an effective sense of three dimensionality.

Holography

At first glance, holograms might seem to be appropriate for interactive three-dimensional displays. Until recently, holography has been a static film technology, but holographic television was developed at MIT in 1990 [5]. The image is about two inches square and is limited to simple line drawings. The problem with computer-generated holograms is that a three-dimensional image must be generated for every possible viewpoint, and the resulting interference pattern must be calculated and then illuminated by a laser for display. Furthermore, with any holographic technology, you always have to look at the hologram itself, even though you may see the image in front of it or behind it. An artificial reality would require a holographic image in every direction, which in turn would require that the current two-inch system be implemented on an environmental scale. We are several revolutions away from such a display.

Three-Dimensional (3D) Glasses

Comfortable 3D glasses now exist that would allow VIDEOPLACE images to be projected in stereo almost immediately. (Surprisingly, the VIDEOPLACE silhouette looks like a solid body when displayed in stereo 3D.) IMAX, the developer of the OMNIMAX theaters, has recently announced a 3D technology called Solido. Solido has a screen six stories high that wraps around the viewer, completely filling his visual field [6]. The projected image alternates between left-eye and right-eye views. Special glasses controlled by an infrared transmitter ensure that each eye sees only the appropriate image.

Goggles

Reality goggles represent the ultimate in display technology in that they completely dominate the participant's vision. It is impossible to see anything but the artificial reality. On the other hand, reality goggles are currently unwieldy and have a texture on the display surface that is plainly visible when the viewer is looking at a solid graphic surface or up at the sky. In spite of these shortcomings, the glasses do take maximum advantage of the three-dimensional graphics techniques that are available. They show perspective, stereo images, and optical flow as you move through a space.

When we look at the world, each eye sees a slightly different view. The brain uses this difference to infer distance. Because our eyes are just a few inches apart, this stereo effect is greatest with objects that are close, and ceases to operate at all with objects that are more than 30 feet away from us. There is undoubtedly a useful class of three-dimensional interactions that do not need two stereoscopic images. (For example, a flight simulator almost never uses graphics to portray objects that are less than 30 feet away.) If the scene changed appropriately as the participant turned her head, there would be adequate spatial cues for some interactions. In these applications, both glasses could show the same image, halving the cost of computing the graphics.

Advances in three-dimensional graphics products permit the artificial-reality programmer to ignore many of the technical problems that used to consume her time and effort. Even more important, the operations required to create three-dimensional views of scenes and objects have been implemented in specialized processors that are faster than the computer itself. There are as many as 50 of these processors in a state-of-the-art workstation. They perform these repetitive calculations so rapidly that the software has trouble keeping up. In particular, these processors perform the calculations required to show what the participant should see from her current location, looking in the direction that her head is facing.

When the computer decides what objects lie in the direction of the participant's gaze, there is one last problem. When you draw two objects in a graphic scene, the one that you draw second will be drawn over the first, making it appear to be closer to the viewer. Half of the time that is the effect you want. But, what if the second object is supposed to be farther away? The naive reaction is to say, "Draw them in the right order"; but determining the order takes a long time.

The current approach to this problem is called *Z-buffering*. This technique would not have been considered before inexpensive memory was available. With Z-buffering, the distance from the viewer is stored with every pixel on the screen. When a new pixel is to be drawn at a particular screen location, the depth value of the pixel in that location is read out and compared to the depth value of the new pixel. If the new pixel is nearer to the viewer, it is written into the screen memory and its depth value is written into the Z-buffer. On the other hand, if it is farther away than the pixel that is already on the screen, it is thrown away, and the write operation is not performed. This technique requires an extra memory, which can be 16 or 24 bits deep for every pixel on the screen. Z-buffering is a brute-force approach, which is why it works. It completely eliminates a tedious operation from the software, and from the programmer's awareness.

With these capabilities, there is a class of three-dimensional scenes that can be produced effortlessly for use in an artificial reality. This class is being expanded as more hardware is added and the speed of each of the components improves. Scenes composed of flat surfaces can be depicted easily in real time. Shaded curved surfaces also can be depicted, but they take longer to render. Out of reach for the moment is a world of realistic graphic techniques that have been developed, but that cannot yet be performed in real time.

Various issues in computer graphics must be solved if artificial realities containing realistic forces, creatures, and humanoid images are to be created. Dynamic interactions of objects, according to realistic physics, have been simulated, but no generalized tools for creating such animations exist. Similarly, realistic animation of graphic creatures that behave with respect to their environments is a problem that has been neglected until very recently.

Creating a convincing human figure is a research topic. Rendering skin, hair, and fabric and animating facial features have been attempted, but the results are not yet convincing. Efforts directed at making a human figure move according to inner volition and with regard to its graphic environment have not yet begun. It will be some time before we can create human forms that could pass for real. On the other hand, computer graphics has always made progress on the problems that it has chosen to address. The animation of human figures is likely to be one of the next hot topics [7].

Once you solve a problem in computer graphics, the solution is available for use in any context without additional effort. For instance, once you have created flowers, you can carpet a room with flowers. When you achieve believable hair, you can use it to cover bodies, trees, and furniture. Convincing stone textures can be applied to a person's face to give her a marble complexion and ruby lips. The public has not seen this new visual vocabulary. When animated and given character and dramatic context, it guarantees novel visual experiences for the movies of the future. In principle, anything that can be achieved in movies can later be accomplished in an interactive experience.

Media

The integration of computer graphics with audio and video technology that started with METAPLAY has recently accelerated to define a new market, *multimedia*. This term has had other meanings in the past, but it currently refers to products that combine live video, stored video, computer graphics, and electronic sound. This repertoire can clearly be applied to VIDEOPLACE interactions. Less obviously, it also holds potential benefits for wearable technologies as the worlds of three-dimensional graphics and computer video merge.

One of the simplest video effects is the recall of stored images. This technique will become more sophisticated. Rather than calling up a complete frame and displaying it, we will be able to key the participant's live image and foreground computer graphics into a video background image. Because the same background can be used for a lengthy interaction, this use of a videodisk breaks one of the constraints of that technology. There are 54,000 frames stored on a disk, which may seem like an enormous number, but they translate into only 1/2 hour of full animation. With an interactive medium, each participant necessarily has a personalized experience because his actions are unique. Thus, each participant will see only a fraction of the total number of frames. On the other hand, if you show the same background for a number of seconds, you expand the value of those 54,000 frames enormously. One disk can now support many hours of possible interactions, ensuring that different participants see different scenes.

It is not necessary to store complete video frames. It is perhaps more interesting to be able to call up video images of real objects that can be placed anywhere on the screen, in what otherwise would be a synthetic graphic scene. The objects displayed in this way need not be static. You could store digitized images of a real animal in many different poses, and make the animal perform a large variety of behaviors just by correctly sequencing through the stored library. This technique would be particularly effective where the animation was clearly responding to events.

Another visual vocabulary is being developed in digital image processing. A live image is transformed according to mathematical functions applied to every point on the screen whose new value is a function of its current value and the current values of the neighboring pixels. Some of the images that result from these transformations are visually very interesting.

VIDEOPLACE Through Reality Goggles

If reality goggles had higher resolution, it would be possible to display a live video image of the participant in a three-dimensional graphic world. The insertion of a two-dimensional video image into a three-dimensional graphic world may seem odd, but some marriage of live video and three-dimensional artificial realities is certain to occur. The video image could be read into the graphic Z-buffer with a depth value associated with every pixel, so that graphic objects could appear to be in front of, in back of, or even penetrating the live VIDEOPLACE image.

One implication of the foregoing is that VIDEOPLACE participants could enter a three-dimensional graphic world created for people wearing reality goggles. Also, graphic images representing people wearing those devices could appear on the VIDEOPLACE screen.

Future Graphics Hardware

Three-dimensional graphic workstations are rapidly increasing in power. Since the needs of three-dimensional graphics are well understood, the strategy of using many specialized processors—as is employed in the VIDEOPLACE perceptual system—has long been followed by designers of graphic workstations such as Silicon Graphics Corporation. More recently, these systems incorporate multiple general-purpose processors as well. The processing power of these systems will continue to improve, but at an accelerating rate. Experimental systems implemented with these general-purpose workstations will be used for most research and practical applications. The military will create huge simulators (containing thousands of circuit boards) similar to those used for pilot training to track the edge of the technology envelope, showing what will be available in the future.

We can also expect that people interested in commercializing artificial realities will abbreviate the three-dimensional graphic experience, and will develop shortcuts while we are waiting for the full capability to become accessible to the masses. It is possible that old-fashioned vector graphics—line drawings of three-dimensional scenes—will be resurrected. (NASA used vector drawings for all its early work in this field.) Videodisk technology is another source of low-end graphics. We may see such toy systems being marketed for a few hundred dollars very soon. For instance, Chris Gentile says that AGE and VPL are working together on a low-cost reality suit and an artificial reality based on black-and-white computer graphics. Mike Miller of Aeon Corporation has shown me lightweight glasses that allow you to watch three-dimensional movies recorded on video tape on your home television. Three-dimensional computer graphics can then be displayed in foreground of the realistic background established by the film.

If these methods are successful, artificial realities may drive graphics technology. (At its peak, Atari was the world's largest user of microprocessors and EPROMs.)

Auditory Expectation and Displays

The conventions of everyday auditory experience are quite different from those of vision. Sounds are less responsible for determining our sense of place. Although a given sound may be associated with a certain environment, if the visual information suggests that we are elsewhere, the auditory evidence will often be overruled and the visual interpretation will dominate. Perhaps this dominance occurs because radios, televisions, and stereos constantly bring us sounds unrelated to our physical environment. Although television, photographs, and films depict other visual environments, they exist as clearly defined, bounded objects. In addition, although there are continuous sounds such as the hum of a fan or the roar of a highway, most sounds start and stop, accompanying dynamic phenomena, such as slamming a door or blowing a horn. Since sounds are often fleeting, we must be able to process them after the fact. Our understanding of speech, in particular, relies heavily on memory. We need to remember in order to understand. We often say, "What?", indicating that we did not understand what a person just said, and then understand what he said before he has a chance to repeat it.

Auditory expectations are less crucial than are visual expectations to our interpretation of the physical world. Thus, toying with them has less effect on our sense of place. In addition, although the computer can theoretically be used to generate any sound and has indeed been used to synthesize almost every instrument, less effort has gone into simulating other real-world sounds. However, we have a well-defined tradition of abstract sound sequences—music. Although an artificial reality need not produce music, musical expectations can be used when auditory feedback is varied. If each footstep is followed by an electronic tone, the participant quickly comes to expect the tones. If the tone after a step is omitted or if two tones are sounded, she is surprised. Complex flirtations with the participant's expectations are possible.

Since we process sound differently than we process visual information, its uses in interactive experiences are also different. Sound can be used to reinforce desired behavior, but this process is slower than the instant visual suggestion used, for example, in the MAZE interaction. Rhythmic sounds will almost certainly lead to dancelike behavior. Movie soundtracks are used to set moods and to enhance the emotional impact of visual events; in an artificial reality, we should be able to communicate suspense, foreboding, or merriment using the same musical techniques.

Sound is important to our sense of self. When we have a cold or laryngitis, we feel not quite ourselves partly because we sound different. Paul DeMarinis has created an installation he calls Alien Voices, in which a person's voice is radically altered in disconcerting and amusing ways [8]. (During the Vietnam era, when then Secretary of Defense Melvin Laird was to speak in Madison, I was going to use his voice to control recorded battle sounds so that when he opened his mouth, machine gun fire would erupt and when he closed his mouth, the war would stop. Unfortunately, he cancelled his trip.) Participants' voices could also be doctored in an artificial reality to alter their identities. In helicopter simulators, an operator can speak to the pilot using one of six different voices. In an artificial reality, participants would have to wear a microphone and headphones so that they would hear only the altered speech while the electronic circuitry received only their normal voices.

Sound Hardware

In an artificial reality, the need for immediate computer-controlled response dictates the use of some kind of electronic sound synthesizer. In 1976, I implemented a Fourier synthesizer. In theory, such a device is capable of synthesizing any sound by adding up many simple waveforms. However, there is an irony associated with its use. Considerable computer power is required to control it, and significant storage is needed to hold the control information.

We have recently replicated this early synthesizer using a digital signal processor. It generates 16 sine waves with controllable amplitude and frequency, as well as an overall volume control. A second signal processor controls the attack and decay as well as amplitude and frequency modulations for each channel on the first processor once per millisecond.

Speech Sounds

Since one of the themes of my work has been experimentation with nonverbal communication, I have stayed away from the use of speech sounds in artistic interactions. A computer responding to footsteps or handwaving, however, might create a new kind of interactive poetry. Verbal response could also be used to create a specific atmosphere within the environment. For example, we could create a hostile atmosphere by letting a buzz of gossip swirl around a room as a person explored it. The computer could coax or warn or congratulate the participant in an unknown tongue.

The use of realistic live or recorded sound is becoming interesting because of the enormous storage capacity of current disk drives and the compact disks with read-only memory (CD-ROMs). A vast repertoire of real-world sounds can be called up at a moment's notice. Thus, the sounds of animals, city traffic, subways, airplanes, ocean, insects, or crowds could be associated with objects and events in the environment, or used to enhance the ambience suggested by the graphic scene.

Spatial Sound

Another technique, originally explored in GLOWFLOW, involved changing the origin of sound by switching among a number of speakers so that sounds moved around the room or bounced from wall to wall. With modern sound-processing techniques, sounds could be made to appear to emanate from any location. Positioning of sound would be useful if several people were in an artificial reality. Each person's sound responses could follow him. NASA has developed a system called the "Convolvotron," which performs the required computations [9]. This device could place the sound of your footsteps away from your feet, so that you would hear your footsteps walking beside you. It can make a mosquito buzz in your ear. If there was a fan in the environment, its sound would stand still as you turned your head, heightening your sense that it was really there. Other sound-processing systems could simulate the acoustics of the graphic space so that your voice would reverberate appropriately. Since these effects require headphones, they are more consistent with reality goggles than with VIDEOPLACE.

A poetic use of spatial sound developed for flight simulators was described by Tom Furness [10]. Apparently, novice pilots often forget to put down their landing gear before landing. They also ignore a variety of alarms that have been developed to alert them to this oversight. The solution was to position a recorded message from a family member such as a small child within the pilot's "sacred space" (within the personal distance that only intimates are allowed to penetrate) saying, "Daddy, put your landing gear down."

Tactile Displays

The sense of touch is not easily addressed in VIDEOPLACE because there is no electronic way of projecting its stimuli. As mentioned in the discussion of VIDEOPLACE in Chapter 3, a participant may perceive a tingling sensation in his finger when he touches the image of another person with his own. Another form of illusory sensation of touch is communicated audibly. When the participant's image touches a graphic object, producing a sound, that sound becomes the "feel" of the object.

The wish to provide realistic touch sensation is a valid reason for considering wearable technologies. If the reality glove and reality suit contained a number of vibrating stimulators, a variety of tactile sensations could be produced. Similar arrangements have been used to bring crude visual images to the blind [11]. These electrically-induced sensations could be used in conjunction with a sensing system that reported the position of the person's body. For instance, if the participant's image's hand touched a graphic object, an electrical stimulation of the hand would emphasize the moment of contact. More elaborate tactile displays could provide sensations of smoothness and sharpness as well as hot and cold.

Psychological research has uncovered a number of tactile illusions that are worth exploring aesthetically [12]. For instance, when two points on the body receive tactile stimulation, it is possible to induce a phantom sensation anywhere between them. Thus, if you are stimulated on the shoulder and on the wrist, phantom sensations can be induced at the elbow or along the forearm. Unbelievably, it is possible to create sensations that are perceived as coming from outside the body by stimulating points on the two hands. Alternatively, these illusions could allow you to experience the sensations of inhabiting a different kind of body. A related illusion, created by vibrating a tendon on the arm, can make a person feel that his arm is bent less acutely than it actually is [13]. Thus, it is possible to feel that you are stretching and flexing your arm, even though you are not moving it. If this stimulation is done while you are holding your nose, you feel that your nose is elongating. In other words, when faced with conflicting sensations, the brain will generate and accept interpretations that are clearly impossible. Obviously, these illusions offer fascinating aesthetic possibilities.

Perhaps the most important aspect of touch is resistance. If we push a wall, it resists. If we push a soft pillow, it yields. If we grasp a block in our hand, its presence prevents our hand from closing. If we lift the block, we feel its weight. It might be possible to stimulate opposing sets of muscles such that, if a participant tried to reach through a graphic object using one set of muscles, the opposing muscles would prevent him from doing so. Virtex Technologies of Stanford, California is working on a glove that will allow the wearer to feel graphic objects. It would also be possible to design an exoskeleton that would strap onto a participant's body and allow or resist any movement of the head, limbs, torso, hands, and fingers under com-

**Figure 7.4
Exoskeleton.**

puter control (Fig. 7.4). With such feedback, the person could climb nonexistent mountains, swing from illusory trees, and grapple with graphic phantasms.

For some reason, this area of research was neglected for years; therefore, there is much preliminary work still to be done. Perhaps the most accessible experience of such feedback is in Atari's video game, *HardDriving*, which provides realistic force feedback through the steering wheel.

Margaret Minsky has been doing research on the perception of tactile textures such as you feel when you run your finger across sandpaper [14]. In her system, you hold onto a stylus while a simulated texture is passed under it. You feel the texture as vibrations in the stylus. For this technique to be available in an artificial reality, it would have to be packaged with the sensors embedded in the reality gloves, which might make the design of comfortable gloves even more challenging.

Movement

Related to force feedback is the problem of moving around in an artificial reality. As mentioned in Chapter 4, Fred Brooks has used a treadmill for simulating movement through a graphic building. A treadmill may be acceptable for walking straight ahead, but there is no obvious way to change direction. On the other hand, in experiences where you are wearing reality goggles, it would be desirable to be able to move in any direction without requiring unlimited floor space. An omnidirectional treadmill could allow you to walk in any direction without really moving.

Rather than project a detailed design for such a device, I will suggest an approach to its construction. The design would be based on a grid of sensors and actuators. The module in each cell of the grid would be capable of detecting the forces exerted by the participant's foot at that point. It would also be capable of rolling the participant in any direction with complete control over the speed and resistance the participant would feel. This device would then allow the participant to start a walking motion in any direction. As he lifted one foot, the other would be rolled in the opposite direction at exactly the rate he would be walking. Since the rolling speed would be carefully controlled, there would be no danger of the participant losing his footing. Assuming the availability of the probably impossible components, such a device would work, at least on paper.

There already are exercise devices that permit a person to climb stairs. They are the vertical equivalent of a treadmill. These could be modified to permit forward movement over varying terrain. It is even possible to conceive a device that could place a support surface at any point in space where the participant's foot should contact graphic terrain. When the participant lifted that foot, the mechanical actuator would move with it, anticipating where it would come down. While the device was tracking the moving foot, it would have to be moving the foot that was pushing off in the opposite direction. The result would be a three-dimensional, omnidirectional treadmill. (Because of the masses and speeds involved, this device would probably dismember a few people before it was perfected.)

As in the case of the treadmill, it is not clear whether the lack of inertial feedback would ruin the illusion. However, it is likely that techniques used in flight simulators could be used to trick the participant into thinking he was running up a graphic hill or leaping a graphic chasm. The perception of acceleration is sensitive only to the beginning or end of a movement; as long as the participant is permitted to move rapidly in the direction of motion and is then slowly moved back to the starting point, he might not notice the trick if his visual perception tells him he is still moving. Of course, the device would have to provide a motion base similar to those used in NASA flight simulators so that the participant could feel that he is standing on an unsteady platform such as the deck of a ship. Even if the experience were not completely true to life, it would be so much more convincing than sitting in a chair and watching someone else's experience that it would qualify as a new level of realism, if not as reality itself.

A similar approach could be used to create a machine that would involve a participant's arms, as well as his legs. A participant would be able to climb a graphic tree or wrestle with another participant. Since their relative strengths could be controlled, a small boy could wrestle his father on equal terms.

It would also be possible to let a participant really fly. Theme parks have used the airflow from motor-driven propellers to elevate people. It is possible to control your movements up, down, and around using the same techniques that sky divers do. If you were wearing reality goggles, you could dogfight with another participant in another flight chamber. Similarly, if you wore the goggles while scuba diving or skiing, you could feel that you were in an entirely different kind of space.

These techniques may seem aggressive, but if artificial realities succeed commercially, such experiences will be created.

Smell

The sense of smell is difficult to stimulate because of the physical behavior of odor-causing chemicals. Odors move through the air slowly and linger for some time, so a wind tunnel would be required to allow rapid delivery and evacuation of smells. Alternatively, especially volatile fragrances might be developed that break down after a few seconds.

It would be desirable to have both a real-time odor analyzer and a real-time odor synthesizer. With such devices, we could analyze the odors in one place and transmit them to another. The sense of being together might be greatly enhanced if you could smell a woman's perfume or a man's aftershave. Another consequence of such a synthesizer would be the possibility of fragrances as a performance medium.

The Other Senses

The remaining senses are difficult to reach by computer-controlled displays. Consequently, they are relatively unimportant in this medium and will be dealt with only briefly. Taste is seldom associated with any behavior other than eating. The sense of balance and momentum could probably be stimulated visually as suggested earlier by the Mystery Ride. Designers of simulators, however, warn that it is very difficult to achieve these effects by mechanical means without introducing unwanted artifacts. These senses are probably best left out of an artificial reality until they can be dealt with more effectively.

Electrode Stimulation of the Brain

The ultimate display might bypass the sensory receptors and go directly to the brain. Past experiments with blind and deaf people have demonstrated the feasibility of introducing coherent sensory information directly to the brain [15, 16]. Cochlear implants are now considered a viable medical procedure. General techniques of connecting electrical circuits to the nerves are under investigation. If such interfaces to all the senses were developed, a total synaesthesia could occur. Smell sensations might arrive in staccato fashion, in counterpoint to tastes and touch. Smells could run down your back. Such possibilities are exciting and disturbing. The courage to take such steps will undoubtedly be found first by those handicapped by the physical loss of these senses.

An ultimate goal of direct stimulation to the brain would be not only to control your perception of the artificial reality, but also to suppress your awareness of your own identity for the duration of the experience. You could be a worm, wriggling through the dirt with no knowledge of a previous existence.

Conclusion

The preceding discussion indicates that we possess a bewildering array of resources for composing new experiences. These experiences will be new not only because they are interactive, but also because they provide access to new sounds and sights that have not yet been exploited in traditional media. These stimuli can be juxtaposed with physical action in totally unexpected ways. Clearly, the responsive repertoire will be more than able to tax the information-processing capacity of the participant as she moves around the space, particularly if the responsive relationships keep changing.

References

1. P. Elmer-Dewitt, "(MIS)Adventures in Cyberspace," *Time* (3 September 1990), pp. 74–75.

2. "Showscan," Showscan Film Corporation, Marina del Rey, CA.

3. N. Max, "SIGGRAPH '84 Call for OMNIMAX Films," *Computer Graphics*, 16, No. 4 (December 1982) pp. 208–214.

4. J.B. Eichenlaub, A. Martens, & T.C. Touris, "3-D Without Glasses Just Flat-Out Better," *Computer Technology Review*, (January 1990), p. 26.

5. "Cartoon Time for Holograms," *New Scientist*, 21 (April 1990), p. 30.

6. P. Elmer-DeWitt, "Grab Your Goggles, 3-D is Back!" *Time* (16 April 1990), p. 77.

7. A. Vasilopolis, "Digital Actors," *Computer Graphics World*, (November 1989), pp. 90–94.

8. I. Sakane, "Alien Voices," Wonderland of Science Art, Kanagawa Science Park, Kawasaki, Japan, November 1989.

9. E.M. Wenzel & S.H. Foster, "Realtime Digital Synthesis of Virtual Acoustic Environments," *Computer Graphics*, 24, No. 2 (March 1990), pp. 139–142.

10. T.A. Furness, "Experiences in Virtual Space," *Human–Machine Interfaces for Teleoperators & Virtual Environments*, Santa Barbara, CA, March 4, 1990.

11. The Neuroprostheses Program, "Data Processing, LSI Will Help to Bring Sight to the Blind," *Electronics* (24 January 1974), pp. 81–86.

12. J.R. Lackner, "Intersensory Coordination," *Human–Machine Interfaces for Teleoperators & Virtual Environments*, Santa Barbara, CA, March 4, 1990.

13. J.R. Lackner, "Intersensory Coordination," *Human–Machine Interfaces for Teleoperators & Virtual Environments*, Santa Barbara, CA, March 4, 1990.

14. M. Minsky, M. Ouh-Young, O. Steele, F. P. Brooks Jr., & M. Behensky, "Feeling and Seeing: Issues in Force Display," *Proceedings of the 1990 Symposium on Interactive 3D Graphics, SIGGRAPH* (March 1990), Snowbird, Utah, pp. 235–243.

15. "C-MOS Implant to Aid Deaf," *Electronics* (20 February 1975), p. 38.

16. "An Electronic Link to the Visual Cortex May Let Blind 'See'," *Electronics* (20 December 1973), p. 29.

8

Controlling the
Experience

Introduction

Most of the discussion in this chapter reflects my experience with and plans for the VIDEOPLACE system. I would take a similar tack if I were working with reality goggles and three-dimensional graphics, although none of the research with wearable technology yet reflects the commitment to real-time processing that has characterized VIDEOPLACE development.

Since I have spent thousands of hours making VIDEOPLACE operate in real time, I am not entirely rational on the subject of performance. Therefore, I invoke the opinion of Ron Reisman of NASA as he discusses flight simulation as it relates to artificial-reality systems:

> "...simulation computing is, above all, real-time computing. It is worth noting that in academia a great deal of time is spent studying techniques of structured programming, high-order languages, and sophisticated operating systems. While it is true that such software technologies may be boons for program "readability" and "software maintenance," it is also true that such techniques are often computationally expensive and thus engender slow, non-realtime performance. Thus, simulation software engineers commonly practice decidedly unstructured programming techniques and use low-level languages; they often avoid powerful, modern operating systems so that the code will be "closer" to the machine; they refine techniques for "control loading" and "real-time executives," which are rarely taught in the majority of computer science curricula. It is worth noting that these simulation computational techniques seem to be rarely found in "virtual reality" systems, perhaps because VR systems are often linked with academic environments. [1]"

As Reisman implies, artificial reality is essentially a problem in simulation and therefore requires a commitment to speed—a commitment from which software engineering has been, inexplicably, forever exempt.

VIDEOPLACE was forced into this commitment from the beginning, because there were no off-the-shelf computer-vision products that analyzed the human image in real time. Specialized processors and a specialized bus structure had to be built. The goggle systems, on the other hand, benefited from 20 years of government and industrial support of three-dimensional graphics. The graphics products that they use already include many specialized processors that perform functions in real time. Thus, researchers working with reality goggles have been content to accept the constraints of off-the-shelf products and to limit their development work to software alone. In some reality-goggle systems, a time-sharing operating system (UNIX) is to operate what is supposed to be a real-time artificial reality. This software-only approach would be understandable if the response rates were satisfactory, but they are not.

The reality-goggle systems have focused on demonstrating artificial-reality concepts, rather than on creating realistic interactions between participants and graphic objects. As people working with these systems focus on specific applications with experienced participants, they will want much more processing. There are many issues that are currently ignored. For instance, these systems often permit participants to fly through walls. Enforcing the integrity of walls and objects requires time-consuming calculations. When you grasp an object, the details of its shape are ignored. Instead, you place your open hand within the object, you close your hand, and the object sticks to your hand. A more realistic grasp is difficult to simulate. A simple act such as holding a graphic block in your hand and turning it over with your fingers to look at the different faces requires amazingly elaborate calculations.

Control of the System

Between the perceptual hardware and the auditory and graphic displays lie the hardware and software that coordinate the behavior of the system as a whole. The hardware includes the processors that analyze the input and generate the output, as well as the interface systems that give the computer control over the harsh analog world that exists outside its benign digital realm.

Since the processing requirements of this kind of system cannot be met in real time by a single processor (if the scope of the interaction is nontrivial), a system architecture that allows a number of processors to work together must be constructed. There are many forms this architecture can take, each of which has strengths and weaknesses. Although much research has been done in parallel-processing architectures, the emphasis has been on creating the generalized supercomputer of tomorrow, rather than on designing systems that are organized to speed up particular applications. When this is the intent, as in the case of an artificial reality, it is necessary to consider the nature of the processing task to judge which architecture is most suitable.

Processing Task

The general goals of a responsive system are to understand as much as possible about a participant's behavior, to devise the most intelligent responses, and to respond with the most vivid displays feasible in real time. Since the potential volume of input and output data is tremendous, and the possible complexity of the artificial reality is unbounded, the computations are beyond the power of any processor— even that of the human brain.

We live in an infinitely complex reality. We are incapable of absorbing all the information available to us at any moment. Clearly, if, as we walked down the street, we tried to attend to the muscular activity of our legs, the movements of our diaphragms as we inhaled and exhaled, the ruminations of our gastrointestinal tract, the sensation of our feet hitting the pavement, and the swinging motion of our arms, we would find ourselves unable to deal with just the information supplied by our own bodies.

Compound this overload with the sounds of human voices, automobiles, birds, or with the sight of pavement, people, buildings, trees, and sky, and it is easy to understand Lawrence Sterne's observation in *Tristram Shandy* that it would be possible to spend an entire lifetime attempting to apprehend fully the events of a single day.

Context

To cope with the potentially mind-boggling amount of information available to us at each moment, we exist in limited, understandable contexts. Within each context, we select information that will help us to function. If we are to cross a street successfully, we must attend to the activities of automobiles, rather than to the inner workings of our bodies.

Context is not solely determined by place. Two people can be in the same place and see it quite differently because they notice different features and interpret what they notice in terms of different goals, different past experiences, and different current trains of thought. A passenger in an airport will notice signs for flights, gates, restrooms, ticket counters, restaurants, newsstands, and gift shops. A maintenance worker in the same airport might see only electrical outlets, trashcans, and burnt-out lights. In other words, each is looking for certain things and ignoring others. The choices are individual, but the necessity for choice is mandated by the limited real-time processing power of the human brain.

We shall continue to call the organizing principle that governs this selectivity a *context*. A context subsumes the currently active filters through which an individual interprets the world and controls her responses. The context includes the physical environment, the state of the person's body, and the activity or train of thought the individual is involved in. The benefit of this principle, from a processing point of view, is that, from one moment to the next, most of the information does not change. All the person has to do is to verify that the context is still the same. Thus, most of the processing and perceptual power of the brain can be devoted to the task at hand.

The concept of a context is not a rigid one. It allows for change. In many cases, our context leads us to expect change and even to predict it. As I drive down the street, my perception is changing, but it is changing according to a set of transformations that I associate with driving. This continuity allows me to predict where objects perceived one moment will be the next, greatly simplifying my brain's processing task. There are also expected changes of context. As I leave one room, I expect to find myself in another space—an office, a corridor, a stairway, or outdoors.

Not all situations are as predictable as these examples. There are surprises and new situations. However, human beings do not function well when they are knocked out of their current context, especially if the new situation is one for which they have no preparation. Most people avoid such experiences completely, or experiment with new contexts in tightly controlled ways. Thus, although not every situation is familiar, it is amazing how much of our experience fits within the idea of a context that provides significance for every perception and a framework for every action.

Context in an Artificial Reality

An artificial-reality system has only a small fraction of the processing capability of the human brain; thus, its designers are desperate for any shortcut that will rationalize its processing task. At any instant, it is assigned a context. That context may be a scene including the participant's image, and several objects, coupled with the fact that the participant's movements generate sound feedback. As the participant moves around the room, the perspective transformations in the displayed scene and the generation of sound responses are part of the current context that is expected to be maintained from one second to the next. Only certain aspects of the participant's behavior are relevant to this framework, and most of the display does not change on a moment-by-moment basis.

If a change does occur, it is derived from the previous display through simple transformations. Thus, at any time, the input is being analyzed with respect to only very specific criteria; the system is condensing the high volume of input data into a much smaller quantity of symbolic information. On the basis of this condensed representation, decisions are made and a compact description of the intended response is created. These instructions are passed down to lower-level processors, which generate full auditory and visual displays (Fig. 8.1). Even

Figure 8.1
The Input and Output Cones.

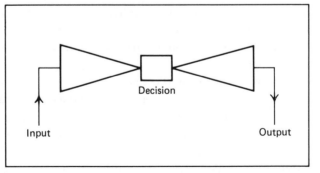

with the constraints that the contexts provide, the processing task is far beyond the capability of any single processor. Although we are accustomed to thinking of computers as "fast," there is little they can accomplish in a small fraction of a second. Therefore, it is natural to use a number of processors, each dedicated to one of the processes discussed earlier.

Parallel Processors

There are many ways that computers can be tied together. Many of these are based on concerns other than speed. Even when processing speed is the stated goal, the emphasis often is on throughput, rather than on response time. Maximizing throughput requires optimum allocation of resources, whereas underutilized resources are acceptable, if they help to get the job done faster in a real-time application. As an example, most cars are used no more than five percent of the time. However, if you were to design a transportation system the sole purpose of which was to effect the maximum amount of transportation with the minimum number of automobiles, you would not allow individuals to have their own vehicles. Yet, any such solution would result in people waiting for cars, because their time would not be considered important. In designing an artificial reality, we should commit whatever resources are required to create a convincing experience. Only then is it appropriate to talk about optimizing resources.

So that we can appreciate the options for parallel processing on an intuitive level, it is useful to consider the ways that groups of people are organized for cooperative effort. One model is the *committee*, an entity not noted for its speed or productivity. Much academic research in parallel processing is enamored of the committee approach. Such systems are considered intellectually interesting. A second organizational approach is a *hierarchy*. Information flows up from the bottom. Command and control filter down. Whether this is a good model for getting things done depends on the degree to which higher levels delegate decision-making authority to the lower ones. Where there is no delegation, the result is a bureaucracy, which is a fair description of traditional operating systems.

Perhaps the most productive organization is the assembly line. The work passes from one worker to the next, with each stop bringing it one step closer to completion. All workers are always busy, and all

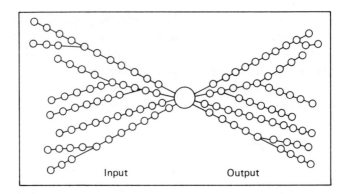

Input   Output

Figure 8.2
The Pipelines in Reflex Cones.

work at the same pace. The assembly line, which computer scientists refer to as a *pipeline*, would seem to be relevant to the reflex level of response processing. The problem with pipelines is that the data at each step in a pipeline is from a different moment in time, and the delay from action to response is a function of the number of stages in the pipeline (Fig. 8.2). Therefore, the only ways to use a pipeline without incurring a performance penalty are to speed up the sampling rate or to have a largely empty pipeline with only one sample in it.

Specialized Processors

Although the number of processors is significant, the type of processors may have a more pronounced effect on the performance. The entire history of computer design has been guided by a single set of principles that has only recently started to yield to new ones. To understand the limitations of traditional computer architecture, we can think of the computer as a factory in which there are thousands of workers. However, unlike any rational factory, the computer has only one workbench and only one set of tools. Only one worker can function at a time. To function, each worker must go to the workbench, perform a simple operation, and move out of the way. The work can be left on the bench if the next worker will be using it. If not, it must be stored somewhere. Even the most militant union would agree that this is a ridiculous way to run a factory.

Although most research in parallel processing has consisted of tying together a number of general-purpose processors, greater speed improvements are gained from specialized processors and those that are inherently parallel in operation. Such an approach may seem less flexible, but a quick look at the anatomy of the human brain reveals many specialized processing structures. The retina of the eye performs an enormous amount of computation before it sends any information to the brain. An artificial reality has similar processing requirements. Therefore, we should expect that specialized processors will be needed to make the system operate in real time, particularly for functions close to the input or the output.

System Architecture

The control of an artificial reality involves at least two levels of function that require quite different architectures and modes of operation (Fig. 8.3). In VIDEOPLACE, these are called the *reflex system* and the *cognitive system*.

Figure 8.3
The Reflex and Cognitive Systems.
The high-level cognitive system will plan strategy while the reflex system controls instantaneous responses.

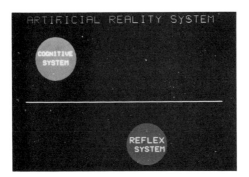

Reflex System

The reflex processing system controls real-time execution within the current context (Fig. 8.4). It perceives and responds in real time. It does not think about or understand what it is doing.

At the lowest level are the drivers, which operate close to either the input or the outputs; for example, feature detectors work on the input, and graphic-element generators produce output. These processors are dedicated to a particular function, which they perform continually, passing any results up to higher-level processors. Their functions may be changed by a superior processor, which instructs them to execute a different portion of their code or loads new code into them. There may be several layers of such processors. Drivers are distinguished by being dedicated to either input or output, but not to both.

Reflex processors operate at a level above the drivers. They determine whether events are within the current context. If the events are in the context, these processors choose the appropriate response and send the commands to effect it to the output generators. The response may be a movement by CRITTER, or a change in the participant's image, or an initiation of a sound response. If the participant's behavior triggers a change in context, the reflex processor directs all subordinate processors to change their operation. It also notifies higher-level processors to stage the next context fully. The

Figure 8.4
The Reflex Processing System.

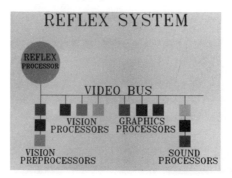

reflex processors are distinguished in that they make real-time response decisions and they deal with both input and output information. Several reflex processors may exist in parallel or in a hierarchy.

Reflex System: Hard-Time Processing
The traditional casual definitions of real-time processing are too lax to work well in an artificial reality. The operating system is banished. An artificial reality requires operating software that does its bidding immediately, not a separate entity of which requests are made. In our system, there are no interrupts and no direct-memory-access (DMA) operations. Both of these techniques lead to probabilistic timing that is difficult to analyze. In the VIDEOPLACE system, we insist on the same kind of hard timing that characterizes synchronous hardware design. Our software modules are similarly timed, and the execution of all processors is synchronized to the video synch pulse.

In standard interactive computer applications, there are fast operations and slow ones. Imagine that the same techniques were used to implement an artificial reality. You might walk down a graphic hallway, encounter another person, and reach out to shake hands. When the system sensed the proximity of the two hands, it would start to consider the possibility that they would touch. If they touched, complex tactile and resistance feedback would have to be generated for both parties. The geometry processing required to determine exactly when and where the hands would make contact and therefore where to apply force feedback is much more demanding than that required when you are walking down the hall. As a result, the system's response rate would slow. Rather than maintaining 60 frames per second, it would suddenly plunge to two. The whole world would go into slow motion.

Cognitive System

The cognitive system is not directly involved in perception or response. Instead, it is responsible for controlling the character of the experience and for meeting the aesthetic goals of the interaction. If an artificial reality is conceived as an art form that seeks to involve participants in a composed experience, an intelligent overseer can adapt the interaction to the behavior of each participant. This function poses both a problem and an opportunity for artificial intelligence.

Most successful artificial-intelligence projects operate in a limited domain of knowledge about which the computer can reason or converse. An artificial reality is such a microworld. In it, the computer must understand human behavior as that behavior relates to graphic objects. Whereas most artificial-intelligence projects are fragmented, with each researcher investigating a small aspect of intelligence and often just one step in its processing, an artificial reality is a complete entity with integrated perception, goals, and behavior. It is a framework within which the control structures become as important as the separate intelligence functions.

Traditionally, artificial-intelligence programs are slow. Their only time constraints are the patience of the investigators and the access that these people have to computing resources. Contrast this with biological intelligence, which has evolved with the requirement that it operate in real time. Reflection and long-term learning have survival value, but only if they are relegated to background status when an immediate threat or need arises. The leisurely intelligence of today's systems would have doomed them to extinction had they appeared in nature.

Furthermore, artificial-intelligence programs often have but one purpose for existing: to produce scholarly publications. Therefore, work continues only until enough functionality has been demonstrated to publish a paper. For this reason, artificial-intelligence systems gain little experience. If we allowed our children so little experience, they would not learn very much either. Therefore, there is a unique approach to artificial-intelligence research that an aesthetic environment can take, because the latter is intended to operate over a period of years.

Dreaming

Although the cognitive system must monitor lightning reflexes during interactions, when there is no one in the artificial reality, it can ruminate about its experiences. It can try to learn from them, and to plan new strategies for the future. Such a function would be the computer equivalent of dreaming. Whether the result would be better performance in some objective sense is not necessarily the most interesting question. If the system were to learn over a long period of time and to consider its experiences from a number of perspectives, the fact that it chose to change its behavior in a coherent way would be as interesting as would be its ability to optimize a specific skill.

Off-Line Intelligence

The only part of the VIDEOPLACE cognitive system that currently exists is an off-line use of artificial-intelligence technology. CRITTER's rules of behavior are specified in Conceptual Dependency Notation, which was developed by Roger Shank of Yale University. This notation is normally used for understanding natural-language texts, rather than for controlling graphic sprites. We represent the objects, spatial relations, and actions that are recognized in CRITTER's world in this notation. Objects include the participants; each participant's head, arms, hands, and fingers; and CRITTER. Relationships include under, over, on, up, down, top, surrounded, near, and far. Actions include chase, avoid, land, climb, cling, jig, dangle, flail, and explode [2, 3, 4].

At any moment, CRITTER is in one of 150 states. In each state, it has a sequence of perceptions to make that are implied by the relations and actions used to represent the state. CRITTER has a sequence of actions that it can perform in the state, and it has a list of adjacent states to which it can make a transition, depending on certain additional relationships that it tests. For example, when it is climbing a participant's silhouette and finds that the participant has moved such that it is now inside the participant's body, CRITTER will move to the closest point on the edge of the silhouette. If it is on the edge, CRITTER will climb. If it is just outside the silhouette, CRITTER will move back to that silhouette and cling without climbing. If CRITTER is more than a few pixels away from the silhouette, it will revert to a chase state.

We do not execute the knowledge representation directly. Instead, we translate it into a form we call FLEX code, which can be interpreted in real time by the reflex system. The attraction of using a knowledge representation was that we thought someday we might want to talk to CRITTER to modify its behavior. CRITTER was the first project anywhere to use a knowledge representation to control a real-time application [5].

On-Line Intelligence

In the near future, the cognitive system will be on-line. Cerebral processors will observe the interaction without participating in the immediate perception and response in order to devote themselves to the goals of the composition as a whole. They must take into account the following:

- Current context

- History of the interaction

- Adjacent contexts

- Expectations

- Goals of the interaction, such as slowing the participant's actions or inducing movement to a new location

- Constraints, such as a time limit in a given context

The cerebral processors are distinguished by the fact that they are not directly engaged in real-time processing. Their responsibilities lie in monitoring the interaction and, occasionally, in redirecting it. They ask, "What kind of participant is this? Has the person been in the current context too long? Should the current context be enriched with some new ingredient or entity?" None of these deliberations need to be accomplished instantaneously; they may require a few seconds. Once a decision is made, it may be enacted immediately, or it may simply change the future path of the interaction.

Context Net

Thus far, we have assumed that the contexts within a composition are joined in a network (Fig. 8.5). The current context is a node that is connected directly to a small number of adjacent nodes, each of which is in turn connected to a few others. Associated with each node are procedures for initialization, normal operation, and exit detection.

Model of Interestingness

In a broader sense, a context is a framework into which new elements can be injected or deleted. The overseer can consider the current state

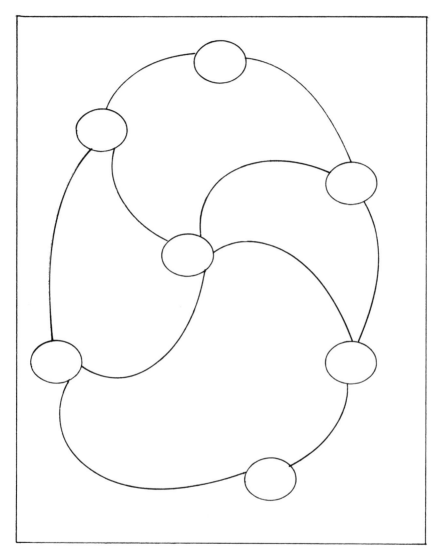

Figure 8.5
The Composition Network.

of the interaction, and can overrule the current script and switch to another one. A more intelligent system could continually improvise the interaction by measuring the novelty and tension available to the participant at each moment. Novel ingredients take time to learn about. Goals take time to attain. Goals that do not motivate behavior or are abandoned by the participant must be removed as soon as possible. Repeating patterns create the possibility of surprise when a response deviates from them. Dramatic effects may require carefully planted expectations. A system that considers such issues will initially behave like an adult playing with a child, trying one approach and then another. Ultimately, the interaction will be like a good conversation, but will be defined with events instead of words.

Software Tools

The needs of an artistic project are different from those of a business organization. Programs are seldom implemented start to finish; rather, they are implemented incrementally and evolve in both form and function over time. Aesthetic criteria are paramount. The purpose of many programs is exploration rather than production, so programs must be amenable to a great deal of tuning. Therefore, our VIDEOPLACE programming strategy is always to provide a wide range of capability that can be explored while the program is running. Rather than tolerate the edit, compile, execute, and download cycle typical in cross-development environments, we choose to provide as much run-time flexibility as possible.

Switching back and forth between the traditional programming environment and the artificial-reality experience can prove awkward, especially when the two are physically some distance apart, as is the case in our laboratory. It is natural to want to change the interaction while you are in the artificial reality. This is not a quixotic fantasy; it is good engineering.

Toward this end, we have created an elaborate tool for editing the 96 waveforms that define a note on our sound synthesizer. This program can be operated from either the VIDEODESK or VIDEOPLACE. As we change a waveform, we hear the new sound immediately. As potentially interesting sounds are created, they can be attached to parts of the participant's body and tested interactively.

We are developing animation tools that we can operate through the VIDEODESK using gesture input. These tools will test the articulation

and interactive behavior of graphic creatures. Both key-frame animation and modeled behavior will be used. These interactive tools for
graphics and sound will evolve into more general tools that will allow
us to define interactive pieces of larger interactions, and to test these
pieces within the same interactive framework.

Neural Networks

There is something fundamentally wrong with the whole idea
of programming. It is apparent that there are far too many eventualities
for us to anticipate every one, or to discover every error through
testing. An old technology that has recently come back into vogue
offers some relief from this problem. *Neural networks* are simulations of
groups of connected neurons. A neural network is a network of nodes
that receives input at one end and generates output at the other. Each
node has a weight associated with it that is multiplied by the sum of
the node's input values. The weights of the nodes are changed
according to the performance of the network as whole on the training
data. Thus, each weight is continually adjusted in response to its
contribution. Unlike in computer programs, logic is not represented
explicitly, and neural networks can learn to improve their performance
through experience. These attributes are ideal for our purposes.

To gain "experience," however, a network must be presented
with thousands of examples. Therefore, training a neural network
could take longer than writing a program. We are adopting the
approach of colleagues at Microelectronics and Computing Corporation (MCC), who train their networks with simulated experience. In
our case, a simulated participant will interact within an automated
artificial reality. Many cases will be generated, the network's behavior
will be tested against listed criteria, and the weights will be changed.
Years of interactive experience can be simulated rapidly in this way.
There are hundreds of small judgments that we would like to ask
neural networks to make for us. Many neural networks would monitor
the artificial reality simultaneously. Unfortunately, software imple-
mentations of neural networks are too slow. We are waiting for
specialized neural-network chips to become available.

Conclusion

The hardware and software systems described in this chapter are the results of a long-term effort to develop the tools required to create and compose within the new medium. Our early emphasis was on hardware, because the needs of real-time systems could not be met by off-the-shelf products. Now that we have succeeded in building a system that functions in real time, we have shifted our focus to examine compositional software.

As the awareness and reflective powers of VIDEOPLACE evolve, an artist should be able to represent wit and intelligence. In the distant future, the artist's goal will be to raise an aesthetic intelligence whose life work is artful interaction with human beings.

References

1. R. Reisman, "A Brief Introduction to the Art of Flight Simulation," Virtuelle Wellen, Ars Electronica 1990, Band II, pp. 159–169.

2. B. Shay, "Real Time Control Through Multiple Levels of State Machines," masters thesis, University of Connecticut, 1983.

3. J. Rinaldi, "Using a Knowledge-Based Artificial Intelligence to Construct Responsive Environments from a Conceptual Representation," masters thesis, University of Connecticut, 1983.

4. T. Gionfriddo, "Real-Time Processing Primitives in a Knowledge-Based Responsive Environment," masters thesis, University of Connecticut, 1985.

9

Applications

Introduction

Artificial realities will have applications in almost every field of human endeavor. Both wearable and unencumbering technologies will be used. This development will not happen overnight, but it will happen.

Human–Machine Interaction

During METAPLAY, we used the computer–video link between the gallery and the computer center to discuss a data-transmission difficulty we were having. Putting concepts designed for aesthetic purposes to practical ends may at first seem surprising. However, there are historical precedents. For example, the perspective techniques that contributed to the beauty of Leonardo da Vinci's eleven paintings also served to make his 2000 technical drawings intelligible.

VIDEODESK

The idea for VIDEODESK came from the METAPLAY experience. We had experimented with the VIDEODESK idea, and had made it the subject of a proposal to DARPA in 1982. We implemented it in permanent form in 1987, when we received a small research contract from the NSF under the Small Business Innovation Research (SBIR) program [1].

The VIDEODESK consists of a light table with a camera mounted above it that is aimed down at the user's hands, which rest on the desk's surface. The silhouette image of the hands appears on a monitor on the far side of the desk. All the VIDEOPLACE capabilities can be duplicated in this format. The light table is a temporary expedient that facilitates the identification of the user's hands. Soon, it will be possible to use a conventional desk with a camera mounted above it.

The image of the user's hands can be superimposed on any application, the user can use the image of a finger to point, draw, or write—or, indeed, to perform any operation that she would normally accomplish using a mouse, joystick, or data tablet. Ordinarily, a mouse is used to control the position of the cursor on the screen. A mouse has one or more buttons that the user presses (clicks) to indicate that the item or command pointed at should be selected. In VIDEODESK, however, the hands are not equipped with buttons, and the "click" function must be simulated; for example, touching the thumb to the forefinger could represent a click, and repeating the action would represent a double click. Thus, the user's hands can be retrofitted to any existing mouse-operated application.

Although gesture control can be used to replace the mouse, it would obviously not be as effective as a keyboard for text input. Our expectation is that this keyboard function will be replaced by speech input. In fact, it is likely that the combination of speech and gesture will be superior to the keyboard for word processing (Fig 9.1). We will position the cursor with one finger and simultaneously use two fingers to indicate the beginning and end of a passage we want to delete or move. We will talk to computers just as we talk to each other. To avoid disturbing other people in the office, we will lower our voices or even whisper. The computer may be able to read our lips to improve its speech recognition [2].

The VIDEODESK interface is intuitive to use and can be operated by a small child or by a technophobic adult who sees the mouse as threatening. It is completely compatible with the traditional work-

Figure 9.1
Word Processing: Moving a Block of Text.

space. In addition, it can be used in public settings where small devices are likely to be stolen.

Floor Space

Personal computers take up space; if placed on someone's desk, they prevent normal use of the desk. Manufacturers therefore have created special desks that have a separate surface for the computer. A significant fraction of office workspace is being occupied by computers. As a result, there is a great emphasis on the desk area occupied by personal-computer systems.

The VIDEODESK will free the desktop. The computing hardware will be hidden. The monitor will become a flat screen that hangs on the wall across from the user. The desk surface will be compatible with traditional use of paper and pen. You will sit at your desk, and be able to look at a mixture of real and graphic papers on the computer screen (PLATE 12). Just placing a real piece of paper on the desk will cause it to be scanned into the system. You will be able to shuffle papers in completely realistic fashion.

Multipoint Control

The intuitive value of a gesture interface may not seem sufficient motivation to replace a mouse—which is, after all, an inexpensive device. However, the use of the human hands for input (VIDEOTOUCH) does more than replace the mouse. The obvious fact that people have found two hands useful, even essential, in daily life has been ignored by the user-interface community, including those working with reality goggles. Although cost is a factor in entry-level systems, there is no justification for the failure to research multipoint-input techniques. (There is almost no scientific literature on how we use two hands.)

There are a number of ways that using both hands for multipoint control could be useful. You could select commands with one hand and point to the place where the commands should be applied with the other. By using two hands at once, you can simultaneously perform operations that are usually performed sequentially.

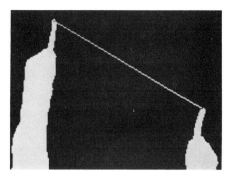

Figure 9.2
Endpoints of a Line.
The user's fingers define the endpoints of a line.

For instance, you could define both endpoints of a line in a single movement (Fig. 9.2). You could position and size a circle in a single operation using your thumb and forefinger (Fig. 9.3). Similarly, you could use two fingers to specify the opposite corners of a rectangle. In these cases, two distinct functions would be combined in a single operation that would be coordinated by your two hands, smoothly and unconsciously (Fig 9.4).

Figure 9.3
Circles.
The user's fingers position and size circles.

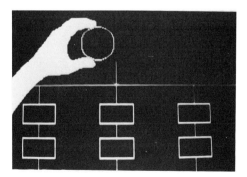

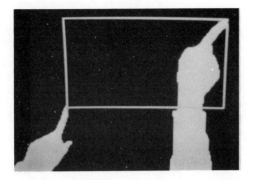

Figure 9.4
Corners of a Rectangle.
The user's fingers establish the corners of a rectangle.

In perhaps the most impressive demonstration of multipoint control to date, the thumb and forefingers of the user's two hands are used as control points for defining a spline curve (Fig. 9.5). Spline curves are used in the design of any object with curved surfaces. We can think of the curve as being attracted by the control points. For example, fingers arranged to form a square define a circle. If the hands are moved farther apart, the circle becomes an ellipse. As the fingers are moved in any direction, different curves are defined. We are developing a series of spline-editing tools based on this technique.

Figure 9.5
Spline Curves.
The user's fingers define spline curves.

Three-Dimensional Applications

The VIDEODESK interface allows you to specify points in two dimensions that are sufficient to operate the vast majority of existing applications. (Even applications that perform three-dimensional functions are universally controlled by input devices that operate in two dimensions, such as the mouse. True three-dimensional input devices, such as the Flying Mouse from SimGraphics, are just starting to appear [3].) To operate the VIDEODESK in three dimensions, we use a sample plane. This plane can be placed anywhere in the volume, in any orientation (Fig 9.6). Once the sample plane is positioned, the live image of the user's hands is projected onto it, where they can be used to perform two-dimensional pointing and drawing in the sample plane.

In PLATE 13, the user's forefingers define the endpoints of a line on a sample plane in a three-dimensional flow volume. The particles that pass through that line define a surface that is deformed as it flows through the volume. They start to flow the moment the fingers stop moving. I developed the flow-visualization component of this software for Pratt and Whitney Corporation. This system is much easier to use for probing a three-dimensional phenomenon than NASA's Plot3D package, which is widely used for flow visualization. One merit of this technique is that the user's hands rest on the desktop at all times. Resting your hands on the desk surface is far less fatiguing than is true three-dimensional input, which would require you to hold your hands in the air without support.

Figure 9.6
Two Views of the VIDEODESK's Sample Plane.

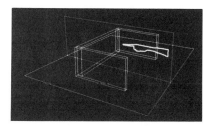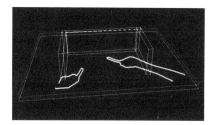

EXTRUSION ILLUSION Graphic Sculpture

The EXTRUSION ILLUSION is another three-dimensional VIDEODESK application controlled by two-dimensional input. It uses multipoint control to define a spline curve that can be thought of as the aperture in an extruding device (PLATE 14). Graphic clay is forced through this hole at a uniform rate. If the curve is a circle, a cylinder will be created. However, if you move your fingers as the graphic material emerges, you can form a much more complex solid (PLATE 15). This is truly graphic sculpture! This technique is hundreds of times faster than any other method of accomplishing the same task.

True Three-Dimensional Input

Although most of our work with the VIDEODESK has used the VIDEOTOUCH technique for two-dimensional input, it is also possible to perceive a participant's hands in three dimensions. By using a second camera, we can locate a single finger in space accurately enough for the participant to be able to draw in three dimensions. We have also implemented simple gesture techniques, including raising a hand above the desk to access a previously invisible menu. If we were to use additional cameras and extensive processing, both hands could operate in three dimensions, completely duplicating the function of the reality glove.

Although the idea of using three-dimensional input sounds desirable, it is worth noting that, unless your hands are unusually steady, you will have difficulty doing precise work in three dimensions without support. There are techniques for working around this problem, but they involve decoupling the image of your hands from your real hands so that your graphic hands are steadier than are your real ones. Note that this caveat applies to the reality glove as well.

Teleconferencing with the VIDEODESK

Artificial reality is fundamentally a telecommunication concept. METAPLAY was a telecommunication environment and the term "VIDEOPLACE" was coined to refer to the satellite project I proposed as the theme of the U.S. Bicentennial. The original VIDEOPLACE experience that occurred during METAPLAY can now be implemented between two or more VIDEODESKs. The image of your hand that appears on your screen as you work at the VIDEODESK can also appear on a colleague's screen 1000 miles away.

If I were talking to my publisher about this paragraph, I could send the text file to him and then run the same word-processing program on both of our systems. Commands given to my machine would be transmitted to his machine to ensure that both of our screens displayed identical information at all times. When I wanted to talk about this paragraph, I would gesture exactly the same way that I would if the two of us were seated side by side at a table with the manuscript between us. For people who know each other and are more concerned about exchanging information than about seeing each other, such a capability would be ideal. Note that the technique is completely independent of the material being discussed. The material could be text or graphics. If eye contact were desired, a second monitor could show the colleague's face, although considerable bandwidth would be required for a live image.

Since VIDEODESK technology uses only the silhouette of the user's hands, full-bandwidth video is not needed. The silhouette can be compacted greatly, allowing the image to fit easily within the capacity of the Integrated Services Data Network (ISDN), a new telephone service that is being installed in some homes and businesses. ISDN provides two bidirectional digital voice channels plus a lower-bandwidth bidirectional data channel for every call. This capability is an acknowledgment that, when I want to talk to you, it is increasingly likely that I also want my computer to talk to your computer.

Local Teleconferencing

We seldom think about the problems we have communicating with people in the same room. If two people are seated on opposite sides of a desk or table, it is common for one person to hold a document upside down so that the other person can see it, and to point a finger to show where the colleague should start reading (Fig. 9.7). Often, a person alternates between reading the paper and holding it for the other person to read. Even when both people have a copy of the text, there is still the problem of guaranteeing that both are looking at

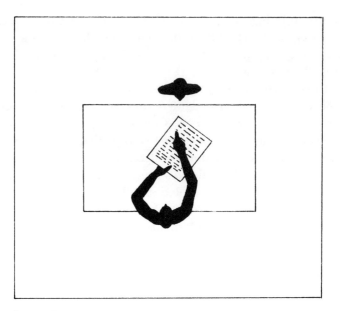

Figure 9.7
Holding a Document Upside-Down.

the same page. These problems could be alleviated if the information were projected so that everyone present could see it. Cameras would look down at each person's hands, so anyone could point to passages of interest (Fig. 9.8). The images of the participant's hands could be

Figure 9.8
Around the Conference Table.

color coded, so that observers could tell whose hands were being displayed. Overlapping hands could be displayed in a variety of ways. One person's hands could always be shown over another's, the hands of two or more individuals could be superimposed and the average of their two colors shown in the area of overlap.

Conferees could point to lines on a budget, boxes in an organizational chart, or nodes in a PERT chart that appeared on a projection screen. This capability suggests a new standard by which teleconferencing techniques should be judged. A teleconferencing system succeeds if people choose to use it when they are together in the same room; that is, when it is better than being there.

Gesture Messages

What would you want to do if you were to call someone and she was not there? You might want to leave a voice message accompanied by an animated image of your hands pointing to graphic or text materials. This kind of gesture message suggests a new form of on-line documentation. A schematic might contain an "explanation point"—a graphic symbol signals the existence of an animated voice and gesture explanation for the indicated part of the circuit.

Three-Dimensional Applications with Reality Goggles

All these ideas mentioned in the discussion of the VIDEODESK could be implemented in an artificial reality experienced through reality goggles when the resolution of these devices has been improved (Fig. 9.9). Indeed, you could crumple a graphic page and toss it in a real trashcan. Since gravity would be strictly optional, you could have stacks of papers floating in mid-air. One page could feature traditional print, another an animated surface, and a third could open a window into another world. The limit is human awareness. If you had complete control of reality, how would you organize it to help you keep track of your projects? Whatever you can think of can be done.

Figure 9.9
The Artificial Reality 3D Desk.

In many domains, we use paper to work on three-dimensional problems. There is a real need for powerful three-dimensional communication tools, to complement those that are being used for design. This need is repeated throughout industry. Anyone in a business that deals with real objects—such as architecture, construction, real estate, auto manufacturing, or computer design—faces three-dimensional visualization problems. In fact, most large businesses have to deal with some three-dimensional problems. All companies have offices and other facilities that they must plan. High-resolution reality goggles would be ideal for presenting such problems. It is easy to imagine a meeting occurring inside a three-dimensional representation of the problem that is to be discussed. For instance, jet-engine designers might meet within the combustion chamber of an engine to determine why the fuel was not burning completely.

An architect who could take her client into a proposed building would have a tremendous edge over one who communicated with print and physical models. The advantage would be multiplied when changes were requested. A physical model cannot be changed without significant cost. A computer model can be changed easily. Indeed, a computer model can be changed interactively. Thus, the carpeting under your feet could be switched, the shape of the room around you could be varied, or hundreds of suggestions for furnishings and accoutrements could be presented in sequence. While you were walking around a space, your voice and footsteps would reverberate exactly as they would in a real room [4].

An artificial reality could be used to create a spectacular presentation on any topic. People could be taken to the mountain top and shown the promised land. All would have good seats. They could move around without blocking anyone's view. In addition, since they would not actually have to be in the same physical room, the need for a separate conference room that is idle most of the time would be eliminated.

Another three-dimensional task that is currently controlled through two-dimensional visualization is air-traffic control. In 1982, I proposed a VIDEODESK system to DARPA and suggested this application. The operator was to sit in a display environment and see a stereoscopic volume of airspace in which planes appeared at their current altitude and orientation, proceeding at their scaled velocity. The controller could select a plane by touching it and then verbally request its flight plan, which would be depicted by a graphic line. By simultaneously selecting two airplanes, she could determine whether the two flight paths were close enough to risk collision. If she wanted to redirect one of the planes, she could trace the desired three-dimensional path in front of the plane with her finger. Although it might be possible for the controller to move her hand precisely enough to specify velocity as well as heading, this information could be provided verbally. Note that a small vocabulary of speaker-dependent disconnected speech is all that would be necessary. This application is currently being pursued by NASA.

Military Applications

Inevitably, there will be military applications. DARPA is considering an artificial-reality version of the $6 million man or Robert Heinlein's Starship Troopers [5]. The soldier would wear a completely sealed suit powered by fuel cells that would add hydraulic strength to his own. He would view the world through reality goggles and could see a variety of computer data superimposed on his view of the outside world.

Tactile and Force Feedback

The real benefit of wearable technologies is that they could be used to feel as well as see graphic objects. The applications described in the next section exploit this capability.

Telerobotics

Artificial reality has been linked to the disciplines of teleoperation, telerobotics, and telepresence, because NASA cites these areas as applications for their technology. Teleoperation has a long history. A person in one location is given controls that can operate equipment in another location. Manipulation of the controls generates signals that are transmitted from the operator's location, and sufficient feedback to perform the task is relayed from the remote site back to the operator's. If the device being controlled is a robot, then it is a "telerobotic" system. The feeling of being in the remote location is referred to as the sense of "telepresence."

There is a growing appreciation of how greater telepresence would make both system design and task performance easier. For instance, auditory cues from a remote site have been found useful for the performance of remote manipulation tasks because their absence is disturbing. In another example, the operator of a remote vehicle could be provided force feedback through a steering wheel to give him the feel of a distant terrain. In general, any deficit in the information available through telepresence should be examined to determine its importance to the task.

The ultimate telepresence interface is the human body and the human senses. By completely capturing the movements of the operator's body, transmitting them to a remote site, and then using them to control an anthropomorphic robot in that location, we could use traditional human controls at the remote site. The operator could wield hand tools in a natural way. All tactile, resistance, three-dimensional auditory, and three-dimensional visual feedback received by the remote robot would be transmitted back to the operator to help guide his work.

Although this prescription may seem utopian, Steve Jacobsen of the University of Utah has produced an exceedingly impressive system that enables the teleoperator to use a hammer to drive a nail, pick up an egg, tighten a thumbscrew, and even bounce a ball on a tennis racket (Fig. 9.10) [6].

There is a fundamental constraint that limits the telepresence that can be attained in telerobotic systems—the speed of light. For most people, the fact that nothing can travel faster than the speed of light is an easy one to live with. For them, 186,000 miles per second is more than adequate. No one complains that it takes too long for their flashlight beam to hit the wall and to travel back to their eyes. However, if you want to be able to look around a remote environment, you will want at least 30 updates per second. You can make do with as few as four updates per second, but then you are quite aware of the delay from the time you turn your head until the world catches up to you. If you want to maintain 30 frames per second, your head position

Figure 9.10
The Dextrous Hand.
Courtesy of the Center for Engineering Design, The University of Utah.

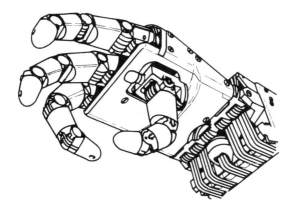

has to be transmitted to the remote cameras, and their images must be transmitted back to you 30 times per second, implying that you can be no farther than 3100 miles away ($186,000 \div (2 \times 30) = 3100$).

For delicate manipulations, the sample rate for the tactile and force feedback must be 1000 samples per second, according to Steve Jacobsen [7]. Thus, the ultimate telepresence can be achieved only at distances less than 93 miles ($186,000 \div (2 \times 1000) = 93$). This argument ignores all delays due to electronics, mechanical inertia, and software processing. The use of tactile telepresence would seem to be limited to local tasks such as controlling an undersea explorer.

Gesture Ahead

An artificial reality could be used to provide the best of two worlds. The operator could perform his manipulations in a graphic world generated locally. Feedback would be received from this simulation. His movements would be transmitted to the remote site, where they would be used to perform the task. As long as the feedback the remote robot received while performing the task was expected by the simulation, the robot would proceed. However, if unexpected feedback was received, the robot could wait for the remote operator to determine the problem before continuing. Since coupling of the operator's actions to the actual performance of the task would not be instantaneous, a sequence of actions could be performed in the artificial reality and later performed as specified in the remote location. This technique would allow the operator to get far ahead of the robot. This is a variation on the 'type-ahead' feature on many computer systems, which allows a user to continue typing commands even though earlier commands have not yet been executed.

This arrangement requires more intelligence at both sites than is needed for pure teleoperation. The artificial-reality system must simulate the physics of the remote manipulator well enough to provide the operator with the appropriate feedback instantaneously. Similarly, the remote manipulator must be able to coordinate the task with the information received from the teleoperator, noting that he will not be in the loop as the action is performed.

It is not yet clear that directly coupled telerobots are easier to implement than are autonomous robots. My own prejudice is that I do not necessarily want to work like a robot in order to control one. I would rather tell it what to do with words and gestures. Such commands could be issued with a modest three-dimensional VIDEODESK input or via a simple reality glove. The robot would then perform the specified operations in very small steps for new objects and new tasks, but in larger bites in familiar domains.

Micromanipulation

A compelling use of these telerobotic techniques will be for manipulations that cannot be performed automatically because we do not understand how we do them. One candidate is microsurgery. Surgeons are already operating on body structures that are almost too small to see. They view their work through stereomicroscopes. As surgery is performed on ever smaller structures, the human hand looms large and clumsy. According to eye surgeon Steve Charles of the Center for Engineering Applications in Memphis, only 25 percent of physicians who complete the medical training required to become an eye surgeon ever develop the manual dexterity necessary to practice in their chosen field [8]. In many cases, the involuntary tremor of their hands is greater than the movements that they must perform. For this reason, he has invented a variety of micromanipulation tools that allow a person with normal dexterity to control the small movements required.

Although miniature tools can make movements much smaller than those of the human hand, we are not close to duplicating the dexterity of the human hand with any mechanical device. We have no idea how a surgeon uses subtle tactile sensations to guide her work. The advantage of tactile feedback for surgery is that the eye cannot see what the hand can feel. Thus, it would be desirable to design microsurgical telerobotic tools that provide tactile as well as visual feedback.

An additional benefit of this approach would be that one of humankind's most celebrated skills would be captured for study. The movements of the surgeon's hands, the sensations received, and the actions taken in response would all go through the computer. We could use this information to model what the tissue tells the hand, and then could create simulators that would allow medical students tc operate on graphic patients and would allow experienced surgeons to rehearse difficult procedures before entering the operating theater. There are electronic-cadaver projects being developed at Stanford, the University of Washington, and MIT for this purpose [9]. The same modeling process would help us to understand how a surgeon performs her task. A long-term consequence of this study could be the development of automated surgeons.

One of the hottest new technologies to arrive in the last few years is nanoengineering. This technology involves the fabrication of ultrasmall devices using the same manufacturing techniques that are employed to make integrated circuits. People working with this technology have already created microscopic gear motors [10]. Assuming that the enthusiasm that these techniques have generated is well placed, we can at least talk about the possibility of miniature robots that would enter the patient's body and transmit video images to a surgeon, who would then perform surgery inside a patient's arteries via remote manipulation (microrotorooter).

On an even smaller scale, microscope designers have reached the point where they can image individual atoms and begin to manipulate them. Perhaps as this capability develops, a researcher will be able to grasp and feel real atoms—not directly, but through an interface that represents both the human and the atom in a common framework. A first step in this direction has been reported by a group at IBM [11].

Scientific Visualization

Scientists and engineers often need to understand dynamic three-dimensional data, such as weather phenomena, heat transfer in nuclear power plants, and the beating of the human heart. However, no single picture can provide complete understanding of events in a volume, because the features in one part of the volume obscure those behind them. Similarly, the many quantities—such as temperature, pressure, and combustion—that can be measured or predicted throughout a volume cannot be combined in a single picture. We need techniques that will help us to integrate such information into a single understanding by allowing us to apprehend more variables simultaneously.

A reality glove fitted with a variety of microstimulators would allow you to feel temperature and pressure on your fingers. You would be able to feel light contact, stretching forces, deep contact, vibration, temperature, and resistance from features you touched in the volume being investigated. Your manual exploration could also trigger complex sounds displaying other quantities that would be correlated automatically by your brain. The resulting discipline could appropriately be renamed *scientific sensualization*.

Fred Brooks, of the University of North Carolina, has been interested in the visualization and manipulation of complex molecules for pharmaceutical research since the original GROPE project in 1971 [12]. The shape of a drug molecule determines that molecule's pharmaceutical properties. The match between the surface of the drug and the receptor site on the surface of the target cell determines whether the former can affect the latter. When I visited Brooks in 1978, he spoke of being able to feel the strength of the molecular forces that acted on a molecule.

Recently, one of his graduate students, Ming Ouh-Young, has adapted the radioisotope manipulator arm used in the GROPE-II project for this purpose (PLATE 18) [13]. The user can bring the drug molecule into proximity to the receptor site and can feel the attractive and repulsive forces acting on the drug. The effect of the surface geometry, electrostatic forces, van der Waals forces, hydrophobicity, hydrofelicity, and hydrogen bonding are displayed in this way. The goal is to find the best fit between the drug and the target. The force display improves the performance of the operator on this task by a factor of two over his performance using the best visual techniques. This task is interesting because tactile intelligence is used to understand phenomena for which vision alone is inadequate. It is the first demonstration that there are intellectual and productivity gains to be realized from using the artificial-reality paradigm.

Programming

In the late 1960s, I was interested in visualizing a different kind of phenomenon—a computer program. I was struck that programmers labored under the worst possible feedback conditions. They were expected to make a plan of thousands of steps repeated millions of times that must proceed from start to finish without error or interruption. It was as though they had to play a round of golf without once seeing the ball.

I sought to enrich the programming environment by providing light and sound displays that reflected the operation of programs as the latter were being interpreted. Programmers came to know the proper sounds for their program to make; if an unfamiliar pattern occurred, it often signaled the presence of a problem. It was this idea of experiencing a program that originally attracted me to environmental computer experiences.

A related issue was that computer programs had no palpable dimensions, no visible structure. If a manager wants another function added to hardware, the engineer can simply point to the circuit board and say, "no room," whereas the programmer is always subject to an escalating specification of her task. When DARPA approached me in 1982, one of the options I offered them was a mechanical metaphor for constructing programs by hand at the VIDEODESK. Modules were to be represented by graphic symbols that looked like pieces of a jigsaw puzzle. Modules that could communicate were identified by interlocking connections. The idea was to make programming a physical task. If the metaphor were extended into three dimensions, a program would be visualized as a dynamic Rube Goldberg mechanism that you could see, hear, and feel.

Artificial Experience

In addition to being used for manipulation and visualization, artificial realities can provide composed experiences for training and education.

Training

Before artificial reality, there was simulation. Whether a simulation system is an artificial reality is a matter of degree. The distinction rests on the nature of the participant's interaction with the simulation. Full-body participation is the hallmark of an artificial reality. The success of training by simulation argues for the use of artificial realities for the same purpose.

A traditional flight simulator contains a sedentary pilot who manipulates limited mechanical controls. However, the designers of flight simulators go to extraordinary lengths to make the sensation on the whole body be exactly that which the pilot would experience in a real plane [14]. The cockpit is mounted on a motion base that can rock in any direction or be accelerated for a considerable distance up, down, left, or right. Special devices jerk the pilot's head, pull down on his hands, pull down his face mask, and squeeze his buttocks to trick him into perceiving additional G-forces as the plane turns or as the tires bounce against the runway.

Simulators have been used to train helicopter pilots, tank operators, and nuclear-power-plant operators for years. Recently, special simulators have been used to teach police personnel when to use weapons. A projected video image depicts a real-world scene and abruptly introduces a believable threat. Trainees must decide whether to fire their weapons. If they fire, they must be accurate. Depending on the action the trainees take and the accuracy of their shots, a different clip of recorded video is displayed [15].

Another simulator is used for medical emergency-room training. A video clip is shown of a patient being wheeled into an emergency room. A nurse rattles off the vital signs and looks out from the screen and asks, "What should we do, doctor?" [16]. Similar tools are also being used for sales training. Recorded video images give the experience verisimilitude. However, because of the storage limitations of videodisks, only a small repertoire of scenarios can be stored. Like VIDEOPLACE, these simulation systems use a single screen. However, as these systems improve, they will be able to synthesize a great variety of situations and to immerse the trainee within these experiences.

We can be sure that the military is developing systems for mission training. Special forces will walk the streets of their objective before the battle. Future presidents will field hostile questions from a graphic Sam Donaldson in rehearsal before they face the real thing. Important negotiations will be rehearsed as realistically as possible because the limitations of any human in a real-time situation are well known. We seek to eliminate the unexpected by anticipating as much as we can, because what we fear most is novel experience.

Design for Trainability

Artificial realities can also be used when designing equipment. The human interface can be tested by having people learn to use the equipment in an artificial reality before it is built. Bill Buxton of the University of Toronto reported perhaps the ultimate low-cost simulation [17]. A paper drawing of the front of a planned oscilloscope was used to train people in the device's use. The trainees were asked to explain their actions and were told verbally what the consequences would be. The result of this exercise was that problems in the design were discovered and corrected—so much for elaborate computer simulations.

The paper process does not necessarily preclude more sophisticated simulations at later stages of design. One benefit of this practice would be that, as people were learning to use a simulation, the training program itself can be tested. By training people in an artificial reality, you capture all their actions—not just the actions that affect the equipment. A person learning to operate any device will often reach toward one control, think better of it, and then reach for another. This confusion is valuable information for the designers of the training process, because it reveals possible defects in the design of the equipment or training program as well as the state of a particular trainee's confidence. Current training systems are too device oriented. If the student does not touch a control, then, as far as the computer is concerned, nothing has happened.

If the artificial-reality interface were used to control a final product rather than to simulate it, there would be no distinction between the equipment used to train and the one actually deployed. Such a system would be self-simulating. Equally important, training by simulation could continue in the field. The air-traffic–control application described earlier would be an example of such a system. Geographically dispersed tank battalions could engage in simulated combat over a simulation network.

Another potential application is driver training. We allow teenagers to take the wheel without first giving them an appreciation of the forces that they will have at their command. In an artificial reality, a variety of driving conditions and situations could be presented. A drunk-driving simulator could simulate the effects of intoxication on your reflexes by inserting delays between your actions and the vehicle's response. I would argue for strong physical feedback, even pain, to make cocky teenage drivers appreciate the effect of momentum on their bodies.

Education

Artificial-reality simulation makes experience a composable medium with implications for education. Rather than simply automating the teaching process, it could radically transform what we teach.

The intent of METAPLAY and of PSYCHIC SPACE was to communicate the essence of the computer to the layperson. The computer needed to be explicated, just as the Renaissance Church used painters to illustrate Bible stories for a largely illiterate public. When my work started, George Orwell's vision of technology was considered prophetic. My goal was to present a benign view, communicating that technology will see us and that computers do not have to be the way they are. We do not have to adapt to technology; it can adapt to us. As well as allaying irrational fears, VIDEOPLACE is intended to convey a child's sense of wonder at the newness of our technological world. It is an invitation to explore—not only the new technology, but also ourselves.

Watch a group of children who are "sitting still." It quickly becomes obvious that children never stop moving. Educators are well aware that the excess energy of young children is a force to be reckoned with. Ideally, this vitality is funneled into the learning experience. However, class size usually demands discipline, which suppresses opportunities for all children to use their physical energy to learn, for the hyperactive child to vent energy constructively, for the passive child to become actively involved in the learning process, and for all children to develop motor skills.

Rather than teaching facts or even concepts, an artificial reality could present a rich variety of causal laws, communicating that there are many ways that objects, actions, and events might be related, that there are many possible ways of looking at them. After a period of such training, even preschoolers could become creatures of considerable abstract, although nonverbal, sophistication; they would be equipped with a rich framework on which to hang specific concepts and details.

Thus, artificial realities would act as preparation for more formal schooling, as well as an adjunct to it.

Experiences could be created in which a child would have to discover the rules in order to succeed, but those rules would be in a state of flux, so that what was correct one moment might no longer pertain to the next. The experience would teach that learning is a continuous process, with results that must be constantly tested and revised. Students would learn to look not for the eternally right answer, but rather for a temporary best answer.

Such a process is not "learning by doing" in the Dewey sense [18]. One consequence of this well-meaning phrase is the prevalence of menial makework exercises that serve primarily to consume the students' time. In an artificial reality, doing is learning—a much different emphasis. If experience is the best teacher, can artificial experience be preferable to the real thing? Although real experience is powerful when it teaches, it is neither efficient nor reliable, in that it may well teach the wrong lesson. It does give us confidence that we can deal with future experiences. The advantage of artificial realities is that compact experiences can be composed that convey lessons more quickly and more certainly than can real life.

Science Education
In 1976, I proposed an alternate form of science education to the National Science Foundation. Rather than teach the vocabulary of science and the mathematical puzzle solving, I proposed that children be cast in the role of scientists landing on an alien planet. Their goal would be to discover the local laws of cause and effect, as well as the nature of the flora and the behavior of the fauna. To eliminate any unfair advantage that adults would ordinarily have, we would design this fantasy world to respond to the kinds of behavior typical of children.

The children would enter one at a time. They would each interact with the artificial reality for an initial period of observation. Since some children would be hyperactive and others almost still, each would observe different phenomena in the graphic world. Afterward, they would discuss what they had seen. They would quickly discover that they each had had quite different experiences. Although some observations would be common to many children, others would be unique to a single child. Still others would appear to conflict.

Children would quickly discover that, unlike the tidy science they read about in the textbook, they faced a muddle of information, just as real scientists do. In their discussions, they would compare notes on what they were doing when certain observations were made. Some children who had made important observations might have no recollection of what their own behavior had been, thereby reducing the value of their experiences. They would learn the importance of careful observation. They would reenter the artificial reality and try to reproduce the observations of other children. They would try to decide how to reconcile apparently incompatible data. They would invent the idea of a critical experiment.

The purpose of this exercise would be to teach what it is like to operate on the frontiers of science. Note that what is most significant about this approach is that the children would be doing the talking and thinking. They would find that some among them have unique abilities in this new world, whether it be capturing graphic creatures or inducing volcanic eruptions. Their teacher would remain in the background, as long as the discussion proceeded on its own momentum. She could step in and rekindle it whenever it started to wane or wander. The result of these investigations would be that children would identify the key ingredients of this reality. They would be able to apply what they learned within the environment. They might discover that a logical consequence of what they had unravelled allowed them to make the rocks levitate or the insects fly in formation. They could also consider what they had learned about this fantasy world that was like the real world, and what was not. It is often difficult to talk about fundamental aspects of the real world, such as gravity, since it is hard to imagine that the world might be otherwise.

Teaching of Content
In addition to teaching general concepts and attitudes, the artificial reality could be used to present specific content. For example, "Sesame Street" uses animated letters to teach the alphabet. The authority of the "Sesame Street" characters could be exploited in an artificial reality. Words could be animated to interact with the child. Numbers, letters, and advanced mathematical symbols could be presented as friendly

Figure 9.11
Animated Number Interacting with a Child.

playful creatures (Fig. 9.11). Children could experience mathematical concepts such as a parameter by letting some aspect of the child's behavior provide values for one of the parameters of a mathematical expression, whose curve could be plotted as he moved. The CAT'S CRADLE interaction lets children play with spline curves without telling them what the curves are. This experience would make it easier for a teacher to discuss spline curves later.

BALLOONACY, the ball-throwing interaction, lets participants play with orbital mechanics. Instead of placing your finger directly in the path of the ball to catch it, you stay a short distance away from the path and use the gravitational attraction of your finger to accelerate and redirect the ball back to the other participant. This technique is counterintuitive at first, because meeting the ball with your finger will capture instead of redirecting it. However, participants adapt quickly to the unfamiliar relationship. One of the goals of education should be to make intuition match reality.

Michael McGreevy, the progenitor of NASA's efforts in artificial realities, speaks of personal simulators [19]. He is interested in using the data from various planetary probes to place the participant at a particular point on the surface of the moon or Mars. His goal is to provide taxpayers, congressional representatives, and children a concrete experience of what we have learned from these explorations. A note on the frustration has sounded such as often accompanies an effort in the real world: Many of the computer tapes used to record the data transmitted back from the planetary probes no longer can be read. They were written on equipment now obsolete, in formats no one remembers. (The time for computer archeology has already arrived.)

It would also be interesting to use real-time data from an electron microscope to place a participant in a landscape where he knows that the mountains that tower over him and the valleys that open beneath him are really smaller than a speck of dust. In this micro environment, a participant and a bacterium could interact on equal terms.

Foreign-Language Instruction
It is difficult to motivate people who live in the United States to learn a second language, since we have little day-to-day need for one and elsewhere in the world many people speak English. An artificial reality provides a means of automating an immersion approach to language training. A student could enter a graphic world and encounter a synthesized native speaker who would start pointing to objects and naming them. The student would be asked to pronounce the words. The student's pronunciation would be replayed alternately with the teacher's. The scenario would progress from the names of objects and body parts to simple relationships, actions, and transactions. Rather than witnessing these graphic skits, the student would participate in them. In VIDEOPLACE, the presence of the student's image would facilitate discussion, as the teacher could interact physically, putting a hat on the student's head or throwing a ball to him. Although such a system would certainly benefit from improved speech-understanding technology, it could be approximated today.

History, Archeology, Anthropology, and Paleontology
Other times and places could be reconstructed and inhabited with graphic characters and creatures living simulated lives. The computer film "Paris 1789" showed a historically accurate view of Paris at the time of the French Revolution. Some time in the future, when artifical intelligence is far more advanced than it is currently, students could enter such a simulation and engage historic figures in conversation

about their times. They could walk the Acropolis or work on the pyramids. In all cases, they would see these disciplines in terms of people living their lives, rather than as abstract dates and concepts.

Experiential Parable

Perhaps the most difficult application to describe is the use of an artificial reality to create an experiential parable. If the interaction is replete with relationships, changes in relationships, and relational ambiguity organized into a coherent whole, the participant's intellect will be provoked. The resulting experience communicates a philosophy of events, instead of one of words. An example is the MAZE, which thwarted the participant's every effort to reach the "goal," yet used that frustration to entertain. His continuing efforts to negotiate the MAZE were motivated by a perverse curiosity about the next frustration. Since this experience could be construed as having meaning as well as interest (if we were sufficiently compulsive about it), it would be easy to envision people discussing the MAZE as earnestly as they might a poem.

Such experiences are, perhaps, the most promising single area of exploration. Ambiguity is an instrument of efficient communication, as several conflicting ideas can be suggested simultaneously. Instruction at this level has been almost completely neglected by the institutions of our culture, with the exception of the churches. Consider the well-known fact that there is a gap between the values people espouse and the values that they demonstrate through their actions. By presenting ethical simulations in which a participant must act and then see the consequences of her behavior, we may be able to teach people to act on their beliefs.

In addition, this technology may allow us to say things we do not already know, for it is fundamentally a tool for altering our own consciousness—for teaching those who created it.

Implications for the Physically Handicapped

Artificial realities have important implications for the physically handicapped. They provide a powerful medium for translating what is limited physical activity in the real world into full participation in a radically different graphic environment.

If the VIDEOPLACE perceptual system were focused on movements of her hand, finger, shoulder, or face, rather than on larger movements of her limbs or the whole body, a handicapped person could use any movement to communicate with the computer. The participant could use these actions to control the behavior of a graphic alter ego. Thus, handicapped persons could participate physically in a graphic environment in which their handicap did not restrict them.

Physical Therapy

Physical therapy is often focused on the movement of a single part of the body. The patient's regimen calls for endless repetition of a meaningless motion. Artificial-reality technology could alter the nature of the task by translating it into a graphic context in which successive movements do not seem repetitious—instead, they are a means to an end within the environment, just as walking is a means of covering distance, rather than lifting the left foot, and then the right foot, and then the left foot, and so on.

We submitted a proposal to the National Institutes of Health (NIH) for automated range-of-motion therapy in 1986. This therapy is often required when a person injures a limb in a way that restricts its motion. During the process, the patient is encouraged to exercise the limb, slightly increasing the amount of movement each day. Without this therapy, it is possible that full use of the limb will never be regained. This therapy is also often indicated for people who are brain injured and physically handicapped.

Our proposal was to provide a motivation for participants to perform the movements required by this type of therapy. Each patient would participate in a sequence of interactions that invite physical action and reward it with interesting feedback. The patient's motives might be aesthetic, playful, or competitive, rather than therapeutic. Indeed, experiences could be constructed to fit any set of motivations that were natural for a given patient. During a session, the system would score the patient's behavior as it occurred, according to the goals of the therapy. Then, it would introduce particularly attractive interactions to lead the patient to perform actions that had been omitted.

VIDIOCY, VIDEOPLACE's shooting interaction, was inspired by a traumatically brain-injured young man who was brought to visit VIDEOPLACE. Although he was confined to a wheelchair, he was tall enough to be able to interact over the entire screen with his one good arm. However, during the DIGITAL DRAWING interaction, he kept trying to make use of his other hand, which had far more restricted movement. After much effort, he was able to make a few marks with that hand and took considerable pleasure in this feat. His mother said he had reacted more strongly to VIDEOPLACE than to almost any other experience in the seven years since his accident.

I thought about his problem and his desire to use his weaker hand. An interaction that would allow him to launch a particle with his finger and to control the particle's direction after it had left his hand seemed ideal. This action could be used for menuing or pointing at letters to spell a message, or, as in VIDIOCY, for having fun.

Artificial Reality as an Experimental Tool

The artificial reality is a flexible tool for presenting stimuli and analyzing behavior; it is a generalized Skinner box. It allows the experimenter to deal with gross physical behavior, instead of the limited button pressing or pencil pushing that characterizes many experiments because such actions are easy to monitor automatically. Quite possibly, findings based on studies that include physical movement in a natural context will conflict with theories of behavior based on sedentary subjects performing isolated tasks. The very language of "stimulus–response" suggests stimuli being presented to a passive subject who responds on cue.

Perception and Behavior

Perception is often studied as though it were an isolated activity. However, it is a necessary part of all physical behavior, and often it provides the motive for that behavior. We perceive, and, based on our perception, we act. We use perception to monitor and control our actions. To improve our ability to perceive, we often move toward the object of perception. For instance, when you are looking for your checkbook, you might enter the kitchen, see something on the floor, walk around the table for a closer look, stoop down to pick up what turns out to be a checkbook, and then open it to make sure it is the right one.

Problems of perception are related to physical behavior. Action cuts down the information-handling capacity of the brain. We filter out most of the information we receive, and attend to only those features of our perception that we need to guide an action. If athletes were outfitted with reality goggles and reality suits, we could fully control their perception and capture their responses to it. If they were given a perceptual task related to their own area of excellence, we would have the means of studying how they do that task. This information could be used to construct a model of human perception and information-handling capacity pushed to its limits. Studying a number of such perceptual specialists might well lead to new insights and generalizations.

Displaced Feedback

Artificial realities will allow researchers to intervene between a subject's behavior and the consequences he perceives. We could reexamine existing theories of perception to see how well they fit in a dynamic environment. For instance, Stratton's classic studies of visual adaptation involved subjects wearing glasses that reversed their vision either horizontally or vertically [20]. The research determined that people could adapt to the influence of such glasses quickly. However, when perception was rotated by 90 degrees, people had much more difficulty adapting.

Displaced feedback is an integral part of the VIDEOPLACE medium. You stand in one place and use your body to control the behavior of your silhouette on the screen. In some interactions, you try to make your silhouette jump or swim by performing a very different motion with your real body. In the SUPERMAN interaction, you may find your silhouette's movements rotated or inverted with respect to your own. Theoretically, this translation should be a difficult one to adapt to. However, people have little trouble making their SUPERMAN silhouettes fly where they wish.

The original displaced-feedback studies could be replicated with much more flexibility in an artificial reality. Rather than using a single feedback relationship for the duration of an experiment, we could change the relationship systematically throughout the study. A host of possible displacements, rotations, and time delays of visual, tactile, and auditory feedback could be tested. Dynamic stereo perception could be addressed with complete generality. For instance, we could vary the distance between the subjects' eyes. Perspective transformations could be varied to define new kinds of spaces and to determine the ones to which we could adapt. Optical flow—the continuous movement of objects through our visual field that we see as we walk, or drive in a car—could also be altered.

An example of a contemporary experiment that could be done more easily with reality goggles, is that described by James Lackner of Brandeis [21]. A subject is placed on a circular treadmill that forces her to walk forward, while visual cues are displayed that suggest she is going backward. Lackner found that subjects did their best to reconcile the conflicting stimuli, and report that they feel that they are pushing themselves backward.

We could also address our mental models of what we perceive with great subtlety. When we perceive and interpret something, how much can it be changed before we notice that it should be interpreted differently? How much could we change a space as a person moved around without offending her sense of place? Changing the dimensions of a room could be useful if the areas she entered enlarged automatically and then reverted to normal size when she left. Her perception of the sizes of the spaces within the room would vary according to the usefulness of those spaces at the moment. Furthermore, as she turned her head, the turning rate could be exaggerated so that she could see directly behind her just by turning her head to the side. This exorcist maneuver has been implemented with telerobotic viewers.

What Is Reality?

Another question that artificial realities pose is one usually left to philosophers: What is reality? What kind of graphic representation and what kinds of causal relationships are sufficient to convince a person to operate within an experience? In VIDEOPLACE, two people on the screen will play catch without complaining about the austere surroundings. It is not that they are confused about which world is real, it is just that they are ascribing greater significance to the illusory world for the moment, as they do when they watch a movie or a play. It is likely that the same result would be achieved with reality goggles. On the other hand, if the effects of your movements on the artificial reality are unpredictable, the environment probably will not be acceptable, no matter how beautifully the graphic context is rendered. Ultimately, the kinds of artificial realities to which we can adapt will define the limits of aesthetic exploration and practical application.

Conversation

Although we seldom think of it this way, conversation has more in common with an athletic event than it does with the cognitive tasks usually considered in artificial-intelligence research. While people are engaged in a conversation, their intellects are consumed with the tension between understanding what the other person is saying with his words, facial expressions, eye movements, and body language and deciding what to say themselves and how to use their body, face, and eyes to communicate it.

Such communication is difficult to study because much of what happens cannot be captured with standard methods. Artificial-reality technology, on the other hand, will immerse people in environments in which all information that passes between them will be available for capture and analysis. With such systems, we could study the techniques of great communicators. We could ask whether it is what these people do, or how they do it, that is most important. With the results of such study, we might be able to measure and improve people's negotiating and sales skills.

Telecommunication in a three-dimensional artificial reality will require a convincing graphic representation of each person. Assuming this representation is possible in real time, the behavior of the graphic figures could be perturbed in ways that people do not consciously detect, but that might nevertheless affect the dynamics of a conversation. The moving-dot experiments described in Chapter 6 show that the analysis of human movement is wired in [22]. The existence of people with brain injuries who cannot recognize faces shows that facial recognition is hardwired as well. A means of altering or delaying facial expressions or of displacing a gaze while a person was engaged in a conversation would be a useful tool for the study of human interaction.

A recent study has shown that children who fail in school are often poor at judging the feelings of teachers and other children [23]. Artificial-reality technology might allow us to measure what these children were attending to while interacting with other people. The results of these studies, in turn, could help us to create therapies that would teach the children how to make better use of the information that is available to them.

Reinforcement

A crucial question in all learning and education is, "How do you encourage a person to continue to learn?" The artificial reality—like computer-aided instruction systems, programmed texts, or indeed any method of teaching—will not succeed unless it gains and maintains the participant's interest. In fact, artificial realities are tools for studying the problem of maintaining interest.

According to the late B.F. Skinner, a person's response to a given stimulus is more likely to recur if it is followed by a positive outcome; that is, if it is *reinforced*. By constantly varying the reinforcers, an artificial reality should be able to encourage participants to persist in activities that would otherwise fail to captivate them. As complex patterns of reinforcers are established, the relationship of each reinforcer to the established pattern becomes a source of interest and is thus reinforcing.

Such an interactive sequence of reinforcers bears a striking similarity to a piece of music. Just as each note might be thought of as a reinforcer that induces further listening, each response by the reality should encourage further action. If this process is to maintain a participant's interest over time, it must involve a subtle form of teaching. If the result of every action either is known beforehand or is completely unknowable, there is little chance a participant will remain involved for a significant length of time. On the other hand, if the reinforcers are regular enough to create expectations about the next occurrence, both the verification and the violation of these expectations will be reinforcing.

Expectations must be taught, however. Each relationship must be introduced, repeated until it becomes expected, varied around the expectation, and finally violated in a way that leads to the next relationship. Once a relationship has been learned, it can be invoked later when an unknown rather than a familiar relationship is expected. Such flirtation with a person's expectations should be studied because it provides a general structure for maintaining interest through varying reinforcers. If this structure were presented in parallel with an independent development of subject matter, the interest would help to motivate people to learn. If the student knows that the response that reinforces each correct answer will be part of a continually interesting pattern, he will be motivated to persist out of curiosity about the next reinforcer.

It is the maintenance of interest that is motivating, rather than any intrinsic value of the reinforcer itself. Consider the well-known fact that intermittent reinforcement schedules lead to more persistent behaviors than do other schemes. (With an intermittent schedule, a subject is reinforced at unpredictable intervals; with a fixed reinforcement schedule, the subject is reinforced after every correct response.) Perhaps, fixed or predictable schedules are inherently more boring than are intermittent ones, and the interest created by variable schedules makes learning more effective. This conjecture might lead to a broader principle: that we should compose sequences of a variety of reinforcers to be provided at aesthetically patterned intervals.

Applications in Psychotherapy

It is our impression that people in VIDEOPLACE often become more playful and flamboyant than they are in almost any other situation. This observation could have important implications for psychotherapists, because this behavior might otherwise be impossible to elicit. In an artificial reality, a person might temporarily overcome a negative self-image by acting through a graphic alter ego. An artificial reality can also be used to prevent a person from withdrawing emotionally. It can focus on motions so small that a person cannot avoid making them, can respond to them, can reinforce these motions, and can gradually encourage more expansive behavior.

Some people with emotional problems have difficulty trusting other people. In certain situations, therapists essentially program themselves to act in a mechanical and predictable manner, to provide a structure that patients can accept. That structure is then slowly expanded beyond the original contract. However, since relationships with people are a source of anxiety, it might be easier to encourage a patient to trust a mechanical environment and mechanized therapy. The ELIZA program, developed at MIT, was originally presented as a tongue-in-cheek offering in automated therapy, but has since been taken more seriously [24]. Its creator, Joseph Weizenbaum, professed horror at the idea that human psyches would actually be entrusted to computers; however, I think his horror was misplaced. A recent study showed computers to be as effective as human therapists in treating depression [25].

A few years ago, a family succeeded in the dramatic cure of their autistic child [26]. The therapy they developed required 10,000 person-hours for this one child. That such therapy is out of the question using professional staff is obvious. Furthermore, the heroic investment of that family is unlikely to be duplicated often. It may be that the only way to accomplish certain kinds of therapy is to take advantage of the endless patience and consistency of the computer. If that approach were to work, the positive ends would certainly justify the means, which seem threatening only if we automatically assume that technology must be dehumanizing.

If an artificial reality were successful in involving an emotionally disturbed person, elements of change could be phased in slowly. As time went by, human images and, finally, human beings might be introduced. At this point, the patient could venture from the responsive womb, returning to it as often as he needed. The possibility also exists that we might permit people to avoid other people in this way. It may be realistic to define realities that adapt to the patients, rather than requiring everybody to adapt to the real world as we define it.

Diagnosis

The artificial reality could also be used to diagnose and classify behavioral disorders. Experiences could be designed that offer subjects unconscious choices among different feedback relations. For instance, a person might avoid areas with overload levels of feedback and favor serene relations. Later, the same person might be bored and seek stimulation.

In another spectrum of options, people might seek positive control of events in preference to situations in which the environment reacts to them, but not in ways they can control. The sequence of choices they made would reveal much about their relationship to the world. Whether different strategies for coping with the artificial reality would correlate with standard diagnoses is a matter for study. It is possible that the environment would suggest new classifications or refinements in existing ones.

Remote Use

Artificial realities are telecommunication environments. Both their educational and therapeutic uses are consistent with remote and distributed function. A student or patient in one location could interact with a teacher or therapist in another. A likely application would be in educational programs for mainstreaming children who have physical or emotional handicaps. These programs place a new demand on the professionals who must look after these children's specialized needs. Where the children might once have been concentrated in special schools, they are now being distributed throughout the regular school system. The support staff may spend substantial time traveling from school to school. As an alternative, the specialist could join the child in an artificial reality for counseling or tutoring.

Conclusion

The applications described in this chapter are but a few of those that will be developed. Indeed, the challenge would be to identify activities where artificial realities are not relevant. Artificial realities could be used almost everywhere.

References

1. M. Krueger, "VIDEOTOUCH: An Innovative System-User Interface," SBIR Phase 1 Final Report, September 1987.

2. E.B. Petajan & D. Bodoff, "An Improved Automatic Lipreading System to Enhance Speech Recognition," *CHI '88 Conference Proceedings* (May 1988), pp. 19–25.

3. SimGraphics Engineering Corporation, 96 Monteray Road, South Pasadena, CA.

4. E.M. Wenzel, "Virtual Acoustic Displays," *Human–Machine Interfaces for Teleoperators & Virtual Environments*, Santa Barbara, CA, March 4, 1990.

5. R. Heinlein, *Starship Troopers*, Berkley, New York, 1968.

6. S.C. Jacobsen, E.K. Iversen, D.F. Knutti, R.T. Johnson, & K.B. Biggers, "Design of the Utah/MIT Dextrous Hand," *Proceedings of the IEEE Conference on Robotics and Automation* (April 1986).

7. S.C. Jacobsen, E.K. Iversen, D.F. Knutti, R.T. Johnson, & K.B. Biggers, "Issues in the Design of High Dexterity, Force Reflective Teleoperators," *Human–Machine Interfaces for Teleoperators & Virtual Environments*, Santa Barbara, CA, March 4, 1990.

8. S. Charles, "Man–Machine Interfaces in Health Care," *Human–Machine Interfaces for Teleoperators & Virtual Environments*, Santa Barbara, CA, March 4, 1990.

9. D. Stover, "Head Shot," *Popular Science*, (May 1990), p. 47.

10. P. Elmer-DeWitt, "The Incredible Shrinking Machine," *Time*, (20 November 1989), p. 108.

11. R.L. Hollis, S. Salcudean, & D.W. Abraham, "Toward a Tele-Nanorobotic Manipulation System with Atomic Scale Feedback and Motion Resolution," *Proceedings of Micro Electro Mechanical Systems* (1990), pp. 115–119.

12. J. J. Batter & F. P. Brooks Jr., "GROPE-1," *IFIPS Proceedings 71* (1972), p. 759.

13. M. Ouh-Young, M. Pique, J. Hughes, N. Srinivasan, & F.P. Brooks, Jr, "Using a Manipulator for Force Dislay in Molecular Docking," IEEE pub. CH2555-1/88, pp. 1824–1829.

14. R. Reisman, "A Brief Introduction to the Art of Flight Simulation," Virtuelle Wellen, Ars Electronica 1990, Band II, pp. 159–169.

15. "Now, 'Artificial Reality'", *Newsweek* (9 February 1987), pp. 56–57.

16. Ibid.

17. W. Buxton, "Drama and Personality in Human Interface Design," Panel Discussion, *CHI89*, Austin, (3 May 1990).

18. J. Dewey, *Experience and Education*, Collier, 1963.

19. M. McGreevy, "The Exploration Metaphor," *Human–Machine Interfaces for Teleoperators & Virtual Environments*, Santa Barbara, CA, March 4, 1990.

---

20. G. M. Stratton, "Vision Without Inversion of the Retinal Image," *Psychological Review*, IV, No. 4 (July 1897), pp. 341–360; IV, No. 5 (September 1897), pp. 463–481.

21. R.P. Burton & I.E. Sutherland, "Twinkle Box—A Three-Dimensional Computer Input Device," *National Computer Conference and Exhibition, APIPS*, 43 (1974), pp. 513–520.

22. J.R. Lackner, "Intersensory Coordination," *Human–Machine Interfaces for Teleoperators & Virtual Environments*, Santa Barbara, CA, March 4, 1990.

23. D. Goleman, "Sensing Silent Cues Emerges as Key Skill," *Hartford Courant* (11 December 1990), p. C1.

24. J. Weizenbaum, "Contextual Understanding by Computers," *Communications of the ACM*, 10, No. 8 (August 1967).

25. "Machine Therapy May Equal Human Kind," *Insight* (5 March 1990), p. 55.

26. "Son Rise, A Miracle of Love," NBC television movie, aired 31 July 1980.

10

Artificial Reality
and the Arts

Introduction

We are living in an age in which technology has transformed many human activities. We might expect that, during such a period, the arts would have changed as much as any other field. Instead, the established arts can be regarded as holdouts against technological change.

In addition to being a new art form in their own right, artificial realities also apply pressure to the traditional arts to redefine themselves or to use technology to pursue their goals in new ways. Artists have made sporadic efforts to bridge the gap between the arts of the past and the capabilities of the present since the early twentieth century, when the Futurists celebrated the machine in their paintings. More recently, in the late 1960s, the EAT (Experiments in Art and Technology) movement teamed established artists with high technologists in an effort to invent the art of the future [1]. Since neither the artists nor the technologists were committed to the enterprise for the long term, the level of technology was not high.

During the late 1960s and the early 1970s, *computer art* was synonymous with *computer graphics*, and was practiced largely in universities. Interactive computer art was represented only by the work at the University of Wisconsin and the outdoor strobe environments of the Pulsa Group founded by Patrick Clancy at Yale.

Art and Technology Today

Today, the art establishment still has not embraced technology. However, a computer art world now exists in parallel with the traditional institutions. This world includes the SIGGRAPH Art Show, Ars Electronica in Austria, Images du Futur in Canada, and exhibits organized by Itsuo Sakane in Japan. In addition, the science museums—especially the Exploratorium in San Francisco—have developed and exhibited technological art work. It is also significant that university art departments now embrace the use of computer-graphic systems for instruction.

Computer Art

When most people speak of *computer art*, they are referring to the use of the computer to create graphics. Although this use can be exciting for artists committed to traditional forms, it is essentially CAD for the arts, rather than a new art form. Thus, there are people who are sympathetic to the use of computers in the arts who nonetheless insist that the result is nothing new. They see the computer as simply another tool, not as a radically different art medium. When the computer is used to create traditional art, they have a point. However, the computer provides possibilities that can alter the process, motivations and results achieved by artists, as well as the way in which the work is experienced by the public.

Computer as Artist

Instead of using the computer to produce pictures, Harold Cohen of the University of California at San Diego created a true "computer artist" named Aaron. His system generates drawings automatically according to a modeled visual aesthetic [2]. Since some of the choices are random, every picture is different. However, all are clearly the product of the same artist.

What is interesting about this system is that it does not simply represent a step in the direction of aesthetic modeling. It works, without apology or qualification. The drawings bear the clear stamp of intelligence. The early ones evoke a feeling of playfulness and whimsy. The later works are more formal drawings of human figures and vegetation that Cohen colors by hand (PLATE 10). The drawings produced in both stages are definitely identifiable as works of art by contemporary standards.

Who is the artist? The computer or Harold Cohen? Certainly, the original aesthetic model was his, and his aesthetic judgment had to be satisfied before he would say the system worked. But that does not mean that the pictures produced are those that Cohen himself would create. Instead, he is constrained by his medium—in this case, his own artificial-intelligence technology. This approach can give human artists a new form of immortality, for their work can continue to be generated after they are gone.

Kinetic Sculpture

I believe much of the art that should exist has never been created. Mechanical art, steam art, and sail art belong in the last century. Although some mechanical sculpture has appeared in this century, created by Tsai, Takis, Bury, and Tingely, much more should have been produced and more new work should be underway. There has been a microscopic amount of art work that targets this void.

In the late 1960s, there were a few cybernetic sculptures that responded to the viewer. One of the nicest of these was the "Searcher" by James Seawright, which scanned horizontally until the light it emitted was reflected back, indicating the presence of a viewer [3]. Then, it gazed up and down, looking the person over, before returning to the horizontal scanning mode. About the same time, Edouard Ihnahowitz created an animal-like sculpture called "Senster" that oriented its head toward people's voices [4]. For some reason, such interactive sculpture was largely abandoned, exactly at the moment when interesting behaviors became possible.

Fortunately, there are signs of artificial life. In 1989, David Durlach of Cambridge, Massachusetts created a piece that uses an array of electromagnets surrounded by iron powder. When he activates the magnets, the powder leaps to the magnetic columns, which then bristle like cacti with spikes formed by the powder. The magnets are activated and relaxed in composed ways accompanied by recorded music. The effect is delightful. It is difficult to look at the work for the first time without smiling. The work has interactive modes that are interesting but are not critical to its appreciation.

Another form of composed movement is illustrated by the leaping fountains at Epcot. These fountains send isolated bursts of water from one place to another in a garden. Where one burst lands, another takes off. The effect is quite whimsical.

A much more elaborate use of water has been developed by Stephen Pevnick of the University of Wisconsin at Milwaukee. Pevnick uses hundreds of computer-controlled valves to control the release of

Figure 10.1
Pevnick's Kinetic Water Sculpture.
Hundreds of computer-controlled valves release water droplet pixels.
Photo courtesy of Stephen Pevnick.

droplets of water that fall in a curtain. The timing of droplets allows him to define graphic patterns in the water as it falls (Fig. 10.1) [5].

Another force is the performance art of the Survival Research group in San Francisco. They build monstrous machines that tear each other apart before an audience. The use of gigantic machines for dramatic purposes is an important idea. I participated in a mock battle involving tanks, vehicles, and aircraft when I was in the Army; I was struck by the theatrical power of the experience and can imagine such scenes being reenacted for aesthetic purposes after we have developed more benign means of settling our differences.

Telecommunication Art

Whereas I believe mechanical art should have started in the last century, telecommunication art is very much a medium of the present. The telecommunication concepts that underlie METAPLAY and VIDEOPLACE have been pursued by other artists. In 1977, Douglas Davis touched the video image of a person that had been transmitted by satellite and declared that this act was "videotouch" [6]. Kit Galloway and Sherri Rabinowitz have done two-way satellite demonstrations. Some of these superimpose the images of people in two different locations to create what they call "composite space" [7]. These demonstrations are similar to the VIDEOPLACE exhibit in the Milwaukee art museum in 1975, except they span a much greater distance and have included performances. Galloway and Rabinowitz have also done two one-way satellite links that allow people standing on the street in one city to talk to their counterparts on the street of another city through video projections in store windows. Finally, they have created the Electronic Cafe in Los Angeles, which is the ongoing focus of their experimentation. From this site, they will do up to five interconnections with local restaurants or with sites around the world.

Interactive Art

Although interactive art is still not widely accepted by the art world, the work of interactive artists is becoming more visible and is influencing younger artists. Several computer artists have adopted aspects of the medium defined by METAPLAY and VIDEOPLACE: a video camera connected to a computer and participants facing a projection screen that displays their images or images controlled by them. Sound may or may not accompany these interactions. David Rokeby of Toronto uses one or more video cameras aimed at participants to control sound with the intent of creating musical interactions. Since his system perceives changes in brightness, instead of in absolute brightness, he can work without a controlled background, and can respond to movements, although not to movements of specific parts of the body. Ed Tannenbaum of San Francisco does installations and performances based on video effects. In several of these, he reflects the image of the participant's body or face horizontally to create a comic effect. He also has used a light wand and stereoscopic glasses to draw in three dimensions. Entrepreneur Vincent John Vincent of Toronto is commercializing an interactive video product that uses the binary perception technique described in Chapter 6. Jeffrey Shaw of Holland creates three-dimensional graphic environments that the participant views from the outside. The participant interacts through controls such as a joystick. In "The Legible City," the participant pedals an exercise bike through a cityscape formed from the words of a poem. Steve Wilson of San Francisco works in public spaces such as escalators in department stores and store windows [8]. In the mid-1970s, Dan Sandin and Tom

DeFanti did live performances of beautiful video-processed computer graphics and recently have created a science-museum exhibit operated with video-game controls that offers a variety of interactive aesthetic media intended to instruct as well as to entertain.

An Artificial Reality as Art

Rather than movement and interactivity being emphasized for their own sakes, concerns about composed interaction might sometimes be subordinated to purely visual goals in an artificial reality. Many early computer films defined a visual space that interested the artist and took the audience on a tour by moving the camera through it. Today, participants could explore these spaces interactively. In 1973, Aaron Marcus did a piece called "Cybernetic Landscape," which allowed a viewer to move his point of view around a three-dimensional graphic environment containing abstract symbols [9]. While working on simulators for Grumman in the mid-1980s, G.Y. Gardner developed techniques for generating landscapes [10]. His painterly treatment of these scenes would satisfy an artist and invite interactive exploration.

It is also possible to imagine an aesthetic form of reality goggle that would alter your perception of the real world such that you see the scene you are viewing as it might have been painted by Van Gogh. (These Van Gogh glasses would be a logical consequence of computer vision. If the computer can see, it can build a three-dimensional model of what it sees. This model together with a model of Van Gogh's painting style would enable the computer to render the scene as he might have.)

Art in Artificial Reality

Within an artificial reality, many of the traditional art forms could be recreated free of the normal constraints of physics. Painting could be done in three dimensions without a supporting surface. (As though anticipating this possibility, Robert Mallory of the University of Massachusetts has painted with light in three dimensions by taking two stereo time exposures as he moves a light through space.) Similarly, sculpture need not be limited to contiguous structurally-stable objects; it could be free of the tyranny of gravity. Fields of particles or

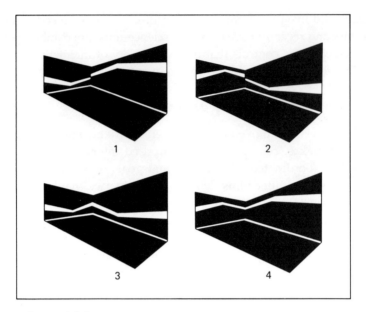

Figure 10.2
Space Dance.

transparent viscous fluids could be attracted and repelled by the participant's body. Karl Sim's film "Particle Dreams" suggests some of the visual excitement that could be injected into interactive experiences.

In addition, a three-dimensional artificial reality could be used to simulate and propose other kinds of art work. For instance, SPACE DANCE is a piece I have long hoped to create. In it, I would use the techniques demonstrated in GLOWFLOW for creating an illusory space within a real one, to create a visual space that changed as the participant moved or in time to music (Fig. 10.2). I have yet to find a satisfactory display for creating the space-defining lines on the wall that could switch on and off at electronic speeds. However, in a three-dimensional artificial reality viewed through reality goggles, this effect would be trivial to simulate.

The fact that a piece has been simulated in an artificial reality does not mean that it should not be created in the real world. A real

object may always have authority over a simulated one. The truest artificial-reality art will focus on works that cannot exist in the real
world.

Audience Arts

Performance would seem antithetical to interaction, since it
usually assumes a passive audience. However, interactive relationships could be established between performers and their stage environments to create new aesthetic possibilities.

The Dancer in Control

Traditionally, dancers have moved to music, responding to the
patterns established by sound. In an interactive performance, the
process could be reversed, so that the music responded to the dancer's
movements. The dancer would play the environment like an instrument, using body movements to create music and to control a variety
of visual displays. Graphic patterns on the floor and walls could dance
around the dancer. Or, a large number of laser beams could automatically track movement, causing the dancer to appear to be the center of
a radiating web of light. If different-colored beams were used, with
each color following a different body part, the result would be a
breathtaking undulation of swirling light. Far from being dominated or
upstaged by technology, the dancer would control it.

Such capabilities might well be the subject of the performance,
rather than special effects within them. The dancer would enter a new
reality, discover its secrets, react to them, slowly gain control of it, and
finally learn to compose and express herself through it. What began as
a potentially threatening external reality would ultimately become an
extension of the dancer. Appreciating this type of dance would require
a new attitude on the part of the audience, which could expect not a
slickly choreographed piece, but rather intelligent and graceful behavior in an unknown situation.

VIDEOPLACE provides opportunities for unique dance performances. In the two-way interactions between the VIDEODESK and
VIDEOPLACE, the desk participant is knowledgeable about the system. A

similar strategy could be employed with a dancer in one VIDEOPLACE environment and a visitor in another. The dancer could interact with the participant, using her knowledge of the current composition. For instance, a tiny dancer could swing on the visitor's fingers, using them as gymnastic apparatus. She could dance on a participant's head as CRITTER does, or slide down an arm using it as a banister. Although having a dancer perform for an audience of one may seem expensive, I would like to do such experiments.

Dancing Through Goggles

Since the graphics computers that drive reality goggles are expensive, it is prohibitive to provide them for each member of an audience at the moment. However, if a dancer were wearing reality goggles, she could dance in an artificial reality. The audience could view the performance in the imaginary world on a projection screen. The projected image would be an external view of the dancer, rather than the view the dancer sees. An additional graphic system would be required to create the new image. The audience would choose, moment by moment, whether to look at the dancer on the stage or to look at the "real" performance on the projection screen. An interesting variation would be to show the dancer moving in two different realities simultaneously. Each movement would have different consequences in the different worlds. Further in the future, each member of the audience could have his own reality goggles, enabling him to change his viewpoint as the dancer performed.

The graphic representation of the dancer could be completely realistic, with the added capability of leaps and levitations impossible in the real world. Or, the dancer's body could be capable of bizarre articulations. Elastic limbs, disconnected or nebulous bodies, and liquid movement controlled by the dancer's actions would be easy to attain. The liquid alien in the movie "The Abyss" suggests an appearance for a transparent performer (PLATE 11). The dynamic magnetic fields portrayed by artist Donna Cox offer another. The concept of dance would be generalized to include the aesthetic movement of any entities or shapes inhabited by a human dancer (Fig. 10.3).

Video dancer joins human dancer

Figure 10.3
Pseudo Dance.

Dance Training

For several years, I took a modern-dance class with my children, partly so that I could better understand how dancers thought. I was struck that dancers were taught different ways of moving as different ways of thinking about your body. One part of the body could be used to lead the other parts, or the whole body could define a space. Attention might be focused on the weight of a body part, or on sustaining a part's momentum from one movement to the next. Such exercises are educational tools designed to give dancers new ways of thinking about their bodies and, therefore, new ways of expressing themselves through those bodies.

An artificial reality can define many such relationships by responding to particular aspects of movement, such as footsteps, the movements of the left foot, the elapsed time since the last step, the force of each step, the overall shape created by the dancer's body, the rate of movement, or the distance between two dancers. Auditory feedback for displaying details of movement might prove as important to dance as the oscilloscope is to electronics. It would allow dancers to observe themselves as they moved, and thus to attain more sensitive awareness of each action. It might be possible to develop an auditory or tactile code that would be transmitted to each dancer to guide her through her movements like a radio-controlled marionette. Whenever her body deviated from the specified position, she would feel a pressure nudging her toward the proper posture.

When dancers came to see PSYCHIC SPACE, their initial reaction was to dance normally, even though visual posturing was irrelevant in the dark room. As time went by, their focus shifted. Since the sensors were in the floor, their movements became more and more floor-centered, until they forgot how they looked.

More recently, the REPLAY interaction found spontaneous application as a dance tool in our 1988 installation at the IBM Gallery in New York City. Dancers learned about this interaction by word of mouth and came in individually to work with it, often for 40 minutes or more. They would make a movement. Watch it. Make another. Watch that. Make another. And so on.

Theater

Interactive technology could also be applied to traditional theater or the concept of theater could be expanded to include the idea of artificial reality itself. Traditionally, theater has included a passive audience, identifiable actors, a fixed script, and an isolated stage, permitting little room for audience participation. As long as the physical separation of audience and cast exists, it is difficult to involve members of the audience in the performance. However, seats in the audience could be wired with sensors so that each person's squirming could be detected by a computer. If these movements triggered auditory or visual responses, the actors could talk about these events, weaving them into the dialogue and perhaps reinforcing the person for making these sounds. Ultimately, the individual would realize that he was being talked about and, finally, that he had inadvertently become a character in the play.

I used this technique when explaining PSYCHIC SPACE to a group of people who were seated on the floor within it. By focusing the computer's attention on a small part of the floor, and reinforcing movements sensed by the floor with subtle sound responses, I was able to get one individual rocking back and forth without his being aware of it. After a while, his motions became so extreme that everyone else noticed that he was not only moving in an exaggerated way, but that it was he who was responsible for the sounds they were hearing. At this point, the computer was redirected to another part of the floor and another group of people became involved in creating the sound. Soon the entire audience was crawling around in an attempt to create sounds, trying to find the active part of the environment. What had started as a staunchly passive audience became quite a different group. In fact, the audience ceased to be an audience, thus ending the talk.

Distributed Theater

Future theater could be designed to lift an audience out of its seats, to involve people physically in the performance. The action could occur in a number of different rooms simultaneously, requiring the audience to wander through the physical space to try to learn as much as possible about what was happening. (Moses Znaimer of Toronto produced a play, "Tomorrow," in which the audience followed the cast around a house.)

With VIDEOPLACE technology, actors no longer need to be in the same physical space to act in the same play. It is feasible to create a geographically distributed theater, in a video space composed of images from widely separated sources superimposed to form a single image. Each actor would enter this VIDEOPLACE through a local camera, in much the same way as people enter a room through different doors. The audience at each of the VIDEOPLACE installations would see the live actor alone on a stage, and also as a presence in the VIDEOPLACE scene that would be projected. This form of theater might be most interesting if there were a mixture of real and electronic scenes. The question would always be, "Is this event happening in video space or in real space?"

If a performance were to take place completely within an artificial reality, the audience would have to wear reality goggles. Since the image seen would be computer generated, there would be no distinction between live and automated performances. Although you would still be a passive viewer, you could move your viewpoint smoothly around the performance space. Again, there would be no single focus for the action. Instead, the action would be distributed throughout the space. Each member of the audience would have to choose a viewing strategy, knowing that, since simultaneous action might occur in several locations, he would necessarily miss some of it. Thus, different viewers would be armed with different pieces of the puzzle. Intermissions would be an opportunity for people to trade perspectives so as to better understand what had happened.

Story line would become less important. Recent developments in television, starting with "Hill Street Blues," signal the end of the classically structured story. Instead, a rich texture of characters and events is presented with threads and themes that do not have to be carried to completion in a single episode. The result is more mature, more lifelike, and more compatible with interactive approaches.

Forged Participation

Individuals in a theater audience might discover that they had unwittingly become protagonists. A VIDEOPLACE installation in the lobby of a theater could engage participants in interactions constructed to lead them to assume a specific series of poses. This collection of video images would be manipulated and reassembled to make a participant appear to perform a completely different set of actions in a prepared video drama that he would see as he sat in the theater.

Initially, the animation of a spectator's image might resemble the partial animation associated with television cartoons like "The Flintstones." Even with this limitation, it would be an unsettling experience to see your own image take on an independent life. In the future, it should be possible to interpolate from one real image to the next, so that the transition will be animated smoothly. Given a modest inventory of a few hundred still frames, it should be possible to make a person's image do anything imaginable.

Interactive Shakespeare

I recently saw a videotape of an interactive Shakespeare experience produced by Michael Naimark of San Francisco. The participant stood in front of a rear-screen video projection of a Shakespearean actor recorded on videodisk—in this case, Stanford University professor Larry Friedlander. When the actor spoke his lines, a TelePrompTer displayed the lines that the participant's character should speak. The participant in the tape responded appropriately. I would not necessarily have expected this experiment to work well, since I have a general distrust of using new media to reproduce old work, but it did look like fun. This installation suggests a line of development that will someday lead to participatory theater.

Participatory Theater

True participatory theater assumes that actors can improvise compelling dialog and action around the spontaneous behavior of an unrehearsed participant. It is not clear that human talents can make this idea work. The requirement is akin to a jazz group absorbing a nonmusician. On the other hand, there are groups of actors who improvise together over a long period. Such a group easily adapts to the exit of one of its members, or to the entry of a new member. Before entering, an actor watches from the sidelines to get the gist of what was going on, and then enters in a manner consistent with the action.

If such a group developed characters, situations, and plays (in the athletic sense), they could then try to impose a role on a naive participant. Their lines would inform him of his character, as well as requiring him to respond. With such a structure and a cooperative participant, an interesting theatrical experience should be possible.

Would not such a form of theater be prohibitively expensive? Absolutely! It is exactly that fact that empowers people who have no money. Any group of actors with time to commit could accomplish this investigation.

The payoff would be working examples of interactive theater that could be used to inform theory. These works could be used to implement automated artificial realities inhabited by intelligent graphic characters capable of engaging participants in dialog and creating the social context within which interactive drama could occur.

My own approach to interactive experience stops short of intelligent dialog because I confine my conjectures to ideas that I am confident I can implement. (Meaningful dramatic dialog coordinated with an intelligent understanding of social context, body language, and facial expression in 1/30 second subsumes artificial intelligence and is too difficult to achieve at the moment.) This preference may make my work akin to movies before the "talkies." However, speech understanding will inevitably become available. It is required as a natural complement of gesture for practical applications. According to interactive theorist Brenda Laurel, when you speak to the computer and it speaks back to you, the conversation that results can be understood best in theatrical terms [11]. Laurel argues from Aristotelian aesthetics that a good interface or a good interactive fantasy must obey the same rules as a good play. It must possess a beginning, a middle, and an end. It must introduce a set of potentialities, allow them to interact in a consistent way, and provide a resolution or catharsis, with no loose ends remaining [12].

Poetry

It is odd that, in a day when film is probably the most accepted contemporary art form, people have not done more to animate the visual representation of poetry as is done in film credits, which often make inventive use of words in motion. It seems lamentable that no poet has seriously taken up the idea of expression through the animation of words, for such an extension of poetry seems inevitable and would be a riskless experiment. Even the movement of words on a computer screen during word processing suggests poetic opportunities.

Interactive Poetry

Traditional poetry is unique among written forms in that it is not necessarily experienced in a linear way. Words are written down on the page in a fixed order, but as a person reads and rereads a poem, the tendency is to jump around to appreciate the relationships that are defined. Unfortunately, an animated poem, like a film, would start at the beginning and would progress inexorably to the end. Therefore, it would be desirable to maintain the participation of the reader by making the poem interactive. The reader would enter into a relationship with the words, which would become entities moving about the screen, each with its own rules of behavior. These rules would be based on the aesthetic of the poet and on the words themselves. The intent of such an interaction would be to create a poetic experience, rather than to duplicate exactly the function of poetry.

I have taken a few small steps in this direction, which I revisit from time to time. One was the WORD DANCE system I developed for Joan Sonnanburg to make animated words into characters in children's stories. More recently, I created an interaction called "LIBERTE, EGALITE, FRATERNITE" for an exhibit at Images du Futur in Montreal in 1989. An initial explosion sent particles flying across the screen. An open hand attracted the closest particles. In the absence of an open hand, the particles went about their business, except that some of them might clump together. As the interaction progressed, a particle might veer away from its current path to join another that was passing by. Later, these clumps of particles became recognizable as letters. The letters occasionally exhibited purposeful changes in behavior that mated them with missing parts. The participant tried to push letters together to make words. Eventually, completed letters started to link up with their neighbors. Finally, the last letters traveled considerable distances by very odd but still purposeful trajectories to form the word, "liberte." This word exploded, and the process was repeated to form "egalite," then "fraternite."

This program suggests a whole new approach to the creation of poetry. Essentially, poetry could become a semantic dance. The words and letters would be in a state of constant flux, moving around the screen, juxtaposing with other words, transforming themselves into new words, picking up new letters and disbanding, in ways limited only by the imagination of the programmer poet. A sequence of such interactions would constitute a poem.

This form of poetry need not be confined to a graphic display screen, but rather could become the basis for an environmental experience. Graphic words and computer-generated word sounds could move around the walls, floor, and ceiling, interacting with the participant or with a representation of the participant. The origin of the sound could move around the room during enunciation of a single word. Words displayed on a lighted graphic floor could follow or be chased by a participant. Footsteps could leave letters on the floor that assembled themselves into words that were spoken by the computer when stepped on. An outdoor environment could speak a word for each footstep of a passing pedestrian. The sequence of words would depend on the spacing, timing, and path of the footsteps.

If a participant were wearing reality goggles, a word could appear as an apparently free-standing object. With tactile feedback, words in an artificial reality could be grasped as solid objects. They could pull toward or repel other words. Although these effects are trivial, it is probable that a poet could make powerful poetic statements if he committed himself to exploring this new semantic universe.

Allowing a word to interact physically with a participant is a symbolic statement, for the written word is then no longer solely a vehicle for communicating meaning, but rather is an entity behaving on its own as well. Given the influence of television and film, and the fact that computers are slowly acquiring the ability to speak and to understand speech, the written word may one day be obviated. Thus, it seems appropriate to give the word life, to allow it to leave the page, to interact with the beings who created it, and to leave the scene.

Conclusion

While the pressure for interactive expression on the part of both audience and artist will lead to more experimentation; the seeds for the interactive media of the future have largely been sown. We will have to wait to see which shall germinate.

References

1. J. Reichardt, *Cybernetic Serendipity: The Computer and the Arts*, Praeger, New York, 1969.

2. H. Cohen, "What Is an Image?" *Proceedings of IJCAI* (1979), pp. 1028–1057.

3. J. Reichardt, *Cybernetic Serendipity: The Computer and the Arts*, Praeger, New York, 1969.

4. J. Reichardt, "Art at Large," *New Scientist* (4 May 1972), p. 292.

5. S. Reddy, "Reinventing the Art of Fountains with a LAN," *LAN Magazine* (April 1989), pp. 117–119.

6. D. Davis, "MATRIX/73," Wadsworth Atheneum, Hartford, CT, February 1983.

7. D. Snowden, "An Electronic Kaffeeklatsch," *Los Angeles/Calendar*, 28 October 1990, p. 7.

8. S. Wilson, *Using the Computer to Create Art*, Prentice-Hall, Englewood Cliffs, NJ, 1986, pp. 34–35.

9. A. Marcus, "Experimental Visible Language," *Proceedings of the Apollo Agonistes: The Humanities in a Computerized World*, SUNY Albany, (April 1979), pp. 349–357.

10. Y.G. Gardner, "Simulation of Natural Scenes Using Textured Quadradic Surfaces," *SIGGRAPH Proceedings* (1984), pp. 11–20.

11. B. Laurel, "Interface as Mimesis," in D.A. Norman and S. Draper, eds., *User-Centered Design: New Perspectives on Human–Computer Interaction*, Lawrence Erlbaum Associates, Hillsdale, NJ, 1986.

12. B. Laurel, "Toward the Design of a Computer-Based Interactive Fantasy System," doctoral dissertation, Ohio State University, 1986.

References

Cybernetic Society

11

Introduction

During the balance of this century, responsive technology will move ever closer to us, becoming the standard interface through which we gain much of our experience. It will intercede in our personal relationships and between us and our tools. The appearance in our homes of isolated devices—such as smart appliances, video cassette recorders, video games, personal computers, and two-way cable television—augurs the knitting together of a single interactive network that we will encounter through every effective device in our environment. As expected, the computer has become as ubiquitous as electricity. In the future, every object that uses or distributes electricity will contain a computer to regulate its operation.

Telecommunication

An artificial reality creates an illusory space in which remote participants can interact as though they are together. The effectiveness of the communication medium depends on the strength of this illusion—the sense of really being together in the graphic world.

Telepresence

Artificial realities are related to the idea of telepresence, the sense of being in a distant real place. An industrial manager might wear stereo video glasses to look around a remote plant site. Movements of her head would control the movements of a pair of cameras mounted on a robot platform in the distant location. She could steer the robot and converse with the people her mechanical representative encountered. The robot platform might sport a video display of the teleparticipant, so people at the scene could see the person with whom they were dealing. At the other end of the corporate hierarchy, factory workers could operate telerobots from their homes, instead of commuting to a factory.

A long-shot candidate for teleoperation is the domestic robot. It may turn out that we can build a mechanical robot long before we can provide the perception, manipulation and intelligence to handle the home environment automatically. Parents who want to stay home with their children might operate telerobots that clean other people's homes.

Informal Teleconferencing

Discussions of teleconferencing often focus on formal communication. Yet even business travel is often dictated by more subjective considerations. It is important to create a personal relationship between salesperson and customer, manager and subordinate, contractor and client. It is therefore desirable for people to be able to relax together at a distance.

VIDEOPLACE was the first communication medium to provide a way for people to do things together at a distance. Instead of talking on the telephone, which is not always satisfying with small children, traveling parents and grandparents could play with the children in a fantasy world. In this vein, one idea proposed for the Bicentennial was that astronauts in orbit and children in science museums could interact in a VIDEOPLACE in which both appeared weightless. Adult friends who live far apart could compete in video sports or relax over a drink at a video nightclub. Such communication would require far greater bandwidth than that used by the telephone, but a subset of the capability can be implemented over the new data services that are starting to appear. In the long run, video cable, fiber optics, and direct satellite transmission will easily supply the required communications capacity.

Tourism

Sightseeing is another kind of travel that could be accomplished in an artificial reality. People considering traveling could previsit possible destinations using systems inspired by MIT's Moviemap project. Reality goggles could be used to look around scenic locations thousands or millions of miles away. A special camera, possibly consisting of many video cameras mounted on the surface of a sphere, would capture and transmit every view of the remote location. Viewers would receive instantaneous feedback as they turned their heads. Any number of people could be looking through the same camera system.

Nanotechnology might allow tiny robot insects, wearing stereo cameras, to fly around a site and to transmit images to receivers nearby. This technique would increase the number of people who could visit these locations and would minimize the impact of tourism on the site itself. Thus, there could be swarms of these viewers hovering over the Serengeti, watching a lioness stalk her prey.

State Street Mall

In 1975, Madison, Wisconsin was planning a downtown mall. I proposed placing a large number of video cameras around the mall. By dialing the system's telephone number, anyone in the city would be able to gain control of a camera and to see what was happening in the mall on his home television. By using additional dialing or touchtone commands, viewers would be able to move their vantage point from one camera to another, as though they were walking about the mall (Fig. 11.1). There also would be areas in the mall where a person could

Figure 11.1
Moving Through State Street Mall Using Different Cameras.

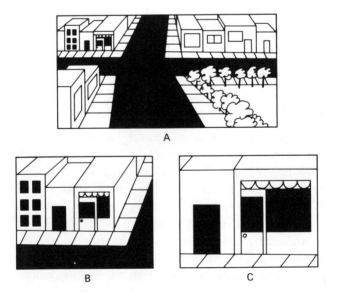

A

B   C

call friends and speak to them through the friends' home televisions. The idea was that the mall would be accessible at all times to everyone, even to shut-ins. In this way, the spontaneous events that occurred in the mall would be part of the fabric of the community.

On-Line Services

Data services such as The Source, Compuserve, and Prodigy are another beachhead for future artificial realities. These services have bulletin boards and conferences that create a new kind of public forum for interaction. Interaction with these services is currently limited to text and low-resolution static graphics, but it is just a matter of time before they offer animation as well as voice and gesture interaction.

Lucasfilm developed a dial-up program, called Habitat, which was implemented by Randy Farmer and Chip Morningstar (now of Amix Corporation) that runs on the Commodore 64. Habitat defines a two-dimensional world containing thousands of connected subspaces within which thousands of callers can participate simultaneously using traditional devices. Each space can be occupied by no more than five or six participants. Additional individuals can observe what happens in a space as nonparticipants. (Since the Federal Communications Commission (FCC) considers them to be eavesdropping, their presence must be signaled by the display of a graphic ghost above the space.) What is interesting is that this simple graphic world operates as a society with a simulated economy. There are lively debates among participants about such issues as whether unethical behavior should be forbidden by the programming or whether it should be punished on a case-by-case basis. (It was decided that, without moral choice, there is no morality, and immoral behavior is permitted but not condoned.)

Global City

The Habitat capability and the participation it provides will evolve. The ultimate result will be an artificial-reality commons that people can visit to encounter other people. Initially, the commons will be inhabited almost exclusively by the technical people who are implementing it. The population will expand as new services are conceived and new needs expressed. Each new service will create an influx of immigrants who do not know the language but who by their numbers may change it. Possibly, the different groups will not interact that much. Instead of a global village, this will be a global city, the distinction being that a city contains enough people for groups to form around affiliations that are too diffuse to reach critical mass in more thinly populated areas. There will be a geographic metaphor for this space. The city might be laid out according to a two- and three-dimensional descendant of the Dewey Decimal system.

Much of the time, most people would stay in the standard space, which would be operated by the most widely accepted conventions. Within specialized communities, there would be additional conventions. In part, these would be required by the people's particular interests; in part, they would evolve in the form of a local culture. There would be more radical variations of the rules in specific chambers of these specialized spaces. In addition, there would be private spaces that are created as needed for special events of all kinds. Even something as mundane to a nonparticipant as a teenage slumber party might have a space of its own.

There also would be elite spaces for experiences that require special terminals at the home or special computational capabilities to run. If there are elite spaces, there will also be slums, to which people who have only alphanumeric terminals will be confined. In the academic community, access to the research networks has long operated as an obvious class distinction among scientists. I know because I have never had an electronic-mail address.

We may be leaving the golden age of democratic entertainment, when a self-appointed elite could fume because their viewing was dictated by the masses and could demand welfare for themselves in the form of public television. At the moment, it is not so clear how this delicious irony can be perpetuated in this new medium. Broadcast television was originally free because there was no efficient way to know what viewers watched in order to charge them for it. Artificial-reality networks will be eminently chargeable, because a participant's every action will be known by the computer.

Experience Society

Although the culture I have been describing will take years to develop, its early evolution has been underway for some time, with the steady march of technology moving from accessing information toward providing experience. We speak of televisions, video cassette recorders, camcorders, and stereos as objects, but they are media of experience. The future holds a dematerialized world, because the resources employed are not the kind we run out of. The primary material is silicon—sand. We tend to do more and more with less and less silicon, so current supplies are effectively unlimited. If we spend much of our time in artificial realities, we will place less of a premium on owning artifacts. The acquisition of experience will be more important to us.

Computer Paper

Our experience with knowledge is also changing. In the future, more information will be accessed through display terminals and less through hard copy. The paperless office has been predicted for a long time. It has not happened because paper is inexpensive, high-resolution, portable, permanent, storable, disposable, and transmittable. Paper can be large or small, requires no capital investment, and can be used anywhere. Perhaps most important, paper is an object and writing and the other operations we perform with paper are physical tasks. Handing a person a piece of paper is a concrete transaction, whereas sending him a file does not have the same psychological affect.

If you look at the long list of paper's advantages, you can see that many of them are starting to be duplicated or surpassed by electronic media. In addition, computers provide many advantages when you are creating and editing documents. Very few people would give up their word processor. Once a document is stored in a computer, it can be printed, transmitted, excerpted, searched, reformatted, merged with other information, and so on, whereas information on paper often must be copied by hand from one piece of paper to another.

In terms of storage, there is no contest when large amounts of information are involved. One optical disk can replace tons of paper. If the paper in a battleship were replaced by optical media, the ship would float three inches higher in the water [1]. Portable computers with the dimensions of a book but with the storage capacity of a small library will soon make the bound volume seem unwieldy by comparison. It is odd that, in our discussions of renewable resources, waste disposal, and the devastation of the world's forests, so little is heard about infinitely renewable electronic media.

Paper and computers will merge. Computers with the dimensions of paper are dead ahead. Flexible computers and screens will follow, and may bring with them animated magazines and books. Computer newsprint may receive live television to illustrate its stories. We will see animated business cards in a few years. In fact, the necessary technologies exist today. We will each have our own soft copies of what we read—complete with marginalia, underlinings, and verbal notations—as well as individual information systems structured to fit personal needs.

The advent of an antique technology, the facsimile (FAX), as a mass application, shows that traditional paper has staying power. However, I have participated in the irony of creating a document on a computer, printing it, and FAXing it to a colleague who typed it into his incompatible computer. Therefore, I believe that FAX demonstrates an appetite for electronic mail if the latter becomes as easy for the user to operate. The FAX experience demonstrates that paper will not be eliminated by fiat. Instead, paper and computers will become more compatible. Electronic pencils may digitize what you write on paper and transmit it to your computer. (In conjunction with goggles, a wireless pen could be used on any surface, since its result would need to be visible only through the goggles. In addition, the same device could be used for three-dimensional pointing, for voice input, and as a telephone.) Special electronic inks might make real paper electronically printable and erasable. Gradually, as electronic media mature, the use of traditional paper will decline without fanfare. I realized recently that is has been years since I have printed out my programs to work on them. My computer tools make it so much easier to look at large programs that paper is useless.

Physical Knowledge

As we combine text, hypertext, and multimedia with verbal and animated graphic presentation, will we continue to be constrained to communicate in the same black-and-white typography that has carried our intellectual freight since Gutenberg? It seems clear that the old alphabet may no longer prove adequate. We may over time evolve new solid symbol systems that employ color, position, movement, and interaction in three dimensions to represent ideas. Instead of reading a book by a left-to-right, top-to-bottom scan, as we now do, we will enter its knowledge space and travel through it. This tendency toward ever richer representation is appropriate for problems of such complexity that they can be attacked only with the total physical as well as intellectual involvement of the problem solver, who may effectively have to live in the represented world. She would spend each day exploring the problem space, learning about it, and intellectually and physically seeking a solution.

These systems will not only organize the information we already have; they also will filter the information available through the media, selecting those movies, articles, editorials, and recipes that are likely to interest us. They will actively query the world's databases, seeking answers to the questions we pose. We will all be executives served by electronic agents who anticipate our desires based on those we have expressed in the past. These agents will not only seek raw information, but also will have models of our current knowledge, and will develop personalized strategies for presenting information to us.

Eyeglass Computers

Our physical relationship with computer knowledge will also change. Today's terminal is an update of the typewriter. To use it, you must sit upright. Using it is not as convenient as reading a book, nor as flexible as writing with a pencil and paper. As I pointed out in 1982, reality goggles could present two-dimensional information, thereby replacing the traditional terminal [2]. You could lie in bed comfortably and read in any position. If a tiny camera were inserted in these goggles, your hands could be seen by the computer, allowing them to be used in a VIDEOTOUCH word-processing system while you were sitting on the beach or under a tree. Or, if you were feeling energetic, you could "read" through an audio presentation and "write" using voice input while you were taking a walk.

Head-tracking systems that allow you to look around in a three-dimensional world might also be useful for scanning two-dimensional information. If you were reading a large schematic, blueprint, or newspaper that did not fit on your goggles' image, you could see more of it by turning your head (Fig. 11.2). Your hands would be free; if you

Figure 11.2
Reading the Newspaper with Goggles.

were working under your car, you could consult the owner's manual without putting down your tools. Three-dimensional information could also be superimposed on the real world. A surgeon could see a CAT scan overlaid on a patient's brain while she operated on that organ.

Interpersonal Communication

Consider the role of graphics in interpersonal communication. Graphics are seldom used because they are awkward to access. The most common use of graphics for communication with people is the use of prepared visuals during a presentation. The traditional presentation is a one-way broadcast of sequential material. Even responding to questions generated during a talk must be done without visuals. Until recently, there has been no rapid means of random access to visuals. The use of computer-based graphics during presentations is a relatively recent and immature technology. As these techniques improve, the speaker will be able to access information and images easily as he is speaking.

Typically, there is one screen, one projector, one set of controls, and therefore one speaker. It is relatively straightforward to imagine each participant having the ability to display information during a conversation or a meeting. The problem is not finding the technology—it is the means of control. To make the problem tractable, we can confine it to the case where the agenda is known ahead of time and each participant comes armed with prepared material which he can access quickly if needed.

As this process matures and takes place in three dimensions, the techniques for doing this may be much like magic. Each presenter will speak and gesture to create and position an object, making maximum use of the audience's field of view. The visual impression created by such a conversation will resemble nothing so much as a sorcerer's duel from fairy tales, where each sorcerer in turn conjures up a more spectacular apparition than the one that preceeded it. As these techniques are honed by high-level professionals involved in complex negotiations over expensive propositions, they may filter down to the point where they become part of every person's repertoire.

Repetitive Work

Although more and more people will work with computers, there will still be a need for assembly-line workers. Mass production, in refining each task to optimal efficiency, has impoverished the worker's experience by not providing enough variation to maintain interest. In many cases, a human is used for a function only because we cannot yet make a machine to do the job as inexpensively.

Interactive technology could be used to enliven such work, or even to provide a sense of community. Even within a well-defined movement, there are variations of articulation, speed, and pressure available to the human body that do not conflict with the task and that might provide as many degrees of freedom as are provided by a piano keyboard. Feedback generated by a task could be reinforcing, and, if the responses were varied, repetitive work might well become more interesting. A person would approach each repetition with a curiosity about what its consequences would be. Throughout the day, as the feedback relationships developed and unfolded, workers would have a sense of progress.

Personal Expression

If workers were able to define their own feedback relationships, they could express themselves while they worked. If the sounds generated by a worker's movements could be heard by other people, everyone could all know what each person was doing. Thus, each person could declare her individuality, even while they all performed identical tasks, or they could weave their feedback together, "jamming" on the job.

Typists endlessly striking the keyboard might enjoy more varied feedback. Each key could emit a different sound as it was struck, telling you what you had typed without your having to look at the result. However, the characteristic sound of each key would be varied according to how it was struck, to keep the feedback interesting. If each user could define his own sounds, offices might murmur with highly individual voices, rather than echo with the consistent rattle of today.

Putting Labor Back into Work

Although technology has failed to relieve tedium, it has all but eliminated physical labor from most jobs. However, because our bodies require physical exertion for health, we face the irony that doctors ask us devote an hour to exercise after we get home from work. Since our labor-saving devices have in this sense lengthened rather than shortened our working day, we must find ways to reintroduce physical effort into our jobs, so that we can at least get paid while we satisfy this need.

VIDEOPLACE's Kung Fu typewriter, which a person can operate by punching and kicking, meets this criterion (Fig. 11.3). This form of typing may not be as fast as the usual method, but by maintaining the health of a valuable person while allowing the performance of a useful task, its output might arguably be greater. Moreover, there are many

Figure 11.3
VIDEOPLACE's Kung Fu Typewriter.

applications—such as spreadsheets, symbolic mathematics, and CAD—where the speed of data entry is not a primary consideration.

The Kung Fu typewriter was one of the first VIDEOPLACE inter-actions implemented, and we have developed a number of tools for our own use that can be operated in this way. Although this idea is easy to laugh at, I have long resented the fact that intellectual labor in general and computer use in particular impose a sedentary lifestyle. At the very least, it should be possible to use a computer while standing, as we can in VIDEOPLACE. Having alternative ways of performing re-petitive tasks also addresses another issue. At a recent conference, one of the researchers who came in to see VIDEOPLACE had his wrist and hand bandaged. When asked what had happened, he replied that it was a mouse injury—carpal-tunnel, or repetitive-motion, syndrome. Since that time, I have met other people with this affliction and have found them to be enthusiastic about the VIDEOPLACE option.

Exercise

As long as jobs fail to provide a workout, artificial realities could be used to make home exercise more interesting. Techniques much like those suggested for assembly-line work could encourage people to exert themselves harder and longer. The computer could provide more satisfying levels of reinforcement, as long as a given level of perfor-mance was maintained. A stationary bicycle wired to interact with a video game is being marketed. Autodesk has connected its artificial-reality system to an exercise bike that enables you to look around a graphic world as you pedal through it. If you pedal fast enough, your bike takes off and flies. In the same vein, the climbing machine discussed in Chapter 6 could provide programmable resistance to specific movements. Instead of weight lifting, participants would struggle to work their will against the complex and unwilling behavior of the load.

Responsive Environs

Every effective object in our environment will one day be capable of perceiving its surroundings so it can perform its function as needed, rather than waiting for instructions. (Joy Mountford, Human

Interface Manager at Apple Computer, calls these objects *Smartifacts*.) As the economics become favorable, many people will be tempted to give their most expensive possessions—the car and the home—the appearance of life and self-expression.

The Home

The computer's usefulness in the home is diminished because it can be operated only in one room and then only from a sitting position. Since needs arise throughout the house, the computer is in the wrong place for most of the tasks it might be asked to perform. It would be desirable to control the computer through voice and gesture, without breaking your current train of thought and action, wherever you happened to be in the house. Since a small number of people live in the typical house, the computer would be able to identify your voice and use speaker-dependent techniques to determine what you were saying.

Assume you are in the basement and discover you have lost yet another Phillips head screwdriver. You would tell the computer to remind you to get one by addressing it directly, "Hey, Computer . . . ." The computer would tell the car, which would remind you when it discovered that it was near a shopping center. (Auto manufacturers have already developed navigation systems that can pin down your location. That location could be accurate within inches if military satellites were used.) Similarly, if you are in the bathroom and discover you are out of shaving cream, the computer could put this item on your shopping list, which it would lay out in the order that you will encounter the items in the store. (Your reality goggles could highlight needed items on the shelves as you looked down the aisle.) Or, if you were in the shower and a thought occured to you about a problem at work, you would tell the computer, which would tell the car, which would tell your briefcase, which would tell your office machine. Tactful software will have to be created so that this reminder process does not seem like automated nagging.

The home's computer capability could include an intercom that would let you talk to anyone else in the house, to leave a message, or to monitor a sleeping baby without carrying an intercom around with you. The average family with a household income of over $35,000 has only 1.3 children. Whether the reason why these families have so few children is the increasing ambitions of the parents or the fact that the three-generation farm household has splintered into as many as four households for divorced parents and grandparents, is impossible to tell. Without older siblings to watch younger children or an extended family to share the burden, technologies that allow a parent to work at home while monitoring a child will be increasingly welcome.

Very small video cameras could be distributed throughout the house to perform this function. A parent wearing reality goggles while working could check on a child in another room without moving. If there were no problem, he would continue working with a free mind. A side benefit of this capability would be that in situ picturephone and VIDEOPLACE interactions could take place anywhere in the house. Home movies could be taken automatically, like security tapes in banks. Every moment of a young child's life would be available for com- memoration. In addition, the computer could tell you where you left your glasses or your keys.

Almost certainly, the house will be given a voice with which to greet the family or to scare intruders. When the house is empty, the computer might talk to itself in different voices, from one room to another, to create the illusion that it is occupied. Keys will be obsolete because the house will recognize its occupants. When the family is home, the house will mediate much of the business that goes on within. The house may become a benign Big Mother, programmed by the parents to control which television programs children can watch, to scold children who make forays into the refrigerator, and to reassure children who awaken in the night. It will monitor all hazards, warning children away from a hot stove or from the medicine closet.

The Automobile

Many people view their car as an expression of themselves. This phenomenon is somewhat surprising since, in its current manifesta- tion, the car is a limited means of expression, confined to a single statement, made at the time of purchase, that becomes less strong as the car ages.

There are times when it would be desirable to be able to express the immediate feelings of the driver, such as embarrassment on inadvertently cutting someone off, or annoyance when the situation is reversed. If the car were coated with an electroluminescent phosphor, it could blush or turn livid. Colors could also be contingent on the direction the car was headed or on vibrations from the road.

The harbingers of personalized cars already speak to their drivers. Since existing military technology could allow the car to know its location to within a few yards, voice maps could tell us what landmarks to expect and where to turn. Voice input will also replace some of the familiar driving controls. The gas pedal will disappear. We will tell the car how fast to go [3]. (Back-seat drivers could cause schizophrenic cars. To whom should the car listen?)

The car of the future will be fitted with radar and other sensors that recognize rain or ice on the road and that detect other cars through fog. At first, these devices will only give the driver feedback about road and traffic conditions. A highway autopilot akin to cruise control could be engineered today. However, at some point, when it becomes apparent that driving has become too hazardous an activity for distractable humans, the car will assume responsibility for driving and navigation. Cars will form caravans, so that only the lead vehicle needs to monitor the road. The followers will maintain their distance, just as in a military convoy. The behavior of each car will be synchronized with a larger transportation system that optimizes traffic flow and the speed of each vehicle through intersections. These systems will be developed for electronic instead of human reflexes. A busy intersection will represent a split-second choreography of hairbreadth escapes performed with aplomb and orchestrated by a nearby traffic computer.

The Mobile Mind

What will the passenger do with his time? The cellular tele-phone already permits workers to be productive while traveling. Freed from the need to drive, the passenger could focus all attention on work, participating in a cellular artificial reality with the same status as his stationary colleagues. The trend of allowing a person to apply his mind while his body is in transit will be extended to people who are in airplanes as well. It may become common for a person walking down the street or sitting on a bus to carry on an animated conversation with a phantom colleague. The mind–body problem will have taken on a new dimension.

In this spirit, nomadic technologist Steve Robertson has implemented a solar-powered bicycle that is independent of the power grid but connected to the world of computer-based information. He has a radio antenna that will allow him to log in on a Sun workstation in Mountain View, California. He views the screen through a Reflection Technology Private Eye display and inputs by typing in binary using buttons on the handle bars. While on the road, he can read electronic books, listen to CDs, and write of his travels.

Shopping

One unfortunate result of our lifestyle has been the removal of all drama from the acts of buying and selling. If you visit the souks of Morocco, you see animation and vitality as buyer and seller compete. In this country, the vendor is almost completely passive. Instead, interactive techniques could be used to gain and hold pedestrians' attention at shopping malls. An advertisement could attract a shopper with one display and then, when the computer sensed that viewer interest was flagging, switch to another. The laser floor can be used to present messages at the shoppers' feet—staying just one step ahead of them. Initially, just the presence of a responsive display would guarantee a crowd of onlookers.

A sales robot could also make shopping more interesting. Counterfeits of these devices already exist—promotional robots controlled by remote operators who converse with the people they confront. At the very least, we can expect to see mobile vending machines stalking their prey.

The distinction that now exists between catalog and store shopping will disappear. Artificial-reality stores could have infinite inventories, constrained only by the shopper's attention span and the width of his gaze. Products could compete for shelf space, just as they do in the real world. However, your preferences could be used to construct a store in which only the goods in which you are likely to be interested are shown. This kind of store could cater to much smaller markets than are economically justifiable today. Artificial-reality networks will permit greater fragmentation of the marketplace, will provide more variety for the consumer, and will create niches for small businesses.

In an artificial-reality showroom, all attention could be focused on a single customer. If the shopper's attention was caught by a fashion show, a computer-generated model, cast in the shopper's own image, could be shown wearing the latest style. Since the outfit would not actually be manufactured until the shopper decided to buy it, she could request modifications in the design. Buttons, belts, pleats, and hemlines could all be adjusted to taste. Voice commands could alter the model to show how the shopper would look in the new outfit if she were to lose a few pounds. Once a wardrobe had been chosen, the graphic mannequin could model different hairstyles. The beginnings of these capabilities already exist. The rest are under development.

Shopping for the Home

Shopping for the home requires shifting attention between two realities: the store containing the merchandise and the shopper's own home. Through reality goggles, furniture, curtains, and carpets could be viewed in the environment in which they would be used. Fabrics, patterns, and colors all could be changed in place. Animated and interactive wallpaper, rugs, and upholstery might even be considered for a party. If this were the case, the interactive relationship between the shopper's new dress and the behavior of the other objects in the home would require careful consideration.

Throughout the entire experience, encouraging mood music could be generated in response to the shopper's movements. When a purchase was made, ceremonial fanfare could erupt in congratulation. No cash, no credit card, and no signature would be required. You would be your signature. The same information that allowed the computer to create a graphic model of your image would confirm your identity.

Leisure

Artificial reality will affect our instruments and rituals of pleasure. Idle games, competitive sports, and musical instruments could all be influenced heavily by the new electronic interface. Even our pets may put on goggles and join us in artificial realities.

One obvious candidate for artificial-reality simulation is skiing. In the short term, VIDEOPLACE has an advantage for this simulation because it could use high-quality video images stored on a videodisk. Three or more projection screens, arranged in an arc, would show you a view of a ski slope. As you traversed the hill, you would feel the slope beneath you, transmitted by mechanical transducers. As you rose to the top of a mogul, you would unweight and turn to face the opposite projector. Fans would blow wind in proportion to your simulated speed. The images shown would be real footage of a ski trail organized on videodisks. You would get a score based on the time it took you to cover the simulated course. At the moment, high-quality real images would be more effective than graphics. Ultimately, we can expect to ski down graphic slopes with our friends on our lunch break. However, there is no reason to be literal about fantasy. We could mix our metaphors. Instead of snow, our slope could be undulating surf, enabling us to ski for an hour down a single perfect wave.

Golf has already been the subject of simulated play. However, although the technology to track the position and angle of a clubface with great precision was developed years ago by Acushnet, it has not yet been applied. With this technology, it would be possible for a foursome of geographically separated individuals to play a convincing round together.

Team sports could benefit greatly from artificial-reality technology. Football players will learn their plays by visualizing them in three dimensions, rather than looking at diagrams with Xs and Os. Practice will include drills against graphic opponents, diminishing the traditional role of the second team as props during the instruction of the first team. Using reality goggles, the fans at home can sit on the line of scrimmage and look around the stands as well as at the field. They can choose to follow whatever part of the action they want, rather than being prisoner of the decisions of the person operating the camera. New sports will be created that permit athletes to perform impossible feats, creating spectacular visual experiences for participants and spectators. Alternatively, athletes could control robots that engage in contact sports even more vicious than those we see today.

Play

The electronic sandbox and the digital doll house are but two of a host of astonishing recapitulations of traditional toys that will be realized in artificial realities. Sand offers a child a rich assortment of tactile sensations, a variety of mechanical manipulations, and a universe of imaginative interpretations. But sand is just one material. The electronic sandbox would allow many nonexistent materials to be simulated, each with its own novel physical properties and sensory impressions. The digital doll house would be more than an architectural model furnished with static figures; it would be a living theater inhabited by magical creatures directed by the child, who could enter the world she created.

Musical Instruments

Until recently, the control of all traditional musical instruments has been directly determined by the mechanical system producing the sound. Piano keys cause hammers to strike metal wires. Fingers stop the holes on a flute or oboe. A bow causes a violin string to vibrate. With electronic instruments, however, the means of control are independent of the means of sound generation. Thus, for the first time, the only constraint on the keyboard system is the human body. Each control system may well have its own distinctive sounds, its own range of possibilities. Control of a set of sounds through frets and strings is likely to provide a different idiom from control of the same sounds through a keyboard. Therefore, we could think of each kind of control as defining a class of music. Certainly, a rock musician would like an instrument with a distinctive sound and a unique appearance that required a dramatic set of gestures to control. The instrument would be conceived for its contribution to the visual spectacle, as well as for the sounds it made. I am amazed that this type of instrument has not been made—it is overdue.

Electron Arts Cabaret

An electron arts cabaret could be a number of real establishments linked by VIDEOPLACE or one that existed only in an artificial reality. In either case, people could interact within it whether they were in the same room or in different cities. By catering to clientele who are geographically separated, such establishments could bring together people with similar interests who do not live in a single location in sufficient concentration to support an establishment there. Whereas any one location might not attract a critical mass, the aggregate crowd of all the connected spaces would be large enough to keep people interested. If people could interact from near their homes or even from their homes, they would lose less time in transportation.

Entertainment would be based on experimentation, rather than on rehearsed performance. The audience would be involved in the experimental process, witnessing rehearsals rather than productions. The strategy would be not to offer continuous passive entertainment, but rather to dim the lights periodically, interrupting conversation with brief presentations lasting no more than 15 minutes—a reasonable maximum for experimental forms.

The audience would be part of the electronic environment. There would be arrays of lights in the floor, tables, and ceiling, as well as keyboards, microphones, and speakers at every table. Thus, the performing artist could control the light and sound displays that moved among the audience. Or, the audience members could control these displays with their keyboards, competing or cooperating with one another. Games would be invented to create a community composed of strangers. Video records of idle chatter or exaggerated gestures could be used later in the evening as part of improvised skits in which people's behavior was edited and comic additions and comments were inserted by the artists.

Intimate Technology

Although we seldom think about it, technology is already intimately involved in our emotional lives. How many times have you told people that you love them over the telephone? If VIDEOPLACE and reality goggles represent future forms of telecommunication, it is reasonable to ask how well they will transmit emotion.

Suppose you were separated from someone you cared about, someone who needed comfort—for example, a small child who was upset. Suppose you were speaking to the child on the telephone and had a device that you could squeeze, that in turn would squeeze the child's hand reassuringly. Would you use it? If you could take a romantic walk along a moonlit beach with your arm around your distant partner, would you do it? Most people to whom I have talked think that they would, if the transducers were aesthetically pleasing. (In a way, acceptance is not surprising, if you consider that between the hand and the brain all sensation is transmitted as electrical signals. All that is being proposed here is an extension of the way nature does it.) Once this intellectual step is taken, it is easy to extend the idea in small and acceptable increments. The communication could be made two-way, so that each party could respond to the other, and the concept could be expanded from one to two hands. There would be a continuum of such small increments that could even lead to full telesexual communication [4].

Telepresence

We usually think of telecommunication as being a brief verbal communication. In fact, most conversation includes lengthy pauses by one or both parties. Transatlantic telephone lines take advantage of these pauses to use the cable for other transmissions. Thus, although what you say is transmitted, you never have a dedicated channel for your communication. Rather, your conversation is broken down into packets that are interleaved with the packets of other conversations on the transmission line. It would be possible to stretch the time frame to provide a new type of communication.

One of the pressures that modern life places on the family lies in the separation of couples because of travel. The telephone provides contact, but only that—a brief contact. Perhaps more important would be a less concentrated communication that would provide a continuing sense of presence even when nothing was being said would be preferable.

Thus, even at night, a couple would be aware of each other's stirrings as they slept. Voice communication would always be available in the infrequent event that one of them spoke. Tactile communication might be included to provide a physical as well as auditory presence. The telephone network would establish a communication path between the two sites, not as a physical connection, but rather as routing instructions, so that the occasional transmissions from each location would reach the other by whatever line was available at a given moment.

Architecture

Both the design of future buildings and the appearance of existing ones could be affected dramatically by responsive technology, perhaps challenging our basic concepts about what a building is. Practical considerations have led us to create buildings with some of the most sterile interiors imaginable. The evenly lit, endless tunnels found in airports and apartment buildings provide an unbroken monotony so rigid as to be upsetting.

There are ways that we could relieve the tedium of a physical space by defining an alternative visual space. In the 1970s, Wisconsin artist Abraham Rothblatt used tape applied to the floor, walls, and ceiling of an existing space to define another, often ambiguous, visual space. If electroluminescent tape were used, such a display could be made dynamic, allowing the same boring hallway to appear to be different each day. Patterns could change in response to the people who moved through the hallway. With a powerful display system, visual organisms could be defined that would effectively haunt the building's corridors, making the halls seem a little more lively even when empty. Each species might have its own habits, seeking or avoiding people according to its nature.

The exteriors of buildings are often monotonous as well. An exception are those whose surfaces are completely consumed with advertisements. In Las Vegas, the buildings have been completely transformed into animated signs whose primary function is simple communication. As usual, the twentieth-century idea of communication is one-way broadcast or dissemination, rather than interactive dialogue. In a world where people wore reality goggles, physical signs might not be permitted. Instead, each person could decide to what kinds of signage he wanted to be open according to his immediate needs. When traveling, you would see signs for gas only when your tank was low, and you would see signs for motels only as night began to fall.

In 1971, I proposed a responsive building for the Outdoor Sculpture Competition that was held that year at the University of Wisconsin. The university administration was housed in Van Hise, a monolithic 21-story building that contained the president's office at the top. The building is somewhat intimidating, but its wide flat sides seemed to me to offer a unique surface for display. I proposed to take over the circuits in the building to allow it to acknowledge people below and to respond to their control. If the fluorescent lights in each office were controlled by a computer, the exterior of the building could be used as a giant display. A television image of a person standing outside the building would be used as input. As the person waved at the building, it would metaphorically wave back with the patterns that flowed over its surface, controlled by the person's motions (Fig. 11.4). Technology would thus be used to expand the power of the individual, rather than to create a sense of impotence.

Figure 11.4
The Responsive Building.
Lighting patterns in the Van Hise building at the University of Wisconsin are controlled by the participant's motions.

Rather than publicize the project ahead of time, I wanted to do it quietly. Then, late at night, when only one or two people were walking by, the building would respond. Initial reports would be treated as less credible than UFO sightings. Then, over a period of weeks, the rumors would spread, until people began to hang around waiting for something to happen. The finale would be an outdoor happening in which audience, rock musicians, and dancers would interact with the building.

Binary Icescape

When the administration failed to hand over the building, and the competition committee said they wanted something for the Union Terrace overlooking Lake Mendota, I proposed a more modest gesture: a one–mile-long light display on the frozen lake, comprising 256 strings of Christmas lights. Participants could control the interplay of lights from the top of the boathouse, or from an airplane flying overhead (Fig. 11.5). I have proposed a much larger version of this idea for the World's Fair to be held in Seville in 1992. The display would be designed to be viewed from the air. It would be the first thing visitors would see as they arrived, and would become the symbol of the event.

Figure 11.5
A Binary Icescape.

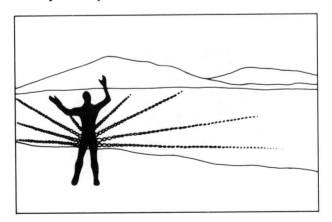

New York Interaction

For years, I have gone to Times Square and imagined taking control of the electronic sign on the old Times building. I approached the company that owns the sign about allowing someone down the street to control it by waving her hands [5]. In the "Digital Visions" show curated by Cynthia Goodman at the IBM Gallery in Manhattan in 1988, one of the VIDEOPLACE interactions was in fact a proposal to implement this idea on a monumental scale [6]. The New York skyline appeared on the video projection screen. Participants could turn on the lights in the buildings with the image of their fingertips (PLATE 11). Each time the image of a silhouetted finger reentered a particular building, the previously defined pattern disappeared and a new one could be created. These patterns were stored, not forgotten. Later, the lights in each building stepped through the sequence of patterns that had been defined for it. The skyline was animated. One day, the people of a great city will create such a monumental interaction.

Artificial Entity

A computer can already understand sizable vocabularies of spoken English if there are pauses between words and the system is trained to recognize the patterns of the speaker. As the computer speaks and understands speech, a permanent confusion will arise about just how intelligent the computer is. We will certainly see systems that will be able to pass for human in a brief telephone conversation. (ISDN will allow the caller's identification to be known. Therefore, the caller's voice templates can be available to the computer, allowing speaker-dependent techniques to be used.) Products based on such intelligent systems will be chosen not just for their competence, but also on the basis of how well they please us. Ultimately, wit and charm will be desirable selling features.

Robots

It may be some time before we see mobile humanoids. Surprisingly, computer processing may not be the technology limiting the development of such devices: we have not been making the required advances in the very small portable energy sources or miniaturized mechanical controls that would be required.

If we were able to duplicate the articulation of human limbs, the problem of creating a mechanical face that could express human emotion would be likely to yield as well. The mechanically-animated historical figures at Disneyland were convincing 25 years ago. More recently, the cinema's Yoda and E.T. both evoked powerful emotional responses. Researchers have recently developed elastomers that constrict when a voltage is applied [7]. These devices could be used to construct the muscles of a robot's face. The movements of these muscles should create expressions identical to those of humans. If they do, the only details that would remain in the creation of a convincing human counterfeit would be the look of the skin, the tears in the eyes, and the software to create an engaging personality.

There will be no limits on the physical beauty of such creatures. Is there a reason to build them? Are there reasons not to? The answers do not matter; these robots will be built. How widely they will be used will depend on whether people like them, as much as on whether they are effective. There is no reason to think we will choose our computer companions any differently from the way we choose our human ones.

Identity

Our view of the world is shaped by our experiences, which are shaped by the genetic hand we have been dealt. In the ultimate artificial reality, physical appearance will be completely composable. You might choose on one occasion to be tall and beautiful; on another you might wish to be short and plain. It would be instructive to see how changed physical attributes altered your interactions with other people. Not only might people treat you differently, but you might find yourself treating them differently as well. Perhaps empathy will be an educational goal in the future.

We are used to thinking of our appearance as a central ingredient in our identity. At the same time, most of us can think of something we might like to change. Now that we can modify the genetic makeup of an embryo, we may be able to make some changes in an adult organism as well. As we do this, we will become less attached to every detail of our genes and we may start to think of the genes we would like our children to have. The act of conception may even include editing a child's DNA at a terminal.

More and more, we are integrating ourselves and our machines. Already, medical technology allows the replacement of a host of mechanical body parts with artificial substitutes. Prototypes exist for artificial eyes and ears that bypass the original organs and stimulate the brain directly. Artificial hearts, kidneys, and pancreases have been developed [8]. A hybrid organ of human cells and artificial materials has already been tested as a substitute for the human liver [9].

At the moment, we simply replace faulty original equipment, but brand-new organs for dispensing medication or suppressing pain have already been developed [10]. At some point, it will occur to someone to include a few discretionary organs. Surgeons may insert the first calculator, cellular telephone, or electronic database in someone before the end of the century. A special organ that breaks down cholesterol would certainly be welcomed by many people. A direct interface from the speech center of the brain to a radio transmitter would provide a functional equivalent of telepathy to its recipient. The body sensors of the reality suit might be surgically implanted using nanoengineering techniques, or artificial-reality interfaces might be embedded in the central nervous system.

The minute we think of ourselves as made up of components, we are less attached to any particular organ and are more interested in the utility of the overall system. Thus, faced with the loss of a body part, most people would willingly accept a prosthetic device that was indistinguishable from the original. I have asked many people if they would accept an artificial arm, leg, kidney, heart, or eye. In every case, they said "Yes, if the alternative was handicap or death, especially if cosmetic problems were solved." Following this line of reasoning leads to the inevitable question, "Are there parts of the body that you would not allow to be replaced, even if form and function were preserved?"

If we fully understood the structures of the brain and their specialized functions, we could probably talk about replacing each of the processing parts of that organ just as we do the rest of the body, especially if all memory and personality were preserved. Would you allow the replacement of your reticular formation or corpus callosum if the alternative were death? In fact, such an incremental approach is not necessary. Having just acceded to the idea of mechanical replacements for every other part of the body, most people sigh and acknowledge that, if they had no other chance for survival, they would accept a mechanical brain.

If these observations are true, we are faced with an astonishing result. Where we might expect greater resistance to mechanical replacements of vital and intimate organs, we find that what sounds like the ultimate philosophical question, "Am I human or machine?" is answered by many people, "I don't care, as long as I am." At the personal level, the mind–body question has been answered. Apparently, identity does not lie in the "hardware." The consensus seems to be, "As long as it's my program, I don't care which processor it runs on, if I cannot tell the difference." At every step, the key concerns are "Would I feel the same?" and, perhaps even more important, "Would other people see me as being the same?"

Conclusion

The examples given in this chapter represent only a few of the infinite number of possibilities that may be realized. Some of them have been deliberately trivial, because our future lifestyle will no longer be characterized by a few economically compelling uses of computers. Instead, it will be permeated by a welter of ancillary applications implemented simply because they are pleasing.

References

1. S. Ditlea, "Grand Illusion," *New York* (6 August 1990), pp. 26–34.

2. M. Krueger, *Artificial Reality*, Addison-Wesley, Reading, MA, 1983, p. 215.

3. "Tokyo Motor Show Heads for the Smart Car of the Future," *New Scientist* (11 November 1989), p. 34.

4. T. Kozol, *The Cult of Information*, Pantheon, New York, 1986.

5. A "Bottom Line" American Businessmen, Unable to Divine His Own Self-Interest.

6. C. Goodman, *Digital Visions*, Abrams, New York, 1987.

7. E. Edelson, "The Strangest Plastics," *Popular Science* (June 1990), pp. 90–93.

8. "An Insulin 'Pacemaker' for Diabetes Sought," *Electronic Design* (6 December 1973), p. 25.

9. L. Oliwenstein, "The Power of Plastics," *Discover* (December 1989), p. 18.

10. *Medtronics Annual Report*, Medtronic, Inc., Minneapolis, MN.

Conclusion

What's the Big Idea?

Artificial reality. We have always thought of reality as natural and immutable. We say a person is realistic if he is aware of how reality will resist his desires. A teenager will tell a friend to "get real" if he is naive about what is possible. Artificial reality offers us a new version of reality that can be composed to suit our whims, promising that fantasy can be made real, physical, shared, and even practical. Artificial reality reintegrates the mind and the body, which have been estranged since the printing press created the sensory-deprivation, black-and-white world of the intellect, and offers a knowledge environment in which the mind, the body, and the full sensorium are employed.

Artificial reality is a scientific instrument, an enormous business opportunity, and an artistic medium. Because the concept touches every aspect of life, it is an intellectual feast to which everyone is invited. It is likely that artificial reality will be the key metaphor of the immediate future—not just in computer technology, but in intellectual discourse as well.

While artificial realities are implemented with computer technology, the concepts suggest new ways of looking at the world at large. For instance, we have been shocked to discover that our actions dictate most of what happens on Planet Earth. For better or worse, we find that we must foresee the ramifications of every action and be responsible for the consequences. This is not only a naturalist argument, but also an engineering one. We are now charged with the design of our entire physical environment. Certainly we will choose to preserve what we can, but the status of what is saved has already been changed forever. A preserve can never be the same as a natural habitat. A protected species is no longer a natural one. In short, the physical world is fast becoming an artificial reality.

What Are the Limits?

While the capabilities of current technology are minimal and technological limitations will always exist, there are also philosophical constraints and restrictions imposed by human nature. For instance, can we live out our fantasies? In a personal fantasy, you effortlessly control the behavior of other people as the experience unfolds. While it is possible to cause anything you want to happen in an artificial reality, you would have to explicitly direct the graphic characters and script their lines. It seems likely that this process would take the fun out of it.

In the foreseeable future, we can expect artificial realities to provide extremely realistic visual and auditory experiences. Eventually tactile and olfactory sensation will be added. Gradually, both the experiences themselves and the graphic creatures that inhabit these worlds will become more intelligent. The problems of robotic perception and action are easier to solve in a synthetic world than in the real one because a computer can be completely aware of the physical context in which a simulated creature finds itself.

These artificial realities could be independent worlds with a continuity of experience. The creatures that inhabit them can have ongoing identities. Since it is unlikely that computer intelligence will operate at exactly the same speed as human intelligence, events in a synthetic world could proceed at a human pace or might even advance at a rate faster than real time. This would allow a human manager to delegate a task to his computer agents and return the next day—his time—after they have worked on it a simulated year. If these creatures are indeed intelligent and if they lead realistic simulated lives, our social integration with them will include the familiar pleasantries. We will form relationships with them. We will face a moral dilemma if we pull the plug or erase their memories. If a person dies, should his personal agents be buried with him?

We may reach the point where the interface to artificial reality technology will be routinely implanted. We may even modify our DNA to facilitate such an integration of human with machine. The techniques for creating and acting in artificial realities may become as natural as speaking is today. In fact, we may learn about artificial reality concepts at the same time that we learn about the physical world—as infants. While such a vision may be disturbing, the steps leading to it will likely be taken for the most prosaic reasons. We will be motivated by convenience rather than some evil plot. The worlds we create may more accurately reflect our nature than the world we now inhabit but perceive so imperfectly. Indeed, we may see the natural world more vividly because we will have ways of visualizing our knowledge of natural forces at the same time that we perceive the physical world.

In the long run, it is likely that conventions will arise and that much of our interaction in artificial realities will be ordinary, even mundane. At the moment, however, we are entering an experimental period during which a host of visions can be explored.

Will There Be Negative Consequences?

Will artificial reality make us completely happy? No, of course not. Nothing ever has and nothing ever will do that. Our nervous systems have evolved to keep us dissatisfied. Will simulated experience dominate real-world experience? One of the points of this book is that simulated and symbolic experience are already well-established staples of the human diet. It is likely that artificial realities will substitute physically active, participatory simulations for sedentary, vicarious ones.

If people interact through graphic simulations, will they cease to interact directly? I expect that in-the-flesh contact will always be preferred to telecommunication experiences; however, it is notable that talking on the telephone is currently the fastest growing use of leisure time [1]. Artificial realities will merely allow us to improve the sense of being together when we must do so at a distance.

Certainly, errors and abuses will exist. Artificial-reality experiences may be much more compelling than film and potentially more disturbing as you become the protagonist rather than simply identifying with one. The actions of any adventure hero include violence. Some people will want to play the part of the villain. The possibility of inflicting realistic mayhem as Jason in an interactive version of *Friday the 13th* seems dangerous. The unthinkable must become more thinkable if you actually rehearse it, even in a simulated experience.

In a totalitarian society, it is possible that a person could even be imprisoned in a graphic world and brainwashed by inescapable experiences. However, recent history suggests that tyranny has more to fear from technology than does democracy. I am not confident that this is a universal truth, but I am old enough to be living in the future I was warned about. On the whole, our system has worked. Relatively few evils have been perpetrated. There are enough alarms set to go off if abuses occur that I think we are more likely to err on the side of excess caution than to commit irreversible errors.

Reality Everywhere

As we develop artificial realities for many applications, we may reach the point where the boundary between artificial reality and physical reality blurs. For example, the telephone started out as an object located in a specific place in the house. It has recently become portable. Soon it will become as much a part of your person as your watch, glasses, or purse. The same may happen with artificial reality. Like air-conditioning, once you have it in the office, you may want it everywhere. Physical reality will be like the backwoods—a nice place to visit, but you cannot get anything done there.

Obviously, if people live a significant part of their lives in artificial realities, art will be created within them. There will simply be no other way for artists to reach their audience. If spaces are created, they will be like any other. They will be decorated. They will be covered with commercial, political, and religious messages. They also will be used to exhibit traditional art that will continue to exist but be updated to take advantage of the new freedom from physics that artificial realities provide.

Most importantly artificial reality offers a new aesthetic option, an important new way of thinking about art. Currently, it lacks the visual impact of film, the narrative capability of the novel, and the complex expectations of music. Ultimately, it should be possible to match these art forms in those dimensions. But the success of artificial reality lies in the importance of physical interaction. It depends on the discovery of new sensations and new insights about how our bodies interact with reality and on the quality of the interactions that are created.

At the same time, the creation of a new view of reality is, in itself, an exciting step in human evolution. It is a fit subject for aesthetic commentary. One of the original goals of my work was to convey the essence of this vision, to make it concrete, much like a painter might try to capture a landscape. I wanted to convey not just the practical or even the playful promise of a new technology, but also to celebrate the artificial.

We are beginning to understand some of the simplest laws of nature as they are manifest in the creatures and environment around us. But we are also discovering that there is a complementary process that may be even more challenging. Once we have apprehended these laws, we see that they can be used in new ways. We move from analysis to synthesis. Rather than dissect, we create. In this process we discover a new set of laws that govern how things can be put together. These laws, the ones that govern how a computer or car can be built, are as natural as gravity. We like to say we invent them, but in fact they are there, waiting to be discovered.

When I look at a powerful new technology, I see it as an expression of natural laws, a new vocabulary, and a new syntax added to humankind's repertoire. As I anticipate its impact on a hundred applications and foresee its effects rippling through human culture and human nature, I feel a sensation not unlike the one stirred by contemplating the cosmos on a starry night. Upon seeing my work at a conference in Boston, one woman sat down, sighed, and said, "It's so joyful!" I thought, "That's what I meant."

References

1. S. Brand, "Social and Cultural Implications of Virtual Reality: Part Two," Cyberthon, San Francisco, CA, 7 October 1990.

Glossary

Adage A vector-graphic display system manufactured by Adage Inc., of Boston, Massachusetts.

AI The abbreviation for artificial intelligence.

Amplitude The magnitude of an electronic signal. The greater the amplitude, the higher the voltage, the louder the sound, or the brighter the image.

Analog Analog signals vary continuously with an infinite number of possible values. Digital values are discrete. (As opposed to *digital*.)

Analog-to-digital converter A device that converts an analog signal representing some real-world quantity into a binary number that approximates the quantity's current value.

Architecture The high-level organization of a hardware or software system.

Artificial intelligence (AI) The effort to automate those human skills that illustrate our intelligence (e.g., understanding visual images, understanding speech and written text, problem solving, and medical diagnosis).

Artificial reality An artificial reality perceives a participant's action in terms of the body's relationship to a graphic world and generates responses that maintain the illusion that his actions are taking place within that world.

Associative memory A sophisticated form of memory that combines logic circuitry with each item of memory. This feature departs from the tradition of separating processing from memory, and can greatly accelerate memory searches.

Attack The onset of a musical note.

Automata theory An area of mathematical theory related to formal representations of computers.

Batch processing The practice of running a stream of programs through the computer such that each is executed start to finish without interruption. (As opposed to *multiprogramming* or *time sharing*.)

Binary Having two values. A binary digit is either a 0 or a 1. In a silhouette image, every point is either the silhouette or the background.

Bit A unit of binary information containing either a 0 or a 1.

Bus A means of distributing a set of signals so that the computer can be interfaced with memory and external devices. Any device that is physically compatible with the bus and observes the protocols that it demands should work immediately after being plugged in.

Byte Eight bits of binary information. Can be used to represent a single character (e.g., 01000001 = A).

Capacitance A measure of the ability to store electrical charge or to resist a change in voltage.

CD-ROM The abbreviation for compact disk, read-only memory.

Cathode ray tube (CRT) A vacuum tube like the one in a television set, a computer monitor, or an oscilloscope.

Central processing unit (CPU) The part of the computer that controls the fetching of instructions from memory, the interpretation of those instructions, and their execution.

Clock A square wave that is used as a source of synchronization in a digital circuit.

Clocked A circuit, signal, or event that is controlled by a clock.

Closed-circuit television system A local (i.e., not broadcast) television system, such as might be used for security purposes.

Code The text of a computer program readable either by people or by machine.

Colorizing A method for arbitrarily assigning colors to image data. For instance, a different color can be assigned to each gray level in a black-and-white image.

Compact disk, read-only memory (CD-ROM) A compact disk similar to those used for recording music that can be used to store any kind of digital information. In ROM, information is stored on the disk at the time of manufacture and cannot be rewritten during use.

Compiler A program that translates a program written in a human-readable programming language into a binary form that can be read and executed by the computer.

Concatenate To place end to end, or to link together. The result of concatenating "dfdfdf" with "abab" is "dfdfdfabab."

Conceptual art A recent movement in art where a work is intended to be appreciated for its conceptual qualities as well as, or in lieu of, its perceptual ones.

Counter A digital device whose outputs count in binary each time a clock pulse occurs on their clock input.

CPU The abbreviation for central processing unit.

CRT The abbreviation for cathode ray tube.

Cyberspace A global artificial reality that can be visited simultaneously by millions of people (coined by the science fiction author William Gibson in his book *Neuromancer*).

Cybernetic Pertaining to the combination of humans and machines into cooperating systems.

DAC The abbreviation for digital-to-analog converter.

Dada An art movement in the early part of this century that poked fun at the traditional view of art.

Data tablet A device for putting two-dimensional information into the computer. The position of a stylus held by the user is digitized and is fed to the computer continually as the user moves it about a special surface.

Decay The end of a musical note, during which the note fades away in a characteristic manner associated with a particular instrument.

Digital Having discrete, as opposed to continuously varying, values. (As opposed to *analog*).

Digital-to-analog converter (DAC) Device for translating a digital quantity, represented as a number of binary bits, into a voltage or current whose magnitude is in some way equivalent.

Digitize To convert an analog quantity into its binary equivalent.

Direct memory access (DMA) A technique for transmitting information across a computer's bus by taking control of the bus, making the transfer, and relinquishing the bus—all without interrupting the program.

DMA The abbreviation for direct memory access.

Doppler shift The shift in frequency perceived when a frequency source is moving with respect to a fixed observer. The classic example is a train whistle, which appears to increase in pitch as the train approaches and to decrease in pitch as the train moves away.

Driver A low-level routine for controlling a hardware device.

Dual-port device A device that can be physically connected to two computer buses simultaneously. Access to the device by one bus does not require the loss of bus cycles on the other.

EEG The abbreviation for electroencephalogram.

EKG The abbreviation for electrocardiogram.

Electroencephalogram (EEG) A recording of the electrical signals generated by brain activity.

Electroluminescence Phenomenon in which the emission of light is stimulated by an electrical signal. (Related to luminescence and phosphorescence.)

Electromyogram (EMG) Recording of electrical signals generated by muscle activity.

Electrocardiogram (EKG) Recording of electrical signals generated by the functioning of the heart muscle.

EMG The abbreviation for electromyogram.

Envelope The waveform used to control the amplitude of another waveform.

Femptosecond One-quadrillionth of a second.

Field Half of a video image, consisting of either the odd-numbered or even-numbered scan lines.

Filtering A technique for culling out some kinds of features from an image while permitting others to remain. Used to remove isolated pixels that are not connected to the silhouette.

Fractal A self-similar pattern generated by using the same rules at various levels of detail.

Frame A complete video image consisting of two fields.

Frequency The number of cycles per unit of time. Corresponds to the notion of pitch in music.

Fundamental The lowest tone in a complex sound. See *harmonics*.

Galvanic skin resistance (GSR) Skin resistance to electrical current, which changes in response to stress.

Gesture A hand movement that conveys symbolic information. By this definition, a static hand position is not a gesture—nor is a mark made by performing a gesture.

GSR The abbreviation for galvanic skin response.

Hard-time Hard-time means what real-time was supposed to mean. There is a hard-timing requirement that must be met. Intuitively, the requirement is that a response to a participant's action must seem instantaneous. In VIDEOPLACE, the response to an action has to be generated within 1/30 second.

Harmonics Components of a complex sound other than the fundamental. The frequencies of the harmonics are integral multiples of the fundamental.

Hidden-line removal The process of eliminating lines that would be invisible to the viewer because they are occluded by surfaces that are closer to the viewer.

Hologram A film image created and viewed with the help of a laser beam. The hologram records a window in a three-dimensional scene. By moving her head, the viewer can change her point of view on the three-dimensional scene.

Impressionists A group of painters of the late nineteenth century who sought to capture the dynamic art of perception, as opposed to the static photographic recording of a scene.

Incremental compiler A compiler that translates only those instructions in a program that have been changed. A traditional compiler translates every line in a program, even if the program is unchanged.

Infrared The part of the electromagnetic spectrum characterized by waves of lower frequency and longer wavelengths than those of visible light.

Infrasound Sounds whose frequencies lie below the range of human hearing.

Interface The interconnection between two pieces of hardware or software. A device or piece of software that accomplishes such a connection.

Interlacing The practice of dividing a television image into two fields, one with odd-numbered lines, the other with even-numbered lines. The two fields are transmitted and displayed sequentially.

Interpolation The process of using known values to calculate unknown values that lie between them.

Intersection In set theory, points that are contained in two sets comprise their intersection.

Interrupt A hardware feature that permits an external event to interrupt the execution of a program, causes some code unrelated to the program to be executed, and allows the program to be resumed without altering the results.

Light emitting diode (LED)

Liquid crystal display (LCD)

Logic Digital circuits are designed in terms of primitive functions that are identical to those used in the formal logic of philosophers and mathematicians. Hence, collections of such circuitry are often referred to as logic.

Loop A programming construction that allows a programmer to tell the computer to execute a particular sequence of instructions a specified number of times or until a particular condition is met.

Mainstreaming The practice of putting children with various disabilities into classrooms with fully functioning children, rather than confining them to special schools and classrooms.

Mass storage High-capacity tape or disk storage.

Megabyte A million bytes.

Megahertz A million cycles per second.

Microprocessor A computer implemented as a tiny integrated circuit, smaller than a fingernail. The small size, low-power requirement, and low cost of microprocessors have revolutionized computer applications.

Microsecond A millionth of a second.

Microsequencer A primitive control unit that is not as general as a computer. Today, most computers are implemented with microsequencers.

Millisecond One thousandth of a second.

Modulation The use of one signal to control the frequency or amplitude of another.

Monitor A video display that accepts video, as opposed to radiofrequency, input; that is, a monitor that has no tuner and cannot receive broadcast signals. It can receive only signals that are generated locally by a camera or videotape recorder.

Moog The first commercially successful electronic sound synthesizer, designed by Robert Moog.

Multiprogramming The practice of running several programs simultaneously on the same computer. The advantage is that, while one program may be waiting for a slow input–output process, another can be executing.

Nanoengineering The design of miniature and even microscopic devices.

Nanosecond One billionth of a second.

National Television Standards Convention (NTSC) The television standard used in the United States. It scans 30 frames per second and contains 525 lines per frame. The red, green, and blue components of a color image are encoded into a single chrominance signal which is then combined with the luminance (brightness) and audio signals to create a composite signal that can be interpreted properly by both black-and-white and color television sets.

Navigation In an artificial reality, the techniques used to move the body or the point of view around the synthetic world.

Nearest neighbor A type of algorithm that is applied to every point in an image and to that point's immediate neighbors to arrive at a new value of each point, and therefore at a new image.

Neural network A hardware or software technique inspired by efforts to simulate the behavior of neurons. A series of inputs are fed through a series of nodes, and the output of each node is a function of the values of the inputs and the weights currently associated with each input. Weights are adjusted as the network is trained.

Neutral background A uniform background of a single color, such as black, white, or blue that contains no features of interest, making it easy to distinguish the person from the background with simple circuitry. With additional hardware or software, a static background can be treated as neutral.

NTSC The abbreviation for National Television Standards Convention.

On-line A system that responds to demands from devices that are directly connected to the computer—contrasted to early batch-processing systems, which accumulated requests on punch cards or magnetic tapes. The accumulated data would then all be processed at once in batch mode.

Operating system A master control program that allows other programs to run and provides them with utility services as they are running.

Oscilloscope An instrument for displaying electronic waveforms.

Partial animation A crude form of animation that employs as few as two or three frames per second, as opposed to the 24 frames per second required for full animation.

Passive art form In this book, art in which the audience does not contribute to the realization of the work. Even though dance involves activity on the part of the performers, people in the audience are passive consumers of the performance.

Passive sensor A sensor that simply accepts incoming signals. In contrast, an ultrasonic burglar alarm is active, because it transmits a signal that is reflected off the participant's body and then sensed.

Pattern recognition The branch of computer science that deals with the interpretation of visual images and other patterns.

PDP-11 A 16-bit minicomputer manufactured by Digital Equipment Corporation throughout the 1970s.

PDP-12 A 12-bit microcomputer manufactured by Digital Equipment Corporation in the 1970s. The PDP-12 combined the earlier PDP-8 and the LINC (Laboratory Instrument Computer) into a single chassis.

Phase A particular point in the period of a periodic waveform.

Phosphorescent A material that absorbs light when exposed to it and then continues to emit light after the exciting source is removed.

Photocell An electrical device for detecting light.

Picosecond One trillionth of a second.

Pipelining The practice of creating an assembly line of processing elements. The output of one processor becomes the input of the next, and so on. All processors are continually in operation.

Pixel A point in a raster-graphics image.

Programmable read-only memory (PROM) A device that can be used to store binary information in a form accessible to digital circuitry. The information is stored permanently and is not affected when power is removed. It is programmable only in the sense that it is blank when purchased and must be programmed by the end user. Once programmed, it can never be changed.

PROM The abbreviation for programmable read-only memory.

Proprioceptive Related to stimuli that are generated within the body, such as the sensors that tell us how much our arms are bent.

Random access When a device can directly access desired material without reading all of the material between the current location and that of the desired material. (As opposed to *serial access*.)

Raster The organization of a television image into scan lines.

Raster graphics A display technique in which the computer is used to generate raster images which are shown on devices based on television technology. In a raster image, a line may be shown as a series of dots on consecutive scan lines that are intersected by the line. (As opposed to *vector graphics*.)

Real-time system A system that computes its results as quickly as they are needed by a real-world system. In this book, a system that responds quickly enough that there is no perceptible delay to the human observer. In general use, the term is often perverted to mean within the patience and tolerance of a human user.

Rear-project To project an image on one side of a translucent screen, with the viewer standing on the other side. Thus, the viewers are unaware of the projector and cannot block its beam with their bodies.

Red–Green–Blue (RGB) signal One alternative to NTSC. Three color signals that are generated separately, carried on separate wires, and finally displayed separately.

Register A collection of one-bit storage devices that are used for temporary storage inside a computer or some other digital circuit.

Resolution The number of discrete values available for displaying, perceiving, or storing any quantity.

RGB The abbreviation for red-green-blue signal.

Sample plane A two-dimensional plane in a three-dimensional volume. A two-dimensional input device, such as a mouse, can be used to point in the sample plane. Or, it can be used to reorient and reposition the plane in the volume.

Sample rate The number of discrete samples that are generated or recorded in a given unit of time.

Scale of a graphic object To make a graphic object smaller or larger by multiplying the coordinates of each of the points that define the object by some constant value.

Scale of a waveform To increase or decrease the amplitude of a waveform by a constant factor.

Semantic Having to do with meaning and significance. (As opposed to *syntactic*, which has to do with pure structure.)

Serial access A serial-access device must read all of the information between the current position and that of the desired information.

Skinner box A device invented by B. F. Skinner for shaping animal behavior.

Soft copy Information stored in the computer that can be used to generate a display on the computer screen or to print a hard copy on paper.

Solid state Employing transistors (the product of solid-state physics), instead of vacuum tubes.

Spectrum analysis The breakdown of a complex waveform into its constituent frequencies.

Spline A mathematical curve whose shape is defined by a small number of control points. The curve can be thought of as being attracted by the control points.

Sprite A small graphic creature, such as is found in video games, which is defined by a two-dimensional array of pixels.

Square wave A periodic binary waveform that is always either 0 or 1.

Staircasing The visual effect created when a step function is used to approximate a continuous waveform.

Strain gauge A sensor that detects deformations of a piezoelectric crystal.

Synaesthesia A combination of stimuli and sensation that breaks down normal boundaries of perception.

Syntactic Having to do with the grammar or structure of information, as opposed to its meaning or significance. (As opposed to *semantic*.)

Telepresence The feeling of being in another location.

Telerobotics Control of a robot in one location by a person in a different location.

Time sharing The practice of allowing a number of people to use a computer simultaneously. For certain functions, such as word processing, the computer is far faster than the human user. Thus, it can handle the needs of one user while the others are moving their fingers to type the next character or scratching their heads to decide what to do next.

Topologists Mathematicians concerned with the most general properties of surfaces.

Track ball A graphic input device that the user controls by rolling a stationary ball mounted in a box. To move a cursor on the screen, the user rolls the ball in the direction he wants the cursor to move.

Transducer A device that translates one kind of energy into another. A speaker, a doorbell, a light bulb, and a hairdryer are all examples of transducers.

Transformation A mathematical operation applied to a point, or to a series of points that comprise an object, that cause it to be moved, scaled, rotated, or deformed on a computer screen. Accomplished by multiplying the coordinates of each point defining the object by the transformation matrix.

Triangulation A method of pinpointing position by computing direction with respect to three known locations.

Ultrasound Sound at higher frequencies than humans can hear.

UNIX A time-sharing operating system that was developed at Bell Laboratories in 1971 and is commonly used on workstations.

Vector graphics A graphic technology in which the electron beam draws only the lines that are to be displayed. (As opposed to *raster graphics.*)

Waveform The shape a signal has when its amplitude is plotted with respect to time.

Workstation A standalone computer system with enough computational and human-interface power to serve professionals, such as engineers. The distinction between personal computers and workstations is becoming fuzzy.

Videotouch The manipulation of a graphic object by touching it with the image of your hand. Also, the sensation that you feel when you touch another person with your image, or when you are touched by them.

Virtual reality Another term for artificial reality that applies only to systems implemented with goggles and gloves.

Zoom Changing the size of an image (which can make the viewer appear to move closer to or farther away) by changing the focal length of the lens. The same visual result can be accomplished by means of computation in computer graphics.

Index

1   2

Plate E (1–4)
INDIVIDUAL MEDLEY Series.
During this series, VIDEOPLACE silhouettes from consecutive moments in time are color-
ized according to their overlaps. The image created by placing succeeding silhouettes

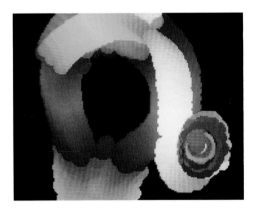

Plate F
FINGER PAINTING Image.
To create the image, each of the VIDEO-
PLACE participant's fingers is used to
apply graphic paint.

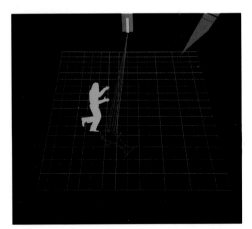

Plate G
An Interaction in the STEP LIGHTLY Environment.
A sensory floor tells laser-projected
graphic fish where to chase the
participant.